The Americas in the
Spanish World Order

The Americas in the Spanish World Order

The Justification for Conquest in the Seventeenth Century

James Muldoon

University of Pennsylvania Press

Philadelphia

Publication of this volume was assisted by a subvention from the Program for Cultural Cooperation Between Spain's Ministry of Culture and United States Universities.

Library of Congress Cataloging-in-Publication Data
Muldoon, James, 1935–
  The Americas in the Spanish world order : the justification for conquest in the seventeenth century / James Muldoon.
    p.   cm.
  Includes bibliographical references and index.
  ISBN 0–8122–3245–3
    1. Solórzano Pereira, Juan de, 1575–1655. De Indiarum jure.   2. Latin America — Politics and government — To 1830.   3. Spain — Colonies — America — Administration.   4. Law — Spain — Colonies — History.   5. Christianity and politics.   I. Title.
F1411.S6973M85   1994
325'.346098'09032 — dc20   93–50529
                                                                         CIP

Cover: Columbus Welcomed to Spain by Ferdinand and Isabella. From Arthur Gilman, *A History of the American People* (Boston: D. Lothrop and Co., 1883), p. 19. Used by permission.

For Judith
Who Held My Hand Along the Way

Contents

Preface ix

Introduction 1

1. The Law of Christian-Infidel Relations: The Spanish Title
   to the New World 15

2. To Civilize the Barbarian — The Anthropology and
   the History 38

3. The Mechanics of Political Evolution 66

4. The Mechanics of Political Evolution — The Natural Law 78

5. A Legitimate Claim to the Indies — The Theory of
   Papal Power 96

6. A Legitimate Claim to the Indies — Papal Jurisdiction
   over the Infidels 110

7. A Legitimate Claim to the Indies — The History of
   Papal-Royal Relations 127

8. Order and Harmony Among Nations 143

Conclusion 165

Notes 177

Bibliography 219

Index 235

Preface

As I finish this book dealing with the way in which one important seventeenth-century Spanish lawyer and imperial official justified the Spanish conquest of the Americas, the United States and the nations of western Europe find themselves asking questions about their role in the world that echo the questions that dominated Spanish intellectual life several centuries ago. Should American troops remain in Somalia in an attempt to establish stable government? Should the major powers of Europe stop Serbian expansion? What justifies military intervention in other countries? Is it legitimate to seek change in another state's policies by employing economic sanctions? In the United States, the federal government has engaged in a variety of actions, military, diplomatic, and economic, to force changes in other societies. Even state and local governments have passed laws forbidding the investment of public pension funds in the securities of countries that pursue policies, such as apartheid, that are repugnant to U.S. standards.

But what is the legal or moral basis for such intervention? Pronouncements of the United Nations are sometimes used to justify intervention in countries that fail to live up to what are seen as world standards of political behavior. In other cases, proponents of intervention simply assert that the need to intervene in another state is obvious to any right-minded observer. When state and local governments in the United States condemn South Africa's racial policies, they generally do so from the perspective of domestic politics.

What is lacking is a coherent body of thought underlying late twentieth-century judgments about correct or legitimate state behavior. Critics often point out the inconsistencies in these judgments, where behavior condemned in one society is tolerated or ignored in another, again for reasons of U.S. domestic policy. There is a general sense, however, that it is the responsibility of the developed nations of the world, especially the United States, to encourage all nations to adhere to a high standard of human rights for all their citizens and that, when governments fail to act according to such standards, the developed nations have the right to intervene on behalf of those being oppressed.

Juan de Solórzano Pereira (1575–1654), the subject of this book, and his contemporaries would not necessarily assert the same bases for intervention that twentieth-century government officials would, but they would agree that what we now call developed nations have a responsibility to assist less-developed nations in the process of developing modern state institutions. Twentieth-century governments no longer declare that they have a responsibility to Christianize non-Christian societies, but they would argue that the international community should impose sanctions on governments that oppress their own citizens. Unlike Solórzano, we do not look to natural law to provide guidance when seeking to determine whether a government is oppressive, but we do speak of universal human rights as a basis for judgment. In other words, although the language has changed, five hundred years after Christopher Columbus reached the Caribbean and began the European encounter with the previously unknown peoples of the Americas, Europeans and their American heirs are again wrestling with fundamental questions of international relations and world order.

Furthermore, in the late twentieth century, as in the sixteenth and seventeenth centuries, the debate about intervention in other societies pits moralists against realists. Those who defended the conquest of the Americas centuries ago generally did so on the ground that Christians had a moral responsibility to eliminate the evils that they claimed characterized American societies. These evils included cannibalism, human sacrifice, and idolatry. When Solórzano and other Spanish writers defended the conquest in moral terms, they were consciously reacting against the contemporary Machiavellian thinking that denied any role for traditional morality in politics. At the end of the twentieth century the political realism that has characterized much of U.S. foreign policy for the past forty years appears to be giving way slowly, as moral arguments are again heard. Ever since the war in Viet Nam generated opposition on the ground that it was not simply the wrong war at the wrong time in the wrong place but was rather an immoral war, moral language has been heard more and more in foreign policy debates. To be precise, several moral languages are being heard as Americans debate public issues from a variety of moral bases, with the result that there is little agreement on what constitutes behavior that would justify U.S. intervention in the internal affairs of other states. At the heart of the problem is the question of the relation of morality to politics. We find ourselves now asking the questions that concerned Solórzano and his contemporaries and looking for an intellectually coherent moral basis that will enable us to act effectively and legitimately in the international arena.

The present book continues a line of research that I have been pursuing for almost three decades. It started with the study of the way in which a few medieval canon lawyers began to consider the relationship between Christians and non-Christians. The next stage dealt with the way in which the Spanish scholastic philosophers of the sixteenth century developed these rudimentary concepts to create a kind of Christian theory of international relations. Solórzano represents the fullest development of these ideas. The next phase of this work will be a general book on the Christian theory of world order from the thirteenth to the seventeenth century.

A major theme of this work is that medieval ideas and institutions continued to shape the way in which Europeans operated long after the supposed end of the Middle Ages somewhere in the fifteenth century. To a medieval historian, much of what was happening in the sixteenth and seventeenth centuries has a very familiar ring. This is especially true in the realm of political and legal thought, as Brian Tierney has forcefully argued in his Wiles Lectures.[1]

A medieval historian crossing the line from the medieval to the modern world in pursuit of medieval ideas and institutions requires the guidance and assistance of those who work in the early modern period. The result is that this book owes a great deal to a number of individuals in a variety of disciplines. In the first place, I owe a great debt to all my colleagues in the History Department at Rutgers-Camden for their patience in answering questions and listening to parts of this work as it progressed. Rodney Carlisle has been especially helpful over the years as I moved cautiously, and sometimes incautiously, into the early modern world and then to the Americas. He has suggested books and articles to consider, read the entire manuscript, and proposed a number of very helpful revisions. Loretta Carlisle, our department secretary, has also been very helpful in dealing with the multitude of details involved in completing this project as well as providing encouragement when things were not going well.

I am also obliged to the sponsors of conferences who have allowed me to develop this work in stages and who have brought me into contact with others who have related interests. Two individuals are of particular importance in this regard. The first is Professor Otto Gründler, Director of the Medieval Institute of Western Michigan University and host of the annual Congress on Medieval Studies where I have given several papers on Solórzano. The second is Professor William R. Garrett of St. Michael's College, Winooski, Vermont, who invited me to attend two conferences on

Religion and World Order, where I was able to discuss a variety of issues with a very knowledgeable group of sociologists of religion.

In the course of developing this book, I also benefited enormously from two fellowships that provided time to read and to write without interruption. The first was a National Endowment for the Humanities fellowship at the Institute for Advanced Study in Princeton, where I had the great advantage of working with Professor John H. Elliott, then at the Institute but now Regius Professor of History at Oxford University, and with Professor Giles Constable of the Institute, as well as with a wonderful group of visiting scholars who provided guidance and advice that has proved very helpful. The second was a National Endowment for the Humanities fellowship that took me to the John Carter Brown Library on the campus of Brown University, where the Director, Norman Fiering, has brought together one of the world's finest collections of materials dealing with European expansion into the Americas and specialists in history, anthropology, literature, and related fields in an extraordinarily hospitable atmosphere. I especially benefited from conversations with Professor Karen Kuppermann of the University of Connecticut and Professor Fermin del Pino of the Consejo Superior de Investigaciones Científicas Centro de Estudios Históricos in Madrid.

As usual, the University of Pennsylvania Press has been very helpful. The readers of the manuscript for the Press examined the text with great care, eliminated repetitions and tightened up the writing, and suggested points to develop further. I also wish to express my appreciation to the Research Council of Rutgers University, which provided a grant that has underwritten some of the costs of publication.

Finally, there are two people without whom this and my other work would not have seen the light of day. The first is Professor Edward M. Peters, Henry Charles Lea Professor of Medieval History at the University of Pennsylvania, who for almost thirty years has been a source of great encouragement and support, believing in this project when my own faith wavered. The second is my wife, Judith Fitzpatrick Muldoon, whose love and support has made everything possible.

Introduction

The Spanish discovery and conquest of the Americas had a number of historic consequences.[1] To critics of the conquest of the Americas, the line of adventurers, beginning with Christopher Columbus, who sailed to the West brought with them only death and destruction for the indigenous peoples of the New World. From sixteenth-century missionaries such as Bartolomé de Las Casas to twentieth-century critics such as Kirkpatrick Sale and the National Council of Churches, a continuous series of critics have condemned to varying degrees the consequences that followed Columbus's successful first voyage.[2] Above all, the critics have pointed to the undoubted reality of the demographic catastrophe that struck the peoples of the Americas. Some small populations were completely wiped out and, among the larger populations, some scholars have estimated that up to 90 percent of the indigenous people died in the first century of Spanish occupation of the Americas.[3] As a direct result of the demographic catastrophe that struck the Americas, the Spanish introduced African slaves into the New World. This action in turn increased the market for such slaves, thus affecting the relations among the peoples of Africa and creating racial problems that still haunt the Americas.[4]

In recent years critics have added ecological disasters, "ecocide," to the list of charges against the Europeans who entered the New World.[5] According to this line of argument, the coming of Europeans to the Americas affected not only the human population of the New World, but also the entire biological system as well. For example, flocks of grazing animals that the Spanish brought to the New World began to flourish in lands where previously there had been none, thus changing the ecological balance. Furthermore, European agricultural methods as well as crops to which the Europeans were accustomed transformed the face of American agriculture.[6]

The efforts of missionaries to convert the inhabitants of the Americas to Christianity have also drawn criticism. From the very beginning of the Spanish occupation of the Americas, there were missionaries who decried the violent methods employed by other missionaries. Some charged that the Spanish were forcing the Indians to accept baptism and then punishing those who continued to practice their traditional religious rituals. Other observers criticized the role of Spanish troops who pacified the countryside in order for the missionaries to preach safely.[7]

Where Catholics vehemently criticized the methods employed in converting the Indians but not the ultimate goal, Protestants condemned the entire missionary effort. To the Protestant Reformers, Roman Catholicism was a corrupt form of Christianity, one that they had first to eliminate in Europe before proceeding to attack it overseas. As a result, they were fiercely opposed to Catholic missionary efforts in the New World, because this work would simply expand the corrupt Roman Church into new areas, making it even harder to eliminate.[8] Furthermore, not only did Protestants condemn the doctrines that Catholic missionaries brought to the peoples of the New World, they also opposed the way in which many Catholic missionaries Christianized the Indians. Specifically, Protestants condemned the rapidity with which missionaries baptized large numbers of converts in mass ceremonies once these individuals indicated a willingness to receive baptism. In the Protestant view, the inhabitants of the New World required a great deal of instruction in Christianity and in the ways of civilized living, as the Protestants saw civilized behavior, before receiving baptism. In seventeenth-century Massachusetts, for example, Indians who wished to become converts had to live in special settlements, the Praying Towns, where they would learn the ways of townspeople and farmers as well as receive instruction in Christianity. This process was expected to take a long time and the Indians' spiritual state would be examined before being admitted to the congregation. Baptism would come only at the end of this education process.[9]

Twentieth-century critics have heaped condemnation on the missionaries for yet another reason, the fact that the missionaries destroyed many elements of the indigenous culture of the Americas. Some scholars have, for example, condemned Catholic missionaries for destroying the written materials of the Aztecs as part of their program of eliminating pagan religion in Mexico.[10] Furthermore, the missionaries sought to wipe out all traces of pre-Columbian American religion by destroying temples, statues, and other physical elements of those religions as well as forbidding the Indians to practice their traditional forms of worship. On the basis of this behavior, modern critics find the Spanish missionaries guilty of cultural genocide.[11]

The air of condemnation that attends much of the current literature about Columbus's voyages and their consequences is, however, only one side of the story. From the end of the fifteenth century to the present there has also been a tradition that has defended the work of discovery and the subsequent conquest of the New World. W. H. Prescott's *The History of the Conquest of Mexico* offered a positive judgment on the effects of the conquest of the New World, a view that reflected Enlightenment optimism about the progress that had occurred in the social and political order since Columbus first sailed. While recognizing that the coming of Europeans meant the collapse of an old order and the death of large numbers of people, Prescott argued that, nevertheless,

> The cause of humanity, indeed, has gained. They live under a better system of laws, a more assured tranquillity, a purer faith.[12]

In this view, European civilization provided a more advanced stage of human existence than the Aztecs and other inhabitants of the New World had reached or would have reached on their own. As Prescott and other supporters of the nineteenth century's conception of progress saw matters, the deaths of so many individuals were unfortunate but necessary if the peoples of the New World were to advance to a higher level of existence. Historians like Prescott and his contemporary Francis Parkman could praise the virtues of the Aztecs and the North American Indians, and even mourn the passing of the unique qualities that marked these societies. For Prescott, the Aztec civilization "was of the hardy character which belongs to the wilderness. The fierce virtues of the Aztec were all his own. They refused to submit to European culture — to be engrafted on a foreign stock."[13] The result was that the decline of the Indian population and the passing of their way of life was, like the subsequent passing of the bison, a necessary, if unfortunate, consequence of the advance of civilization. Such being the case, the Spanish adventurers who followed Columbus to the New World deserved neither praise nor blame, because they were simply the agents of the forces that shape humanity's movement onward and upward.

The major flaw in both the negative and the positive judgments about Columbus and the effects of his voyages on the New World is that they reduce the study of history to the passing of judgment on the peoples of the past. In making such judgments, however, twentieth-century historians are doing what one of the high priests of self-confident Victorianism, Lord Acton, said they should do. In his inaugural lecture at the University of Cambridge (1895), Acton exhorted his listeners "never to debase the moral currency or to lower the standard of rectitude, but to try others by the final maxim that governs your own lives, and to suffer no man and no cause to escape the undying penalty which history has the power to inflict on wrong."[14] Any historian who accepts the reality of continual, inevitable progress therefore becomes a hanging judge, since presumably the present generation is more advanced morally and otherwise than its predecessors. The historian who chooses to follow Acton's maxim has, of course, the advantage of knowing the long-term effects of actions that previous generations took, effects unknown to those who caused them. As a result, historians can easily pass judgment on the defendants who stand before them in the dock.[15]

In fact, however, the historian should not play the part of hanging judge. Rather than rushing to judgment, the historian's first question should be not "How well did the peoples of the past perform according to the standards of my own day?" but rather "What did these people do and how did they perform according to what they knew and believed?" Having done this, the historian can then legitimately go on to determine whether the people of the past lived up to their own standards and only then compare the beliefs and actions of the past with the values of his own generation.

When we turn to Columbus and his successors, men who created the Spanish domination of the Americas, we must ask first what they did and why they did it, what it was that they intended to achieve. How did the Spanish envision what they accomplished? One way to consider this question is to examine the writings of Spaniards who reflected upon the Spanish experience in the New World, an intellectual process that began within a generation of Columbus's first voyage and continued on throughout the sixteenth and seventeenth centuries. The Spanish, and only the Spanish, reflected at length on the morality or legality of what they were doing as they encountered the New World and its inhabitants. From the very beginning of contact with the New World, Spanish officials, guided by a long intellectual tradition, acted to prevent the exploitation of the peoples of the New World. Columbus's attempt to create a trade in slaves drawn from the ranks of the Indians of the Caribbean caused Queen Isabella to forbid such trade as early as 1500.[16] The official Spanish desire to possess the Americas legitimately did contribute to the Portuguese and Castilian request that Pope Alexander VI (1492–1503) issue a bull (eventually three bulls) distinguishing between Portuguese and Castilian spheres of jurisdiction in the newly discovered lands.[17]

The great official concern about the legitimacy of the conquest of the

Americas and about the rights of the Indians who lived there provided a dominant theme for Spanish intellectual life in the sixteenth century. That century, "the Golden Century" in Spanish history, saw an unusually close link between explosive overseas expansion, with its attendant growth of wealth and power, and impressive intellectual development centered on a revival of medieval scholastic learning.[18] As explorers were discovering new lands and new peoples, learned officials, university professors, missionaries, and others were attempting to fit these new lands and peoples within a legal and political framework that would legitimize Spanish domination of the Americas.[19]

One result of this sixteenth-century Spanish interest in the legitimacy of the conquest of the Americas was an extraordinary outpouring of books on political and legal thought that dealt with various aspects of the conquest.[20] In the twentieth century, this material has been studied by a number of authors who have correctly recognized that previous generations of scholars have neglected sixteenth-century Spanish thought.[21] While this work has examined a broad range of topics in Spanish political thought, especially the conception of constitutionalism, much of it has focused on the debate about the New World that attracted the attention of the most important Spanish thinkers.

Within the overall discussion of the implications of the New World conquest for Spain, scholars have for many years focused on the debate about the rights of the Indians and the efforts to protect them from exploitation. This issue, associated above all with the name of the Dominican friar, Bartolomé de Las Casas (1474–1566), reached a climax in the famous debate in 1550 between Las Casas and Juan Ginés de Sepúlveda (1490–1573) at Valladolid before representatives of the Emperor Charles V. This represented the high point of what Lewis Hanke felicitously described as *The Spanish Struggle for Justice in the Conquest of America*, the point at which legal and theological theory came closest to shaping Spanish royal policy in the New World.[22] Hanke's work defended the Spanish from many of the charges against them that stemmed from the "Black Legend," leading to the charge that he was in turn countering the Black Legend with a White Legend that provided too favorable an evaluation of the Spanish efforts to limit, if not to end, the exploitation of the indigenous peoples of the Americas.[23]

A second line of interest in sixteenth-century Spanish thought concerns the role of Spanish thinkers in the development of modern international law. This work, associated with the efforts of James Brown Scott

(1866–1943), onetime Secretary of the Carnegie Endowment for International Peace, led to revived interest in the works of Francis Vitoria (ca. 1480–1546) and Francis Suárez (1548–1617). Scott argued that in order to understand modern international law, the origins of which were usually attributed to Hugo Grotius (1583–1645), it was necessary to examine Grotius's predecessors, of whom, he argued, Vitoria and Suárez were among the most important. His views were epitomized in the title of one of his last works, *The Spanish Origin of International Law: Francisco de Vitoria and His Law of Nations*.[24]

The work of the numerous scholars who have examined the Spanish debate about the legitimacy of the conquest of the New World has obviously followed several paths, yet they share an important characteristic — they all focused on the sixteenth-century developments and rarely gave any attention to the seventeenth century. It is as if the debate about the conquest and about the treatment of the Indians had ended with the death of Las Casas. For Scott, the lack of interest in seventeenth-century Spanish thought arose from his approach to the sixteenth-century thinkers. He saw them as the forerunners of Grotius and the other figures who created international law in the seventeenth and eighteenth centuries. In his opinion, the development of international law was a linear process, moving directly from Catholic Spain in the sixteenth century to Protestant Holland in the seventeenth.

It is easy to understand why scholarly attention to the conquest has centered on the sixteenth century and not the seventeenth. After all, the sixteenth century was the period of stirring deeds, great adventures, empire-building, and all the ancillary activities, including intellectual developments, that accompanied these actions. With the death of Philip II (1556–1598), however, the great days of Spanish expansion were over and Spain had begun its inevitable decline. If Philip's death is taken as a sign of the inevitable collapse of Spain, then it is easy to understand why historians have neglected seventeenth-century Spanish history.

In recent years, traditional opinions about Spain's decline and about the consequences of that alleged decline have been challenged. In particular, questions have been asked about the severity of Spain's decline and when exactly it began. This line of questioning naturally leads to wondering about the inevitability of Spain's decline. Was this decline inevitable? If not, then its history can be traced, and the major turning points in the history of seventeenth-century Spain, the points at which the decline could have been halted or reversed, can be charted. Recognition that the decline of Spain was not inevitable has led to a series of important books and articles that demonstrate that the study of seventeenth-century Spain deserves more detailed attention than has previously been paid.

The most important figure in this reassessment of seventeenth-century Spanish history has been John H. Elliott. His magisterial study of the Count-Duke Olivares (1587–1645), the principal minister of King Philip IV (1621–1665), is crucial to the question of the decline of Spain.

> Decline, then, was not simply the context into which later generations chose to set him. It was also the context in which he and his ministerial colleagues were consciously operating as they framed their policies. Indeed, the Count-Duke's ministerial career can be interpreted as a long and ultimately unsuccessful struggle to find the right responses to a perceived challenge of decline. . . .
>
> Inevitably the Count-Duke was to a large extent a prisoner of these trends, which he and others interpreted as manifestations of sickness and decline. One possible response was to bow to them. . . . An alternative response was to move boldly and decisively in the direction of change, taking risks where necessary. The Count-Duke by instinct was canny and cautious, but he was also by temperament one of nature's activists. . . . His own assessment of the gravity of Castile's condition, his activist temperament, and his burning desire to restore his monarch to his rightful position in the world, all led him to place himself squarely in the ranks of the reformers.[25]

In Elliott's opinion, the decline of Spain was not inevitable or necessary. The problems facing the world monarchy that Philip II left to his heirs were not unsolvable. Olivares understood many of the problems and recognized their solutions. Try as he might, however, he failed to implement these solutions successfully. If nothing else, the size and scope of the problems facing his king and the particular circumstances in which he faced them required, as a frustrated Olivares wrote to a friend not long before his death, a miracle, and miracles were not commonly found in the political order.[26]

In the years since Professor Elliott re-opened the question of seventeenth-century Spanish history, a number of other works have taken up the challenge to reconsider the significance of that century in the history of Spain and in the history of Spain's place in the world.[27] The very existence of a major scholarly debate about the significance of the seventeenth century in the history of Spain indicates that the earlier judgments about its importance, or lack of importance, for historians were too facile. It is true that by the middle of the seventeenth century, Spain was in full retreat within Europe, giving way to France as the dominant power. As Professor Paul Kennedy put it in his 1987 book on imperial collapse, the "conditions of the Treaty of the Pyrenees (1659) were not particularly harsh, but in forcing Spain to come to terms with its great archenemy, they revealed that the age of Habsburg predominance in Europe was over."[28] This statement is correct as far as it goes, but it does not go quite far enough. Above all, it overlooks the survival and even the revival of Spanish power overseas. The Spanish empire in the Americas largely survived into the early nineteenth century. The history of Spain and its overseas possessions from the death of Philip II thus cannot be graphed as a straight line that slopes gradually downward. The line falls and rises, occasionally levels out, and does not end until 1898, reflecting a more complex reality than that which a straight line can describe.

If the story of the Spanish overseas empire is more complex than scholars have often realized, it also means that Spanish political history in the first half of the seventeenth century is worth much more study than it has received. It was an age in which a talented, if flawed, chief minister sought to create the means that would insure the long-term survival of the family and the kingdom that he served. It was also an age in which scores of proposals for reform emerged from the pens of those known as *arbitristas*. While some of these proposals were exercises in fantasy, others were sensible and realistic. All of this was part of "an orgy of national introspection" that marked Spanish intellectual life in the early seventeenth century.[29] Even if one concedes the inevitable decline of Spain, the intellectual history of that period, especially as it concerns the history of ideas designed to encourage the reform and reconstruction of the institutions of government and politics, is especially vibrant.[30]

In this light, the work of Juan de Solórzano Pereira (1575–1654) deserves serious attention. Solórzano was not a university professor, a missionary or a cleric. After studying law at the University of Salamanca, the premier institution for the study of law in Spain, he spent his professional career in the Castilian royal service.[31] For almost twenty years (1609–1627) he served as an *oidor*, a judge, in the *Audiencia* in Lima, Peru. After returning to Spain, he served on the Council of Castile and on the Council of the Indies and, in addition, wrote several books on legal and administrative matters.[32] He also played an active role in organizing and developing the major seventeenth-century work on the laws affecting the New World, the *Recopilación de leyes de las Indias*.[33] His career then was that of the scholar-bureaucrat, one of the most characteristic products of the humanist movement.[34]

While Solórzano is not widely known in the twentieth century, scholars have described him as one of the most important Spanish legal writers of his era, an age that J. H. Parry described as "a great age of theoretical jurisprudence in Spain." Parry described Solórzano's work "as the most outstanding work of Spanish colonial jurisprudence . . . a magisterial and immensely erudite analysis."[35] In praising Solórzano's work, Parry was only restating the judgment a line of distinguished nineteenth- and twentieth-century scholars had made.[36]

It is not simply that modern scholars have rediscovered the work of a man who was neglected in his own day. Quite the contrary. Solórzano and his work were very well known in seventeenth- and eighteenth-century legal and government circles. As a Latin-American scholar pointed out some years ago, Solórzano's *De Indiarum Jure* "enjoyed an unrivalled prestige in the official and legal circles in the Indies for a century and a half."[37] Any historian interested in presenting a positive view of the Spanish role in the Americas and who seeks to examine the laws and policies of Spanish colonial government must deal with Solórzano's work because of his place in the Spanish colonial legal tradition.[38] For Lewis Hanke, the most important critic of the Black Legend of Spanish wickedness in the New World, Solórzano's work was the "most learned and most detailed statement made during the seventeenth or eighteenth centuries on the whole complicated question of Spain's right to America and her method of operations there."[39]

Solórzano's fame was not restricted to his native land and its American possessions. Contemporary writers on international law, colonies, and related topics in other countries occasionally cited him as well.[40] He was even cited by several writers involved in the debates about the right of the English Parliament to legislate for the British colonies in North America.[41] Solórzano's work remained a standard authority on the problems of imperial governance as late as the early nineteenth century, when lawyers in the United States cited him in cases that arose from the acquisition of Florida from Spain between 1810 and 1818. Several pages of his work were made available to the United States Congress in 1833 when Joseph M. White, territorial representative from Florida (1825–1837), arranged for the translation of these pages. Subsequently, White published them, along with a great deal of additional Spanish legal material, for the use of lawyers and judges involved in land disputes in the various territories that the United States had acquired from Spain during the course of the early nineteenth century.[42]

The *De Indiarum Jure*, upon which Solórzano's reputation primarily rests, appeared in two volumes, the first in 1629, the second ten years later.

In addition to the original Latin text, there was subsequently a Spanish version, the *Política indiana*, that first appeared in 1647.[43] Both the Latin and Spanish versions of the text were reprinted several times in the seventeenth and eighteenth centuries.[44] The present discussion of Solórzano's work is based upon the Latin text of the *De Indiarum Jure*, the original version. There are several reasons for the choice of the Latin text upon which to base a study of Solórzano's thought. In the first place, the Spanish version of the text was not simply a translation of the Latin volumes; it was apparently designed for a different audience than the Latin text. It included, for example, material dealing with the monarchy's finances in the Americas, material not found in the Latin text.[45] The existence of different Latin and vernacular editions of important books was not unknown in early-modern Spanish intellectual life. The vernacular version of a work, accessible as it was to a wider audience than a Latin text would be, might be modified to soften criticism of important people. Perhaps the most famous case of this kind of censorship through revision and translation was that of the Jesuit Juan de Mariana, whose history of Spain led, for a time, to his imprisonment. Concerning the Spanish version of his history, Mariana wrote:

> In this translation I have proceeded not as interpreter but as author. I have not tied myself down to words or clauses; I have extracted and written with liberty as it appeared to me to be proper. Certain things are fit for the learned and others for the common people.[46]

A modern commentator on Mariana pointed out that this meant that in the Spanish edition of his history, Mariana

> seems to be very careful not to utter opinions likely to be offensive to the faith or subversive to good order. In the Latin text, on the other hand, he apparently has fewer such hesitations and expresses himself somewhat more freely and critically.[47]

Other Spanish writers contemporary with Solórzano, Cervantes the most famous among them, are also said to have phrased their opinions differently in Latin and Spanish.[48] In Solórzano's case, the Latin text contains a number of very biting observations about the behavior of Spaniards in the New World, echoing the slashing criticisms that Las Casas made almost a century before. As a result, because some "of the most telling descriptions of Spanish cruelty were embedded in royal orders . . . Solórzano was ordered to remove from the manuscript of his *Política indiana* some of the royal orders on mistreatment of Indians to prevent notice of these things reaching foreigners."[49]

Secondly, the Latin text of Solórzano's great work has many of the characteristics of a medieval legal treatise. The format of the volumes is quite traditional, posing questions, arranging arguments pro and con, citing authorities, and, finally, drawing conclusions in the manner of medieval scholastic philosophers and lawyers. This essentially medieval format graphically illustrates the place of medieval ideas and historical experience in Solórzano's thought. Although Solórzano was also well aware of contemporary humanist thought and indeed, as the contents of the *De Indiarum Jure* demonstrate, shows many influences from that tradition in his writings, humanist learning was subordinated to an essentially medieval perspective on the issue of relations between Christian and non-Christian societies. This perspective stemmed from the thought of the medieval canon lawyers who had first dealt with the issue of Christian-infidel relations and upon whose work all subsequent Catholic thinking on the nature of the relationship between Christian and infidel societies was based. It is one of the contentions of the present book that Solórzano developed Catholic thought on this issue as fully as it could have been, given the underlying assumptions upon which it was based. The *De Indiarum Jure*, though written in the seventeenth century, may thus be considered the fullest expression of a medieval Christian conception of religious and social order.[50]

The very traditional nature of Solórzano's work has obscured its importance. As a modern student of Spanish thought has pointed out:

> It is fairly clear that two elements most dear to the hearts of historians are largely missing from the fabric of Spanish political thought: great seminal minds, and those trends which, historical insight tells us, may be identified as precursors of later and important movements and attitudes. . . . Ironically enough scholars have in this manner missed a splendid opportunity to survey a climate of opinion dominated by talented but not exceptional personalities who far better than any seminal mind reflect the attitudes, views, limitations, and insights of the age.[51]

For the medieval historian, especially one familiar with the canon-law tradition, interest in Solórzano stems precisely from the fact that he was not an original thinker. What makes him interesting to the medievalist is the fact that he did not rethink the fundamental problems that arose in the wake of the New World conquest or re-orient the ways Europeans viewed the New World and its inhabitants. Solórzano began with a conception of a legal and moral relationship between Christians and non-Christians that medieval lawyers had first developed and that was then adopted by scholastic philosophers and theologians.[52] To this theoretical framework, Solórzano added enthnological and anthropological materials that missionaries had produced in order to understand the peoples whom they were seeking to convert. This enabled him to place the peoples of the New World and their ways of life within an existing intellectual framework. Finally, he drew upon the materials dealing with the history of Europe that sixteenth-century scholars had produced. Much of this material, generated as it had been by the polemical battles that accompanied the wars of religion, dealt with the history of the later Roman world and with the early Middle Ages, the period in which Europe was, according to Catholic historians, converted to Christianity. Protestant historians looking at the same historical documents saw in the period from Constantine to Gregory I the gradual deformation of the true Church and the rise of the Roman Church, which in fact had led medieval Europe away from the true faith.[53] As a result of this contemporary debate about whether or not Europe had actually been converted, Solórzano's work was not only a defense of the Spanish military conquest of the New World, it was also a defense of the methods that the Catholic Church had employed in the conversion of early medieval Europe and was presently using in the New World. Finally, it was a defense of Catholic Christianity in general and of the role of the pope in particular.

The result of synthesizing various intellectual approaches to the Spanish conquest of the New World was that Solórzano provided what one might term a three-dimensional picture of the conquest. The legal-philosophical-theological tradition was the first dimension and the enthnological-anthropological tradition was the second. The historical tradition provided the third dimension, one that accounted for change over time. It is this last dimension that provides the most interesting element of the *De Indiarum Jure*. It suggests that the experience of the missionaries in the New World was not qualitatively different from that of the missionaries who had introduced the barbarian invaders of Europe to Christianity. There is also the implication that Europeans could expect the Indians to develop socially and politically, as well as religiously, as the Europeans themselves had evolved over a period of a thousand years. In a general sense, the historical dimension in Solórzano's thought provided the basis for comparing the process of religious conversion and socio-political development in the New World with the experience of the Old World. This comparative and historical approach to the problems raised by the conquest of the Americas leads to another significance of Solórzano's work. Embedded within the *De Indiarum Jure* was a rudimentary theory of world order, an issue central to

Spanish thought in the seventeenth century as lawyers, philosophers, and government officials sought to justify the Spanish monarch's possession of a great part of the earth's surface. As Europe generally had evolved over time into at least a religious and cultural unity and as the Iberian kingdoms had moved to a political unity as well, so too might the great mass of Spanish overseas possessions one day be joined into a single political unit that would in turn be a preparatory step toward a Christian world order.

The present study will concentrate almost entirely upon the second book of the first volume of the *De Indiarum Jure*. This volume bore the subtitle *De justa Indiarum Occidentalium Inquisitione, Acquisitione, et Retentione*, meaning a discussion of the just or legitimate Spanish search for, acquisition of, and continued possession of the Americas. The second book, dealing as it did with the legitimacy of the conquest of the Americas, considered the ten basic arguments that defenders of the conquest had offered over the years to justify the conquest of the New World. It is here that Solórzano's traditional approach to the question of Spanish domination of the New World shows up quite clearly. The Spanish and Catholic approach to the debate about the New World was by way of the theory of the just war. This approach assumed that the relations between Christian and non-Christian societies were likely to be warlike, not peaceful. Such an approach tended to limit the terms of the debate about relations among peoples to matters that fell within the purview of the theory of the just war.

Solórzano began the discussion of the conquest of the New World by placing it within the theory of the just war, an approach that Francis Vitoria initiated in his *De Indis*, the first formal discussion of the legitimacy of the conquest. It was within this framework, a narrow and restrictive one, that Solórzano had to develop his ideas about the relations between Christian and non-Christian societies. It is no coincidence that Hugo Grotius, who was writing his *De Jure Belli ac Pacis* at the same time Solórzano was writing and who cited many of the same sources that Solórzano and the other Spanish writers employed in their discussions of the conquest of the New World, took a different approach to the problem and the sources.[54] As a Protestant and as a member of a trading nation, Grotius's interest in the newly discovered lands led him to see the problems posed by the discoveries in different terms than had the Spanish Catholic writers who saw the encounter with the New World in religious terms, in terms of the just war, and in terms of the possession of land.

The analysis of *De Indiarum Jure* will be thematic. The first chapter will consider the legal basis, that is, the ten titles alleged to support Spanish possession of the Americas, that Solórzano analyzed and consider why the conquest of the New World in particular generated such an extensive debate about European relations with non-European societies. The second chapter will examine Solórzano's anthropology, that is, his perception of the social organization of the peoples of the Americas, and then consider his use of historical information as it concerned the conversion of Europe to Christianity from the fourth to the tenth centuries, from Constantine (d. 337) to Otto the Great (d. 973), a period in which, as Solórzano saw it, secular rulers played the dominant role in the conversion of entire societies to Christianity. Chapters 3 and 4 will deal with how Solórzano perceived the manner in which societies evolved from simple to complex levels of organization. Chapters 5, 6, and 7 will deal with various aspects of Solórzano's discussion of the papacy's role in legitimizing the acquisition of the New World by the Spanish. Finally, the eighth chapter will consider how Solórzano believed that a harmonious world order might be achieved.

In the final analysis, the argument of this book is that the most important element in shaping relations between the Spanish and the inhabitants of the New World from the late fifteenth to the mid-seventeenth centuries was the Christian religion, specifically as it had developed ideas and institutions designed to deal with non-Christian peoples who dwelled beyond the borders of Christendom. In the first place, Christ's mandate to preach to all nations provided a theoretical justification, indeed an obligation, for Europeans to enter the New World. In the second place, the means employed to spread Christianity in the New World had long been used both within and along the frontiers of Europe. Furthermore, when Spanish officials and missionaries sought to understand the process of conversion to Christianity, they did so through the lens of the medieval missionary experience. Finally, the response, both positive and negative, of the inhabitants of the New World to the missionary endeavor shaped the course of the Spanish conquest and subsequent development of Latin America even into the twentieth century. Long after the silver mines of Peru were exhausted and long after the extraordinary decline in the indigenous population had occurred, the Christian religion continued to shape the course of events in Latin America.

1. The Law of Christian-Infidel Relations: The Spanish Title to the New World

Juan de Solórzano Pereira's *De Indiarum Jure* was, above all, a legal treatise that dealt with the right of the Castilians to conquer and to retain possession of the Americas. It was, in other words, the application of traditional thinking about the nature of the just war to the situation in which the Castilians found themselves following the discovery of the Americas.[1] The author was not primarily interested in the conversion of the inhabitants of the New World or in the history of Christian relations with them. His primary aim was to defend the Spanish occupation of the Americas, which meant, in effect, to consider the issues that the discovery of the New World had raised in terms of the theory of the just war. The approach that Solórzano took to the issues involved was basically one that intellectuals had taken for a century, one that was in turn rooted in four centuries of debate in legal circles about the basis upon which relations between Christian and infidel societies could exist. This tradition had developed from the fact that the earliest medieval thought about the nature of Christian relations with non-Christian societies grew out of the crusades against the Muslims and from the efforts to blunt by diplomatic means the Mongol assault against Europe.

Thus, consideration of Christian relations with non-Christian societies began with the assumption that Christian societies were likely to be in conflict with their non-Christian neighbors. Contemporary military and diplomatic experience framed within the system of canon law that emerged in the twelfth and thirteenth centuries rather than Biblical teachings and the principles of theology, became applicable to society through the vehicle of the law. Lawyers, specifically canon or ecclesiastical lawyers, then, became the most important figures in shaping Christian society's relationship with non-Christian societies, not theologians or philosophers. As one modern scholar has noted, the opinion of the canonists was that their "science . . . is neither pure theology nor civil knowledge, but absorbs both of them."[2] It was the canon lawyers who would develop the means to implement the abstract theories of theologians and philosophers in the daily life of the Christian world and, subsequently, to develop theories of behavior applicable to Christian relations with non-Christian peoples. In the medieval hierarchy of knowledge, at least as the canonists saw matters, this placed canon law and its practitioners at the peak of the intellectual hierarchy. The fact that canon lawyers and other legally trained individuals formed an important element of the papal curia, a more important element than that provided by theologians or philosophers, reinforced the canonists' opinion of their own importance.[3]

Discussions of the relationship between Christian and non-Christian societies first appeared in canon law during the twelfth and thirteenth centuries in connection with the Crusades. The canonists did not deal with Crusades in and of themselves, however, but rather in terms of the just war and in terms of the rights and privileges of pilgrims. There was no section of canon law explicitly devoted to the Crusades and there is no known canonistic commentary on the Crusades.[4] As James Brundage phrased it: "the crusader was first and foremost a pilgrim, although a pilgrim of a special type, inasmuch as he was pledged to fight a holy war in the course of achieving his pilgrimage goal."[5]

Not until the middle of the thirteenth century did the lawyers attempt to develop a broader base for a theory of Christian relations with non-Christians. This work began with Pope Innocent IV (1243–1254), a noted canonist, who wrote a commentary on a decretal, that is, a papal judicial decision, of his predecessor, Innocent III (1198–1216). The original papal letter, *Quod super his* (X.3.34.8), dealt with the problems that arose when a man who had taken a vow to go on a Crusade found himself unable to fulfill that vow. While Innocent III had simply discussed ways in which such an individual could compound for his vow, Innocent IV took the opportunity to discuss the justice of the crusade, that is, by what right Christians attacked those Muslims who now held the Holy Land.[6] Innocent IV took the position that because the Muslims had taken the Holy Land from Christians in an unjust war, it was legitimate for Christians to wage war in order to regain control of that territory. It was, in effect, a just war of recuperation.[7] At the same time, he declared that other lands that the Muslims occupied, lands that they had not unjustly seized from Christians, were safe from Christian attack because "lands and jurisdiction can be held licitly, without sin, by infidels and not only by the faithful because these exist for all rational creatures."[8] All men have the right also to govern themselves as they see fit as a consequence of the natural order, that is, all men, regardless of their spiritual state, possess what the lawyers termed *dominium*.

If Innocent IV had ended his discussion with this defense of the natural right of all men, believer and nonbeliever alike, to own property and to establish governments, he would not have had a role to play in the development of international law and relations. He went on to further explain, however, that although all men possessed the right to own property and to establish governments, this right was not absolute. In particular, the fact that *dominium* was legitimate did not mean that those who possessed it were exempt from judgment by a higher authority, specifically the pope. Innocent IV saw the world in terms of order, not anarchy, and he saw the pope as responsible for the salvation of all human beings, not just those who belonged to the Church.[9] As a consequence, he argued that the pope, acting as God's agent in certain circumstances, had the right and the obligation to judge all people according to the law to which they were subject. Only in this way could he fulfill his responsibility before God for the spiritual welfare of all mankind. When necessary, he could judge Christians by Christian law, Jews by Jewish law and infidels by natural law. The pope would act thus only if it was clear that the civil leaders of these societies had failed to punish violators of the law proper to their society. In this way, Innocent IV was able to assert both the autonomy of non-Christian societies and the pope's role as judge of all peoples everywhere. For example, infidel societies whose members did not unjustly seize the lands of Christians or otherwise violate the natural law, the law known to all, were secure from invasion by Christian armies.

In the commentary on Innocent III's decretal, Innocent IV did not spell out in great detail the violations of natural law that would authorize the pope to order the invasion and conquest of an infidel society, although he did suggest that sexual perversion or the worship of idols would provide such justification. He focused instead on how the responsibility of the pope for the spiritual well-being of all mankind might necessitate a war. Because eternal salvation was the most important goal that any human being could achieve, any ruler who prevented the entrance of Christian missionaries into his lands was interfering with this possibility and so could be forced to allow the entry and free movement of missionaries within his territories. Innocent IV was careful to point out that this did not entail the forced conversion of infidels. Conversion and baptism required the free and voluntary consent of the individual. The pope was arguing only that since "all men are made for praising God . . . if [their rulers] forbid preachers to preach, they sin and so ought to be punished."[10]

The responsibility for dealing with infidel rulers was the pope's alone. Christian rulers could not attack infidel societies simply because they determined that the infidels were blocking the entry of missionaries. Innocent IV was quite emphatic that it was the pope's responsibility to make this determination, not the responsibility of anyone else. In effect, secular rulers, the "secular arm," as it was called, could act against infidel rulers only under papal direction, the arm acting at the behest of the head of Christian society.[11]

Innocent IV based his conception of Christian-infidel relations on the definition of the pope as the vicar of Christ in all matters on earth.[12] This meant he had responsibility not only for Christians but for non-Christians as well. Jewish-Christian relations in the Christian kingdoms of Europe provided a limited model for relations between the Church and infidels and the role Christian rulers should take. In his commentary on *Quod super his*, Innocent IV argued, for example, that Jews could be forced to attend Christian sermons and that the Talmud could be burned because it contained errors that Jewish leaders had not corrected. Obviously, this would require the use of at least some physical force on the part of a Christian ruler. Such rulers, however, could engage in these activities only under papal license.[13] Furthermore, although Jews could be required to attend sermons and to surrender for burning books deemed destructive of the authentic Jewish tradition as the pope defined that tradition, they could not be forced to accept baptism. Here the pope was distinguishing clearly between the kinds of behavior in which non-Christians engaged that the pope could regulate, by force if necessary, and baptism, an act that required voluntary acceptance. The pope's responsibility for the salvation of infidels was restricted to insuring that their rulers placed no obstacles in the way of preaching the Gospel. Once the freedom to preach existed, the papal role ended and responsibility for the salvation of these souls was theirs individually.

All these activities were under the supervision of the pope as the *iudex omnium*, the judge of all men, in a very specific yet far-reaching way. The secular rulers of Christian Europe were in turn papal agents, the secular arm of the body of the Church, acting under his licence in various matters.[14] The result was a hierarchic conception of the world, a structure that embraced all mankind within three legal traditions, the law of the Old Testament, that of the New Testament, and natural law. The structure provided a theoretical justification for some kind of Christian domination of the world, but only because of the pope's responsibility for preaching the Gospel to all people. In theory, at least, Innocent IV's conception of world order also provided restraints upon Christian rulers who might wish to add to their domains by conquering their infidel neighbors on religious pretexts. Secular rulers, acting on their own, could not legitimately declare war on non-Christians simply because they were not members of the Church. Because a spiritual goal was involved, the preaching of the Gospel in infidel lands, the waging of such a war required papal authorization.

At this point it is worth noting one of the important differences between Christian-Jewish relations and Christian relations with all other non-Christian societies. Innocent IV accepted traditional Jewish law as the proper law for the Jewish people, thus placing the pope in the position of enforcing Jewish law when the leaders of the Jewish community failed to do so. In the case of infidels, however, as in the case of Muslims living under Christian domination, Innocent IV did not appear to recognize the legitimacy of their laws. That is, the pope specifically mentioned the validity of Jewish law, presumably that found in the Pentateuch, but he did not mention the validity of Islamic law based on the Qur'an for subject Muslim populations, nor did he indicate that the legal systems of infidel societies were in themselves valid. For those not subject to Christian or Jewish law, natural law, presumably known to every rational human being, was the only valid law. What this meant, of course, was that when the pope was evaluating the actions of an infidel who was acting in accord with his own legal tradition, he had to evaluate the actions in question not according to the laws of the individual's society but according to natural law as the pope defined it. To act in accordance with one's own legal tradition was not a valid defense if that legal tradition itself was constructed on principles other than those of the natural law. Furthermore, there appears to be no presumption in Innocent IV's thought that the laws of infidel societies would be in accordance with natural law. Under these conditions, even the infidels' possession of *dominium*, the natural right of all men, was subject to papal oversight.

Innocent IV's arguments supporting the right of all men, even non-Christians, to possess property and to govern themselves free of Christian interference was not unopposed. His student, Henry of Segusio (d. 1270), better known as Hostiensis because of his appointment as Cardinal of Ostia, rejected these arguments, a rather surprising stance considering the fact that Hostiensis's works are filled with references to the teaching of "*noster dominus*," that is, to Innocent IV. In his own commentary on the letter of Innocent III, Hostiensis rejected the notion that all men had a natural right to property and power. He argued that the coming of Christ meant the end of the natural right of nonbelievers to possess these. Instead, all legitimate *dominium* was in the hands of Christians.

> It seems to me that with the coming of Christ every office and all governmental authority and all lordship and jurisdiction was taken from every infidel lawfully and with just cause and granted to the faithful through Him who has the supreme power and who cannot err.[15]

In Hostiensis's opinion, the lands of infidels would not be secure from invasion by Christians unless their rulers were willing to recognize the suzerainty of Christians. At the same time, Hostiensis, like his master, would not allow Christian secular rulers to determine the situation regarding infidels. That remained always in the hands of the pope.[16]

The opinions of Innocent IV and Hostiensis became the basis for all canonistic discussion of the rights of infidels and of the nature of Christian-infidel relations for the next several centuries. While one might conclude that the opinion of Hostiensis regarding the lack of *dominium* in non-Christian societies would have been the more attractive position for the papacy to accept, it was, in fact, ultimately unacceptable. The major intellectual obstacle to accepting the Hostiensian view of Christian-infidel relations was that those who would rest *dominium* on the state of grace would be guilty of the heresy of Donatism. The Donatists, against whom Augustine of Hippo (354–430) had written, asserted that only priests in the state of grace could exercise sacramental authority. Sacramental actions of sinful priests had no effect. By the thirteenth century, an English canonist had extended this argument to the civil order, asserting that only rulers in the state of grace could legitimately exercise jurisdiction.[17] It was this position, tainted with heresy, that Hostiensis had espoused.[18] From the fifteenth century onward, critics of the Hostiensian position on *dominium* invariably linked his argument with similar arguments of John Wyclif (ca. 1330–1384) and John Huss (ca. 1372–1415), both of whom the Church condemned as heretics.[19]

The subsequent debate among canon lawyers about the nature of Christian-infidel relations took place between those holding the Innocentian and the Hostiensian positions. Many of the later participants in this debate no doubt acquired their knowledge of these positions by way of the extensive commentary on the *Decretales* that Joannes Andreae (1270–1348) compiled. This commentary, encyclopedic in nature, provided the reader with the widest possible number of opinions on any topic. In the case of the commentary on *Quod super his*, for example, Joannes Andreae included virtually all Innocent IV's commentary and then presented, again virtually in its entirety, Hostiensis's position. The result was that anyone interested in this issue could obtain the full range of opinions simply by reading this one commentary.[20]

The discussion of the right of infidels to *dominium* that Innocent IV began was not simply a matter of theoretical interest. It was linked to the pope's own effort to negotiate with the Mongol khan who had conquered Central Asia and Russia and who appeared ready to absorb western Europe into their empire.[21] When, in 1245, Innocent IV dispatched the Franciscan friar John of Plano Carpini (c. 1180–1252) with two letters for the Khan, he was hoping to establish permanent relations with the rulers of Central Asia. The hope of establishing peace across Eurasia and the desire to find allies in the continuing wars with the Muslims encouraged other missionaries to go to China, a movement that lasted into the mid-fourteenth century and even beyond.[22] The collapse of the Mongol Empire during the fourteenth century, however, made travel across Asia virtually impossible and ended the contacts between the papacy and Asia. While canon lawyers and papal officials continued to cite Innocent IV and Hostiensis on the issue of infidel *dominium* during the fourteenth and fifteenth centuries, there were few opportunities to apply these concepts in concrete situations.[23] Furthermore, the lawyers continued to deal with the issue of infidels and their right to property and governance entirely within the terms that their two mid-thirteenth-century predecessors had created. They did not extend the analysis of Christian relations with infidels beyond the limits that Innocent IV and Hostiensis had reached.

The full significance of Innocent IV's commentary on *Quod super his* was not apparent until the sixteenth century, when the discovery of the Americas revived the question of relations between Christian and non-Christian societies on a much larger scale than ever before. It was at this point that Spanish intellectuals began to draw upon the canonistic tradition in order to develop a theory of peaceful relations between the ruler of Castile and the infidel inhabitants of the New World.[24]

One might ask, at this point, why it was only Castilians, or intellectuals in the service of Castile, who sought to develop a theory of international relations (to use an anachronistic term) and why such a theory was developed only with regard to the inhabitants of the Americas. One reason for

Castilian emphasis on the legality of the acquisition of the Americas in the sixteenth century was that Iberian expansion in the Atlantic and along the west coast of Africa during the fourteenth and fifteenth centuries had always proceeded with papal approbation. A long line of papal bulls addressed to the rulers of Portugal and Castile had marked this gradual Iberian expansion. Such bulls authorized the acquisition of lands not occupied by Christians or not already subject to Christian rulers and defined the areas within which the Portuguese and the Castilians had responsibility for the conversion of infidels. In return for bearing the costs of the work of conversion, the Pope granted the rulers of Castile and Portugal a monopoly of trade with the regions that their agents discovered and settled. Alexander VI's *Inter caetera*, the bull that divided responsibility for the conversion of the inhabitants of the newly discovered lands between the Castilians and the Portuguese, was part of a line of similar papal letters stretching back to the early fifteenth century and was modeled on those earlier letters.[25] Once Ferdinand, Isabella, and their advisers realized that the lands that Columbus had discovered were not the lands that he had anticipated reaching, they requested Alexander VI to issue yet another bull that would provide a legal determination about which European countries had responsibility for the New World and its people.[26]

Another reason for the Spanish interest in the legitimacy of the conquest of the Americas was that as Spanish adventurers were revealing the New World to the Old World, providing Europeans with a legal and moral problem of enormous proportions, the universities of Spain were flourishing, especially in the areas of scholastic philosophy and theology.[27] In addition to philosophy and theology, legal thought was also important, because many Spanish university students planned to make their careers in the royal bureaucracy, where legal training was useful, even necessary, for advancement.[28] The discovery of the New World and the problems that it created fitted neatly into the medieval scholastic framework within which Spanish intellectual life operated. Church-state relations and Christian relations with non-Christians, examined on the basis of medieval legal, theological and philosophical thought, were raised in a new context.

At the core of the sixteenth-century debate about the legitimacy of the conquest of the New World was the legal tradition that had begun with Innocent IV and Hostiensis. Even the famous discussion of the right of Spain to take control of the Americas, associated with theologians such as Francis Vitoria (c. 1485–1546) and missionaries such as Bartolomé de Las Casas (1574–1566), used the language of law to a great extent.[29] In the *De*

Indis et de iure belli relectiones, for example, one of the earliest discussions of Castilian claims to the New World, Vitoria discussed possession of the New World in terms of "the irrelevant and illegitimate titles which may be offered, and then pass to the legitimate titles by which the barbarians could have been subjected to Christian rule."[30]

An incentive for the specifically Castilian debate about the legitimacy of the conquest of the Americas was that the problem of taking possession of the lands of infidels only arose in connection with some of the societies that Europeans encountered. Generally speaking, Europeans only claimed the right to acquire those territories that were vacant or were occupied by people who lived at a primitive level. The debate about the right to acquire infidel societies did not include consideration of more developed societies such as China and Japan. The chief interest of Europeans in these societies was trade, not their conquest and subordination. Christian Europeans had long traded with Muslim societies, and there was no general ecclesiastical prohibition against trading with infidels.[31] Consequently, there was no reason to attempt the conquest of those societies, an activity, even if it could have succeeded, which would have been counterproductive.

When Columbus sailed on his first voyage of discovery, he was primarily interested in initiating trade with the Great Khan and developing a sea route that would provide access to the spice trade.[32] What he found was a new, or at least an unexpected and previously unknown, land that stood between him and the land of the Khan. This was a land inhabited by people who had not developed trade, government, and the other elements of civil society. Rather than being the social equals of Europeans, the inhabitants of the Caribbean islands appeared to be living at the same level as the peoples of West Africa, and therefore Ferdinand and Isabella sought the same kind of papal authorization for their domination of the Americas as previous popes had granted to earlier Castilian and Portuguese monarchs who sought control of the Atlantic islands and the western coast of Africa. Columbus and his Castilian masters required papal approval for taking possession of the newly discovered lands, something that Alexander VI provided in his bull *Inter caetera* of 1493. The publication of this bull and several related ones served as a transition between the medieval and the sixteenth-century experience with infidel societies.

By perceiving the inhabitants of the Caribbean islands in the same terms as they had perceived, for example, the Canary Islanders, the advisers of Ferdinand and Isabella shaped the way in which Columbus and those who followed him dealt with the inhabitants of the Americas. Had Columbus encountered societies at the level of the Aztec and Inca empires, and if disease had not taken so great a toll of the Indians, it might have been possible to work out a different kind of relationship in the Caribbean islands between Castilians and Indians. The Spanish might have been able to take over functioning empires with effective governments or begun trading with them.

As a result, the framework for dealing with non-Christian societies with whom Christians were at peace, a framework based upon trade relations, did not apply to the inhabitants of the New World. How, then, were they to be approached? If European relations with the people of the New World were only to be through the work of pirates or adventurers seeking to acquire American treasure, it might not have been necessary to develop a theory of international relations. In reality, however, the government of Castile was directly involved in the work of conquest and governance, so that a formal theory justifying and legitimizing its role in the New World was essential. Fifteenth- and sixteenth-century governments were accustomed to justifying their activities in legal terms, requiring the Spanish conquest of the Americas to have a formal theoretical base. It was the search for a theoretical base upon which to justify the actions of the Castilians in the new World, that caused numerous Spanish writers, bureaucrats, and royal officials such as Solórzano, as well as professors of law, theology, and philosophy such as Vitoria, to write their defenses of the conquest.

The legal framework of the debate about the conquest of the New World appeared clearly in the full title of Solórzano's work and in the structure of the first volume. It is entitled *De Indiarum Jure sive de justa Indiarum occidentalium inquisitione, acquisitione, & retentione*, that is, *A Treatise on the Justice of the Spanish Conquest of the West Indies, that is, specifically concerning , the legitimacy of the Spanish Discovery, Conquest, and Continued Possession of the West Indies*. In turn, the volume consisted of three sections, labeled books, of unequal length. The first section, approximately 30 percent of the text, provided an *inquisitio*, that is, a survey of the New World, where it was, who dwelled there, and how the Spanish came to find it. The second and by far the longest section, the *acquisitio*, approximately 56 percent of the text, dealt with the legal and moral bases for the Spanish conquest of the New World. The final section, concerning the *retentio*, 14 percent of the text, dealt with why the Spanish have the right to retain possession of the New World.

In terms of the theme of the present work, the application of medieval theories of order to the new world situation that was emerging in the sixteenth and seventeenth centuries, the most important section of the *De Indiarum Jure* was the second book, in which Solórzano discussed the basis upon which the Spanish conquest of the Indies proceeded. In this section, more than in either of the others, he relied upon the medieval experience and upon arguments drawn from that experience to defend the Spanish possession of the Americas.

The opening chapter of the second book of *De Indiarum Jure* offered a broad outline of the debate about the legitimacy of the conquest as it had proceeded thus far and the rationale for Solórzano's tome. The honor and majesty of the Spanish monarchs had been assailed, and it was the responsibility of their subjects to defend them against ignorant critics.[33] Solórzano stressed his own place within the long line of writers who had already come to the defense of the Spanish monarchs. In effect, this chapter provided a roster of the main participants in the debate about the conquest that had been taking place since shortly after Columbus's first voyage.

Solórzano then went on to discuss his method and the approach that he planned to take in the discussion of the legitimacy of the Spanish conquest of the Americas. He pointed out that the nature of the material and the way in which he planned to use it might suggest to some critics that he was more like a historian or geographer than a lawyer. Nevertheless, he structured the book as he did, drawing upon a wide variety of sources, because his goal required the use of more than purely legal materials.[34] Furthermore, Solórzano was, after all, more than a legal technician or paper-shuffling bureaucrat. Like many of those who served Renaissance and early-modern princes, he saw himself as a humanist or as a scholar-bureaucrat. As a result, he could confidently cite the works of ancient Latin and Greek writers, men who long ago had themselves described the importance of drawing on every kind of learning in the search for practical wisdom. Solórzano's knowledge of these ancient writers was not necessarily firsthand. In the course of his studies, he would have read a number of works containing extracts from important ancient writers. The term for such an anthology was *florilegium*, a "little bunch of flowers," from which the reader could extract wisdom, wit, and learning; also, a favorite academic metaphor compared the wise man who seeks wisdom through wide-ranging reading to the bee who draws from a wide array of flowers in order to produce his honey.[35]

The garden whose intellectual flowers Solórzano plucked in order to complete his task was one whose flora consisted of the "many complicated arguments and opinions and legal positions" that had grown up in the course of centuries. In the past, other scholars, recognizing the complexities of the problems created by the discovery of the Americas, had avoided dealing with them or had dealt with them inadequately.[36] Solórzano was going to undertake the task that some had shirked and do it better than those who had already attempted it. Like a gardener faced with a tangled, overgrown flower bed, he would prune, clear, and weed so that the flowers would once again feed those who came to them for sustenance. The honor and reputation of the Spanish monarchs required no less.

Having thus defined the task he was undertaking, Solórzano then went on to survey the basic materials with which scholars had defended the Spanish conquest of the New World, identifying, so to speak, the flowers from which he would draw as he developed his work. The basic works upon which Solórzano drew were "the well known treatises of Hostiensis, Innocent [IV] . . . and others on the decretal *Quod super his* . . . where they treat in general of the *dominium* of things that the infidels possess and whether and under what circumstances such *dominium* can be taken from them." Solórzano also pointed out that the philosophers who were the contemporaries of these canonists had also dealt with these issues. Thomas Aquinas (c. 1225–1274), for example, discussed this issue in both his *Summa Theologica* and in the *De Regimine Principum*.[37] Finally, Solórzano cited a number of more recent scholars who wrote on these issues in the tradition that the thirteenth-century writers had established. These included Diego de Covarrubias (1512–1577), Luis de Molina (1535–1600), and other well-known Spanish Thomists.[38]

Having presented the broad philosophical and legal background of the debate about the rights of infidels, Solórzano then moved to the literature that dealt specifically with the problems arising from the Spanish conquest of the New World. He began with the work of Juan López de Palacios Rubios (1450–1524), whose *De las Islas del Mar Oceano* published about 1512, provided an early discussion of the Spanish claims to the Americas.[39] Solórzano observed at this point that although he knew of this book, he had never actually read it and had not been able to acquire a copy. Palacios Rubios was "an ardent regalist," noted not only for his defense of the conquest of the New World under Ferdinand and Isabella, but also for his defense of Ferdinand's conquest of Navarre in 1512.

Furthermore, although Solórzano did not mention it at this point, Palacios Rubios was also the author of the *Requerimiento*, a formal legal statement issued in 1512 that Spanish officials read to any Indians whom they encountered before attacking them. While from a modern perspective the *Requerimiento* appears to have been a "useless legalism," as one scholar has described it, the use of such formal legal rituals in fact was essential to the Spanish effort in the Americas.[40] The Spanish used this statement to explain to the inhabitants of the Americas why they were there and what they intended to do. The Indians, who in all probability never heard or understood the words of the document, were then expected to allow the Spanish peaceful entrance to their lands and to accept Spanish overlordship.[41] The refusal of the Indians to admit the Spanish would then justify the use of force against them. In effect, the *Requerimiento* enabled the Spanish to occupy the Americas by employing a legal ritual that allowed them to adhere to the letter of Innocent IV's opinion on infidel *dominium* while missing its spirit.

The second writer to whom Solórzano brought the attention of his readers was Bartolomé de Las Casas (1474–1566), the associate of the Columbus family and former colonist in the New World. He had initially used forced Indian labor, but then underwent a religious conversion, became a Dominican friar, and ended up as the most vociferous defender of the Indians.[42] In particular, Solórzano stressed Las Casas's efforts to convince Ferdinand of Aragon and, after his death, his grandson, Charles V, to correct the injustices taking place in the conquest of the Americas.

Las Casas also devoted much of his energy to combating the views of Juan Ginés de Sepúlveda (1490–1573), the leading proponent of the view that the Indians were natural slaves according to Aristotle's definition of natural slavery.[43] This led to their famous debate before a commission set up by Charles V to evaluate the arguments about the legitimacy of the conquest. Solórzano said that he himself did not possess a copy of Sepúlveda's book, because Philip II had banned its circulation.[44] The stated reason for this censorship, curious in that the author provided a strong defense of the conquest, was that the book had not been printed at the royal press. The real reason, according to Solórzano, was that Sepúlveda's work contained material that was not suitable for the general public to hear.[45]

The climax of the dispute between Las Casas and Sepúlveda was the debate held at Valladolid before a royal committee in 1550. In Solórzano's treatment of it, the emphasis was on the active involvement of the royal court in the general debate about the conquest of the New World. Although he did not mention the fact at this point, Solórzano and his readers were no doubt aware that Las Casas had participated in the momentous events that had occurred in the two decades following 1492, so that the debate at Valladolid presented a participant in the earliest days of the age of discovery now criticizing the conquest that followed before the representatives of the successor of the monarch who had authorized the first voyage of discovery in 1492.[46]

Even though the debate at Valladolid was inconclusive and even though the conquest of the Americas continued, the debate about the legitimacy of the conquest did not end. A number of other writers, often priests who had participated in the efforts to convert the Indians, continued to write criticisms of the way in which the Spanish were treating them. These writings reinforced Las Casas's views, and they also contributed to Solórzano's understanding of the situation in the Americas.

Furthermore, Solórzano noted that discussion of the conquest of the Americas was not restricted to angry friars bitter over the exactions of royal officials and over the mistreatment of the Indians. Scholarly tracts also took up the charge that the Spanish conquest of the Americas might be illegal. Lawyers, theologians, philosophers, and even royal officials such as Solórzano himself wrote tracts that examined the conquest of the Americas, often employing the basic lines of argument that Innocent IV and Hostiensis first set down. Perhaps the most famous of these writers was Francis Vitoria, whose classroom lectures on the legitimacy of the conquest, first given in 1532, were eventually published after his death in 1546 through the efforts of his former students.[47]

Solórzano also recognized that the debate about the legitimacy of the conquest was not simply an issue involving the Spanish and the inhabitants of the Americas. It was also an issue that involved the power of the papacy. He cited, to give but two examples, a treatise on papal and episcopal jurisdiction by Francisco à Vargas (d. 1577) and a treatise by Cardinal Bellarmine (1542–1621) on papal authority.[48] These and similar citations emphasized that the debate about the right of the Spanish to conquer the Americas was intimately linked to the debate about the papacy that was central to the Protestant reformers' attack on the Catholic Church.

Solórzano then went on to mention the names of a number of other writers upon whom he would drawn in this section of the treatise because they possessed special expertise on the debate about the legitimacy of the conquest. These included historians like the Mexican-born Dominican Agustín Dávila Padilla (1562–1604) who, in 1596, published a history of Dominican missionary efforts in Mexico, missionaries such as Joseph Acosta (ca. 1593–1600), whose work on the nature of missionary activity was one of the earliest works on ethnography, and royal officials who had

served in the Americas, such as Juan Matienzo (16th century).[49] In addition, Solórzano cited in traditional fashion the authors of legal treatises,
such as Marquardus de Susannis (d. 1578).[50] In effect, this section of *De
Indiarum Jure* provided an index to the literature of the debate on the
legitimacy of the conquest of the New World as that debate had taken shape
in the Spanish intellectual world.

What especially prompted Solórzano to write when he did, however,
was not the existence of a large body of Spanish material on the debate
about the legitimacy of the conquest of the New World. What did inspire
him, he said, was that "in recent years a certain anonymous book has been
published which treated at length the question of the legitimacy of the
conquest of the Indies, the title of which book being *Mare liberum*," published in 1609. Solórzano added that he himself had not actually read the
book, because the Inquisition had banned it. His knowledge of its contents
came from "a learned and pious Spaniard who read it before the ban," and
who had told him of it. On that basis he concluded that "the book reeks of
the hand and talent of an heretical author who raves against our kings and,
more gravely, against the Roman Church."[51] The book that inspired Solórzano to write was none other than the first of Hugo Grotius's treatises on
international law to appear in print, although Grotius's authorship was not
definitively demonstrated until 1868.

Grotius composed the *Mare liberum* as part of an effort to deny the
legitimacy, on the basis of Alexander VI's bulls, of Castilian and Portuguese
possession of the newly discovered lands. Citing the same writers as Solórzano, Vitoria and Aquinas in particular, Grotius argued that the inhabitants
of the newly discovered lands had a perfect right to their lands and government, a right not taken from them by their status as infidels.[52] Further on,
Grotius argued that any claim to domination of the New World based on
papal grant was invalid because the pope "has no authority over infidel
nations, for they do not belong to the Church."[53] Consequently, Castilian
and Portuguese claims to possession of the New World and to a monopoly
of trade with these lands was insupportable in law. As Solórzano pointed
out, a Portuguese canon lawyer, Seraphinus de Freitas (d. 1622) had
already answered the *Mare liberum* in a treatise with the combative title *De
Iusto Imperio Lusitanorum Asiatico*, that is, *On the Just Asiatic Empire of the
Portuguese*. Another Portuguese scholar had also entered the fray, but less
successfully than Freitas had done.[54] Solórzano was inserting himself into a
new stage of the debate about the conquest of the New World. Previously
the discussion had been within the framework of Catholic thought. Now,

for the first time, there was emerging a theory of international law and relations that did not accept some of the theoretical premises upon which Spanish possession of the Americas had rested for over a century, above all the idea that the pope was responsible for the salvation of all people and that on this basis he could deprive infidels of at least the exercise of their *dominium*. As a result, Solórzano's treatment of the debate about the conquest of the Americas would have to consider not only the traditional lines of argument but the newer lines of argument that Protestant writers were developing as well.

The overall impression that this opening segment of the discussion of the legitimacy of the *acquisitio* of the New World offers is that the Spanish in particular and the Catholic world generally were profoundly aware of the legal and moral problems arising from the conquest of the Americas. This awareness, however, was not simply created by missionary polemics, nor simply a humanitarian response to vivid descriptions of the devastation that the conquistadores caused. For a man such as Solórzano, an official of the royal government as well as a humanistically trained scholar, the debate about the conquest was far more than a debate about the damage done to the Indians by the invaders. Above all, it was a debate about the right order of the world. In the first place, it was a debate about the nature of the Christian Church and the relationship between the Church and Christian secular rulers. In the second place, it was a debate about the universal mission of the Christian Church and how that mission was best implemented. In the third place, it was a debate about the nature of relations between Christian and non-Christian societies. In the final analysis, Solórzano's *De Indiarum Jure* was an attempt to define the role of Spain and its overseas possessions within the framework of a Catholic world order.

Having explained the importance of the debate about the conquest of the Americas, having sketched the broad outlines of the debate as it had developed in the sixteenth and early seventeenth centuries, and having noted that Protestants were now joining the debate, Solórzano then devoted the twenty-four remaining chapters of his book to the ten titles by which the Spanish might claim legitimate possession of the New World. The word "title" as employed here has, of course, a double meaning. On the one hand, it simply meant headings under which arguments were arranged and was so used in philosophical and legal texts. On the other hand, during the Middle Ages the term *titulus* also came to mean legal possession of something, as in holding title to a piece of property.[55] When Solórzano, a lawyer by training, used the term *titulus* or title as he marshaled his arguments, he could not have been unaware of the double meaning of the term. As a result, the ten titles presented in this book were not simply the organizational structure of a debate, they represented ten legal bases that might serve, and indeed had often been employed in scholarly debates, as legal justifications for the Spanish conquest and occupation of the New World.

The use of the term *titulus* in the debate about the justice of the Spanish conquest of the Americas, as we have seen, went back at least to the mid-sixteenth century, when Francis Vitoria had organized his discussion of the conquest, his *De Indis*, in terms of seven titles that he defined as illegitimate and seven or eight that he defined as legitimate bases for the Spanish possession of the New World.[56] By doing so, Vitoria was linking the contemporary debate about the conquest of the Americas to the four-centuries-old discussion of the rights of infidels found in the canon-law tradition. At the same time, Vitoria had also warned against believing that these issues could be resolved by lawyers using their professional skills alone:

> I say that it is not the province of lawyers, or not of lawyers alone, to pass sentence in this question. Since these barbarians we speak of are not subjects [of the Spanish Crown] by human law (*iure humano*), as I shall show in a moment, their affairs cannot be judged by human statutes (*leges humanae*), but only by divine ones, in which jurists are not sufficiently versed to form an opinion on their own. . . . Yet since this is a case of conscience it is the business of the priests, that is to say of the Church, to pass sentence upon it.[57]

As a consequence, discussion of the legitimacy of the conquest, of the status of the Indians, and of *dominium*, questions that arose with increasing frequency during the sixteenth century in Spanish intellectual and bureaucratic circles, took place within a framework that was by modern standards highly moralistic, even idealistic, yet also legalistic as well.[58] While Vitoria did not originate the terms of the discussion, he did shape the way in which Spanish writers were to deal with it.[59] For Vitoria, following as he did in the intellectual footsteps of Pope Innocent IV, the foundation of any correct policy toward the New World would have to be morally justifiable if the Spanish were to claim legitimate domination of the Americas. Any title asserted to justify the conquest of the New World would have to meet both a moral standard as defined in philosophical and theological terms, and a legal standard. Vitoria added that such a discussion would not be necessary if the situation in the Americas was not already a matter of dispute. As matters presently stood, some observers judged the Spanish conquest as a clearly just act, while other, equally qualified, observers judged it as being unjust.

> At first sight, it is true, we may readily suppose that, since the affair is in the hands of men both learned and good, everything has been conducted with rectitude and justice. But when we hear subsequently of bloody massacres and of innocent individuals pillaged of their possessions and dominions, there are grounds for doubting the justice of what has been done.[60]

Having determined that the Spanish conquest of the Americas was not so obviously just as to be exempt from any further discussion, Vitoria then broke the issues involved into two categories. The first category contained seven titles to possession of the Americas that various defenders of the conquest had offered, titles that Vitoria determined were unjust:

> [2.1] . . . that our most serene Emperor might be master of the whole world;
> [2.2] . . . that the just possession of these countries is on behalf of the supreme pontiff;
> [2.3] . . . that possession of these countries is by right of discovery;
> [2.4] . . . that they refuse to accept the faith of Christ, although they have been told about it and insistently pressed to accept it;
> [2.5] . . . the sins of the barbarians;
> [2.6] . . . by the voluntary choice of the barbarians;
> [2.7] . . . by special gift from God.[61]

The second list contained seven arguments in support of the Spanish conquest that Vitoria considered legitimate and one that was of dubious legitimacy but not clearly illegitimate. These were:

> [3.1] . . . natural partnership and communication;
> [3.2] . . . for the spreading of the Christian religion;
> [3.3] . . . the protection of converts;
> [3.4] . . . papal constitution of a Christian prince;
> [3.5] . . . in defence of the innocent against tyranny;
> [3.6] . . . by true and voluntary election;
> [3.7] . . . for the sake of allies and friends;
> [3.8] [An eighth possible title, the mental incapacity of the barbarians].[62]

In practice, Vitoria's two lists reflect two competing principles. For the most part, the illegitimate titles to the New World assume that European Christian rulers can act unilaterally toward the Indians. That is, on the basis of European legal and religious standards, the pope or the Holy Roman emperor could take some action against an infidel society without there being any need to discuss matters with the infidels first. This is especially clear in titles 1,2,3, and 7, but is also present in title 5 as well. These titles imply that the infidels have an obligation to act as the Europeans believed they should behave, without any discussion or debate, or face punishment, making European standards the basis for determining legitimate possession of the New World. Even the one alleged title in this category that would seem to involve the infidels themselves in determining legitimate posses-sion, title 6, which would claim that the Indians themselves freely accepted Spanish overlordship, does not actually do so as simply as Vitoria presented it. He pointed out that even if some inhabitants of the New World did appear to have accepted Spanish domination, they did so not freely, but out of fear.[63] As a consequence, their apparently voluntary submission was in fact a unilateral conquest clothed with some actions that would imply that the Spanish had acquired possession of the New World through a legiti-mate transfer of power.

The legitimate titles that Vitoria presented in the *De Indis* focused on the infidels, not on the Christians. Here the emphasis was not upon the right of Christian Europeans to conquer infidels, but upon the right of all people, Christians and non-Christians alike, to control their own political destiny. In a broader sense, Vitoria stressed the rights that all people, Christian and non-Christian alike, shared. The first five legitimate titles emphasized the right of all men to act freely in their own interest, whether it be the right to travel in peace to a distant land for commercial or religious reasons, or the right to protect themselves from a wicked ruler who was preventing them from practicing their new religion, or the right to over-throw a tyrant who ruled them. Titles 6 and 7 would justify Spanish domination of at least part of the New World because the inhabitants, with full knowledge of the consequences of what they were doing, either ac-cepted Spanish overlordship or made an alliance with the Spanish in the course of seeking their own political ends. Vitoria withheld judgment on the eighth title because he questioned the motive behind arguing that the Indians, being uncivilized, required the guardianship of a more civilized people. The danger that he saw was that the Spanish would claim domina-tion over the Indians for their own good, while in reality doing so for the Spaniards' personal interest. Here, the danger to the spiritual well-being of the Spaniards was the central point. He feared, in effect, that the Spanish might go to the New World to do good and wind up doing well at the expense of the Indians, and thereby lose their souls.

When Solórzano wrote the *De Indiarum Jure*, he dealt with many of
the same arguments (titles) that Vitoria had presented, but he organized
them in a different fashion. Vitoria, the Dominican Professor of Philosophy, had organized his argument in traditional scholastic fashion, that is,
using a 'pro and con' technique, lining up the arguments on each side of the
case and then drawing a conclusion reconciling the differences to the
greatest extent possible. Solórzano, on the other hand, organized ten titles
that defenders of the conquest had argued for and set them out in hierarchical fashion. He presented the ten titles beginning with the least effective one
and ending with the most important one. Looked at dialectically, the first
nine titles were illegitimate. Only the tenth title, Spanish possession of the
Americas as the result of a papal grant, was legitimate. His list presented the
titles in this order:

1. (Ch. 2) God gave the Americas to Spain.
2. (Ch. 3) God moved the Spanish to discover and take possession
   of the New World.
3. (Ch. 6) Discovery and occupation created a title to the New
   World.
4. (Ch. 7) The barbarous nature of the inhabitants of the New
   World justified their conquest and subordination by the Spanish.
5. (Ch. 10) The Indians, being infidels, could be legitimately conquered by Christians.
6. (Ch. 12) The actions of the Indians that violated natural law
   justified their conquest by the Spanish.
7. (Ch. 16) The conquest of the Indians may have been justified in
   order to preach the Gospel in those lands.
8. (Ch. 20) The refusal of the Indians to admit missionaries could
   have justified their conquest.
9. (Ch. 21) The Holy Roman emperor had the right to award the
   lands of infidels to Christians.
10. (Ch. 22) The pope could grant the lands of infidels to Christians.

The arguments that Solórzano presented moved from those least likely
to provide a legitimate basis for the Spanish conquest and possession of the
New World, those based on direct divine intervention in the conquest of
the Americas, to the one that actually provided a basis for legitimate
Spanish title to the Americas, a papal grant. One might wonder at this point
why a seventeenth-century royal official would see the papacy as the source

of legitimate Spanish possession of the Americas. The answer to this question lies in the way in which Solórzano understood the debate about the legitimacy of the Spanish conquest of the Americas and what he wanted to achieve.

For Vitoria, the debate about the legitimacy had been, structurally, a simple one. It concerned the conflict between the right of Christians to invade and to conquer and the right of infidels to defend and to govern themselves. He was discussing these questions at the very beginning of Castilian and Portuguese expansion in the Americas, when the two Iberian nations had no competitors in the work of discovery and conquest in the new lands that were opening up to European penetration. For him the debate was a very theoretical one that relied almost entirely upon a scholastic tradition reaching back to the mid-thirteenth century. The inhabitants of the Americas did not appear in Vitoria's *Relectiones* except as presenting a problem that required analysis. They were not people, only the justification for a debate.

By the early seventeenth century, however, the debate about the rights of the infidels had become much broader. Spanish critics of the conquest such as Las Casas had introduced the Indians and their sufferings to a European audience. The Indians were now human beings, not abstractions. Furthermore, as other European rulers had become interested in exploration and conquest, they expressed doubt about the right of the pope to limit such activity to Castile and Portugal. One result was that Solórzano had to defend not only the Spanish conquest of the Americas in itself, he had also to defend the papal authority upon which the Spanish based their claims to the New World. In Catholic circles, while the existence of the papacy was, of course, not in question, the nature and extent of its jurisdiction certainly was. Catholic rulers and their advisers could call upon a long tradition of opposition to papal involvement in temporal matters to reject the Castilian and Portuguese monopolies in the Indies. On the other hand, Protestant reformers were now attacking the very existence of the papacy itself. The papacy and the clerically dominated Church structure that it headed was, in Protestant terms, a deformation of the true Christian Church that was now in the process of being reformed. A Protestant ruler could simply disregard without further ado any claims on possessing land or a monopoly of trade with the New World based on a papal grant or determination. In fact, as early as 1540, even a Catholic ruler, King Francis I of France, expressed doubts about the power of the pope to grant the newly found lands to Castile and Portugal and to exclude the rest of Christian Europe from entering them without permission.[64] Rulers of Protestant kingdoms such as England, would, of course, have no need to ask about the specifics of papal policy in this area, inasmuch as they had already rejected the papacy. Queen Elizabeth and her Stuart successors had no hesitation in authorizing English settlements in North America, which clearly violated the terms of *Inter caetera*.[65]

These contemporary battles, one an old debate stretching back at least to the Investiture Controversy in the eleventh and twelfth centuries, the other a new one associated with the Protestant Reformers, required Solórzano to defend the legitimacy of Spanish possession of the Americas not only against the claims of the Indians to legitimate possession of land and governance but against the arguments of Catholic and Protestant critics of the papacy as well. Therefore, unlike Vitoria, Solórzano had to do more than deal with the scholastic arguments about the rights of infidels. He also had to trace the development of papal power within the Church and defend its legitimacy in order to defend legitimate Spanish possession of the New World.

The nine titles to the Americas that Solórzano rejected have one important element in common — they made no reference to a papal role in determining who should possess the newly discovered lands. Put slightly differently, any one of the nine illegitimate titles, if acted upon, would open the New World to a kind of land rush. There would be no supervising authority to arrange for an orderly process of expansion and conquest, nor would there be any recognized authority to settle disputes arising from conflicting claims to the same property. These titles that Solórzano deemed illegitimate would lead to anarchy in the international order instead of stability, if any Christian ruler could claim that God had destined him to rule the New World or that the barbarous nature of the Indians justified their conquest by a more civilized people.

According to Solórzano, only the tenth title, grounding Spanish possession of the Americas on a papal grant, would provide a legitimate title to the New World. His intention was to justify continued Spanish possession of the Americas and to provide a basis for opposing any attempts by other European rulers, Catholics or Protestants, to acquire territory in the New World without papal or Spanish permission. At the same time, the tenth title, however self-serving, assumed that the European acquisition of the New World would, in theory at least, proceed in an orderly fashion and be guided by the papacy's conception of the right order of relations between Catholic and infidel societies.

By basing possession of the New World on a papal grant, Solórzano was making the continued legitimate Spanish possession of the Americas dependent upon Spanish rulers continuing to accept the papal view of the proper way to deal with the indigenous population. Potentially, the pope could coerce the Spanish into acting in accordance with papal conceptions of dealing with infidels by threatening to take back what he had granted to them and awarding it to another ruler. After all, one of the great themes of medieval political thought was the *translatio imperii*, that is, the removal of imperial authority from the Byzantine ruler by Pope Leo III in 800 and its transfer to Charlemagne and his successors in the West. Charles V's possession of the imperial title was a direct result of this *translatio*.[66] Furthermore, other popes had attempted to remove other European monarchs, with varying degrees of success. Innocent IV, for example, had successfully ordered the deposition of King Sancho II (1223–1248) of Portugal in 1245.[67] On the other hand, Pope Pius V's (1566–1572) bull ordering the deposition of Queen Elizabeth in 1570 failed for the most part to win the support even of Catholic Englishmen.[68]

From Solórzano's perspective, the papacy was not likely to remove the Americas from Spanish control, however, precisely because by insisting that the only legitimate title to the New World came from papal grant, Solórzano and his master were upholding the papacy's conception of its own power. In other words, while all Protestants and some Catholics were denying, or at least seriously undermining, papal power, Solórzano was supporting it, at least in theory. The price of this theoretical support was that the papacy would not exercise its power against the Spanish claim to legitimate possession of the Americas. For the Spanish, this emphasis upon papal grant, not discovery and conquest or direct divine grant, meant that they had to defend their continued possession of the New World in the terms of Alexander VI's bulls, that is, in terms of papal responsibility for the salvation of the infidels.

2. To Civilize the Barbarian —
The Anthropology and the History

Juan de Solórzano Pereira and his fellow Spaniards were not the only early-seventeenth-century public officials concerned with legitimizing the possession of land in the New World. At precisely the same time as Solórzano was serving in the *Audiencia* at Lima, the government of James I of England was arguing that the English had the right to settle in New England because this region was virtually uninhabited. As the Patent for the Council for New England issued in 1620 noted, "within these late Yeares there hath by God's Visitation raigned a wonderfull Plague, together with many horrible Slaughters, and Murthers, committed amoungst the Savages and bruitish People . . . to the utter Destruction, Devastacion, and Depopulacion of that whole Territorye." Clearly God had arranged this state of affairs so that the lands in question, "deserted as it were by their naturall Inhabitants, should be possessed and enjoyed by such of our Subjects and People as . . . shall by his Mercie and Favour, and by his Powerful Arme, be directed and conducted thither."[1] Thus the actions of God, not those of His Vicar in Rome, became the basis upon which English possession of at least some of the New World could rest.[2]

The argument that James I's government was making would make the occupation of the New World a simple matter, at least for some countries. For the Spanish, however, it had two serious drawbacks. In the first place, the papacy, on whose bulls Spanish possession of the Americas rested, had jurisdiction over people, not over land. The terms of *Inter caetera* required that there be people on the lands the pope assigned to the Spanish, people with souls to save. Furthermore, the Spanish desired a monopoly in the Americas. They had no interest in allowing other European nations to acquire a share of the newly found lands. If entry into the New World was limited to those who bore the pope's commission, the Spanish, as the bearers of that commission, would be secure in their monopoly. In the second place, even after the tragic loss of a large number of people after the entry of Europeans, South America still contained a large population the existence of which could not be ignored. Any argument basing European possession on the existence of empty land in the Americas clearly would not work in the Spanish-American context.

There were, however, ways to justify the conquest of the New World that would eliminate any role for the papacy. For example, Solórzano's fourth title, or justification, for Spanish possession of the Americas employed the argument that the barbarous way of life that the inhabitants of the New World followed would justify their conquest by a more civilized people. Like all of the titles that defenders of the conquest could adduce to justify Spanish control of the Americas, this argument had some obvious attractions and one important drawback. If the Indians were so uncivilized as to justify their conquest by their civilizational betters, what was to prevent every European ruler from joining in the scramble for the Americas? Thus, Solórzano had to refute this argument, and in the course of doing so he had to examine what was meant by barbarous behavior and to discuss the ways in which societies became civilized. Furthermore, he had also to consider the relationship between becoming civilized and becoming Christianized. In effect, the long-standing argument about the barbarous nature of the peoples of the New World led naturally to a discussion of anthropology and of history, specifically the history of social, political, and religious development.

Solórzano was not original in considering these historical and anthropological issues. Questions about the nature of the Indians' way of life and about the relationship between being civilized and being Christianized had arisen at the very outset of the Spanish encounter with the Americas, in 1493, to be exact, when Columbus published a letter announcing the results of his first voyage. In this letter, he described the people whom he encountered as simple, timid folk who went about naked, had no metal except some gold, and who apparently did not hold private property. These people did not even seem to have any form of government.[3] Columbus described a society of childlike individuals, where simple people lived simple lives in an environment like that of the Garden of Eden.

The people whom Columbus's letter introduced to Europe did not, however, live in an absolutely idyllic world. They were not Christians, they had as neighbors another tribe that periodically attacked them, stealing what little these simple people possessed, even engaging in cannibalism, and living a very primitive life. As a result, Columbus could justify forcing them to accept Spanish overlordship, because they would have the opportunity to accept the true faith, they would be protected from their fierce neighbors, and they would have the opportunity to develop a more sophisticated way of life.[4]

Columbus's picture of the life of those who lived on the Caribbean Islands found its way into Alexander VI's bull, *Inter caetera* (1493). The pope authorized the Spanish occupation of the New World so that the people, who presently are "going unclothed, and not eating flesh" but who "seem sufficiently disposed to embrace the Catholic faith and be trained in good morals" would be brought to the baptismal font.[5] These words suggest that the Church's position was that people who lived blameless, if simple and even primitive, lives could be baptized and become members of the Christian community. Presumably, one consequence of such incorporation into the Christian world would be a transition from the simple way of life these people had been following to the more advanced one that the Spanish led. The process of Christianizing at least some inhabitants of the New World could thus precede the process of civilizing them.

In Solórzano's own day, the Jesuits were wrestling with precisely this question in the *Reductions* they established in Paraguay, but the issue was not restricted to Spanish Catholic thinkers.[6] In the 1630s, as Solórzano was writing the second volume of the *De Indiarum Jure*, the Puritans in Massachusetts were facing the same issue, eventually concluding that the local Indians would first have to become agriculturists and town-dwellers as part of the process of becoming members of the Church.[7]

At the beginning of book 2, chapter 2 of the *De Indiarum Jure*, setting out the theme of the fourth title alleged to justify the conquest of the Americas, Solórzano dealt with the relationship between being civilized and being Christianized. As he pointed out, there were those who argued that the inhabitants of the New World were

> wild, barbarians, disorderly, and rustic, as is commonly noted, so that they scarcely seem worthy of the name human; and consequently they can and ought to be subjected to our kings and to be deprived of supreme *imperium*, jurisdiction and control of their lands and their persons, so that, finally being brought to a humane and civilized level of existence (*ad humanitatem, & civilitatem*) they might become worthy to be rendered capable of the Christian faith and religion.[8]

In a list of citations of authors who had discussed this issue, Solórzano cited Sepúlveda first, followed by the names of several other prominent writers including Vitoria, suggesting how widespread the discussion was.[9]

Solórzano began his discussion of this argument for the conquest of the New World with a discussion of the term "barbarian." He pointed out that originally the barbarian was simply one who did not speak or understand Greek. Subsequently, the term came to be applied to those who were not Greek and, later, to those who were not subject to the Roman Empire. In this sense, the barbarian was simply a stranger. St. Paul had used the term *barbarus* in this sense when he observed "if I do not know the meaning of the language, I shall be a foreigner (*barbarus*) to the speaker and the speaker a foreigner (*barbarus*) to me."[10] Thus the term barbarian originally lacked any element of moral or cultural judgment, being instead a means of distinguishing "us" from "them" linguistically.

In Solórzano's etymology, the term "barbarian" acquired a judgmental quality because of its application to the people of North Africa known as the Berbers. Their land was known as Barbaria, a word that evolved to "Berberia".[11] "More properly and more frequently, however, it customarily refers to those who are rude and ignorant or dominated by a certain natural fierceness or (moral) blindness, those who deviate from the commonly accepted rule of human existence, those who do not use right reason, and those who do not employ the laws and practices consonant with natural reason . . ." as Thomas Aquinas and others have taught.[12]

Although Solórzano does not appear to have realized it, he had accepted a significant change in the meaning and implications of the term *barbarus* when he identified the barbarian with the individual who lacked reason rather than simply the person who did not know Greek or who was not subject to Roman jurisdiction. In the ancient world, the outsider who learned Greek lost his barbarian status by that very fact.[13] He became a member of the Greek community. Likewise, the barbarian conquered by the Romans who eventually acquired Roman citizenship and manners became a Roman and was no longer a barbarian.

Tacitus (fl. 100) described the Roman technique for dealing with conquered barbarians in his biography of his father-in-law, Agricola, who served as governor of Britain (78–84). Traditionally, one of the keys to Rome's success in dealing with conquered peoples was the willingness to extend the privileges of citizenship to the most sophisticated of those peoples. While the obvious purpose was to insure loyalty to the Roman Empire, the effect of this policy was to influence the development of other peoples, causing the conquered outsiders, the barbarians, to become Romanized. As is well known, Tacitus did not approve of the results of this process of Romanization, at least in the case of the British. He identified the Romanization of the British with their loss of a sense of liberty, surrendering freedom for the fleshly delights of the town and the gymnasium.[14] At the same time, however, he recognized that non-Romans, barbarians, could become just like the Romans, whether for good or for ill.

The argument that barbarians lacked reason, however, was one that could be used to reject the classical view that the barbarians were just like Europeans and just as capable of civilized behavior as Europeans. One consequence of this line of argument was the theory that barbarians could never be just like the Europeans, that they lacked the capacity for civilized life. This could in turn lead to the conclusion that barbarians ought to be subjected permanently to European domination simply for their own good, to keep them from harming themselves and one another. In this view, the peoples of the New World were, at best, thought of like women and children, unable to function in a fully human way without the guidance and direction of men.

Equating the barbarian with nonrational creatures came from identifying the barbarian of Greek and Roman thought with the *brutus*, the wild, uncivilized, and presumably uncivilizable creature found, according to Solórzano, in the Hebrew tradition.[15] The term "brute" he derived from the Hebrew word *Babar*, which he defined as meaning "to act furiously, just as the barbarians also act in a furious manner, and as brutes customarily do, they are led by a furious impulse to those things that they seek. From this, these brutes take the name of wild beasts according to Varro (116–27 BC)." Such people "are borne by their natural impulse, and they rush about, controlled by no intercourse with other men, by no civilized standards or by any government (*imperium*)."[16]

The brute was not restricted to the Hebrew tradition, however. Solórzano pointed out that the ancient Greeks also recognized the existence of nonrational creatures who were not capable of being civilized. The fact that such wild creatures had the external appearance of men did not mean that they were men. Reason, not physical appearance, was the measure of humanity, and it is reason that distinguishes humans from animals. Socrates, after all, referred to "men without reason as apes," that is, as creatures who appeared to be men and who in some ways acted like men but who in fact lacked reason.[17]

For the Spanish intellectuals and royal officials who were dealing with the conquest and governance of the Americas, the Indians thus posed a problem of definition and classification. Were the Indians barbarians in the classical sense, who did not speak and live as the Greeks and Romans did, so to speak, or were they brutes, a lower form of life, human only in appearance? The manner in which the Spanish should deal with these people would be determined by the category of creature to which they belonged.

It was against this backdrop that Solórzano began his discussion of the classification of the Indians.

> . . . it happens that the Indians of whom we speak are to be understood as being within the category of barbarians and wild animals, since, for the greater part, as we have said, they seem to be similar to them, scarcely retaining any human (characteristics) except for the external form of men.[18]

In support of this view, he cited descriptions of the Indians and their way of life from several sources, including the writings of Amerigo Vespucci (1451–1512) and Peter Martyr (1457–1526). Vespucci had described the peoples he encountered as "wild, living according to the practices of animals, openly and everywhere joining with women, worshipping nothing, and going about naked." Relying on the reports of explorers who had been to the New World, Peter Martyr wrote that the inhabitants of Hispanola were "wild, inhabiting caves and woods, living without any exchange with any other human society, naked and without speech . . . without any law to live by, and only in appearance seeming to be rational men.[19]

The major source, however, for Solórzano's view of the Indians was the work of Joseph Acosta (c. 1539–1600). Acosta was a defender of the Indians but, at the same time, saw them and their way of life with a clear eye. In his *Natural and Moral History of the Indies*, Acosta offered the opinion that "this uncivilized kind of men" whom the early explorers saw in the Americas had "developed from barbarians and those who had run away (from organized society)." Acosta also recognized that in the Americas, specifically "in the Mexican and the Peruvian kingdom, some form of organized society and government (*respublica*) had been established." The people who had created these societies were quite different from the bulk of the American population, peoples who "had no kings, no fixed, established republic but who dwelled promiscuously in bands." Instead of "specified kings (*certos reges*)," that is, stable governmental leadership, these other peoples of the New World only possessed war chiefs (*duces*) whom they made and unmade capriciously.[20]

In determining the status of the Indians according to whether they lived in organized communities, Acosta was judging the Indians and their way of life not by religious or moral standards but by rational ones. His criterion was the standard of civilized behavior that Aristotle had meant in his famous observation that "man is by nature a political animal. And he who by nature and not by mere accident is without a state, is either a bad man or above humanity; he is like the 'Tribeless, lawless, heartless one,' whom Homer denounces — the natural outcast is forthwith a lover of war. . . ."[21] On the basis of this argument, then, the people of the New World who lived without social organization were not, presumably, moving toward the stage of stable, orderly living, life in a *respublica*, but rather had fallen away from such a stage. If, then, the inhabitants of the New World, with the exceptions of those who inhabited the Mexican and the Peruvian empires, lacked stable, orderly government, how then were the Spanish to convert them to Christianity?

To answer the question about the relation between being civilized and being Christianized, Solórzano drew on Acosta's other work, the *De Procuranda Indorum Salute*, which provided a lengthy description of the Indians who did not live in organized societies. In the Jesuit's opinion, these people were virtually impossible to deal with on a rational basis. In brief, they were deceitful, inconstant, lacking a sense of honor, and ungrateful. "And not only is their nature servile, indeed it is also in some way brutish: so that you might think that it is easier to tame wild animals than to bridle their rashness or to arouse them from their torpor." They lived not in organized, stable communities "but in rocks and caves . . . scattered about, often wandering without any fixed abode."[22]

This line of argument led to the next point that Solórzano wished to examine. Was the mission of the Spanish in the New World simply the work of converting the Indians to Christianity, or did it include converting them to a civilized way of life as well? Was it possible that the Indians could not be converted until they had undertaken a civilized, that is a stable and orderly way of life? At this point, he drew upon the *De signis Ecclesiae*, the work of Thomas Bozius (1548–1610), to demonstrate that historically the Church had engaged not only in the work of converting barbarous infidels to Christianity but to civilized forms of behavior as well. According to Solórzano, Bozius demonstrated how "barbarians, fierce and wild peoples, had been led to the culture of humanity by means of the church of Christ and the reception of his faith, in order to fulfill many prophesies that foretold that result." Bozius had written:

> Indeed, who can number all of the nations in Africa, Asia, and the East and West Indies that for the most part had nothing except the appearance of humanity: for otherwise they were entirely bestial.

This being the case, it was essential for the Spanish to enter the New World in order to clear the land that had become overgrown with weeds, briars, and noxious and sterile plant life. The image of the Spanish clearing the land was especially striking. Bozius described the Spanish as "purging the land with iron and fire," a description that fitted not only the Spanish treatment of the land but of the people as well.[23]

But the Church did not engage in this dual task of civilizing and converting the barbarous infidels alone. As Solórzano pointed out, following Bozius's line of argument, the conversion of the inhabitants of the Americas was the result of "the concern of the Holy See and the piety and generosity of the Catholic Kings."[24] The obvious question to raise at this point was, of course, whether or not the task of the missionaries really required the assistance of the secular power. Could not missionaries alone have preached the word of God to the peoples of the New World? Solórzano recognized that the tension between preaching and force, between the process of converting and the process of civilizing the infidel, was an old one. Again following Bozius, he noted that the problem had plagued the Spanish mission in the New World from the very beginning. Columbus himself had quarreled with a missionary about the character of the Indians. In the course of this argument, the Indians were described as cannibals, even to the extent of raising their own children in order to devour them.[25]

Solórzano went on to cite a number of other writers whose descriptions of the inhabitants of the New World supported the view that the Indians were primitive, nonrational and savage. One of these writers went so far as to find these people so primitive as to be the most primitive people in the entire world, more primitive even than Ethiopians.[26] Another writer provided a scale for evaluating the primitive nature of the Indian way of life. Antonio de Herrera (1541–1596) claimed that the Indians could not count above ten, and even after many years of instruction could recite only one Christian prayer, the *Ave Maria*.[27] Obviously this line of argument could have only one conclusion, namely that the inhabitants of the New World, even the Aztecs and the Incas, were either too stupid, too primitive, or too inhumanely cruel to have an unchallenged right to their lands and to self-government. People in such a primitive state were, obviously, then not suitable candidates for Christianization either. According to some missionaries, these people "were not true human beings and they did not possess the capacity to understand the Eucharist and the other mysteries of the Christian religion."[28] To drive the point home even further, Solórzano then offered a number of other illustrations of the primitive life of those who lived in the Americas, all designed to emphasize the ignorance and un-civilized behavior of these people, behavior that other writers had educed to demonstrate the justice of the Spanish conquest of the Americas.

Having brought the reader to this point, Solórzano then outlined the most famous argument against the right of the Indians to live free of European, Christian domination, the argument that "if the inhabitants of these West Indies are as stupid, savage and barbarous as appears from the above descriptions of their behavior, it would seem that the Spanish had the best possible right to conquer and subdue them." Citing Aristotle to the effect that some peoples are naturally servile, Solórzano pointed out that it might be argued that such primitive and savage people, barely human in fact, might be better off if subjected to the power of those wiser than themselves. If such people "cannot be led to the good and the right (way of life) by means of teaching and reason, they ought to be placed under a yoke as wild animals are placed under a yoke" and so coerced into behaving correctly.[29]

Although Solórzano cited numerous ancient and medieval writers in support of Aristotle's views on natural slaves, he did not mention at this point Juan Ginés de Sepúlveda, who had defended the conquest at great length on precisely these grounds. Furthermore, it is not clear exactly what the writers whom Solórzano cited at this point meant by the term "servile." While the term *servus* is often translated to mean slave, it could also mean serf, that is, an individual who is legally free but tied in some way to a particular piece of land or jurisdiction.[30] As Solórzano used the term in this discussion, it would seem that the naturally servile ought to be brought under the control of the wiser elements of society for their own good. The suggestion of this line of argument is that the Indians could be brought under Spanish domination only if the Spanish acted for the good of the Indians and not simply for their own interests. This does not suggest buying and selling or otherwise mistreating fellow human beings. It does suggest a paternal sense of responsibility for the less developed members of the human race. To support this argument, Solórzano called upon Aristotle, Plato, and Cicero to demonstrate that "as the body is subject to the soul, so the more savage are to be subjected to the more wise." The result would be the training of these savage people "in virtuous actions . . . (so that) . . . eventually they will turn into good men."[31] Furthermore, Solórzano offered the argument that only the wise could be truly free because the stupid were by nature servile and could not act rationally and sensibly. Put another way, the "barbarous men who are like brute animals . . . ought to be subject to the *imperium* of the more prudent."[32]

Those who argued that according to the natural order of things the wise had the right, even the obligation, to govern the stupid, could conclude that wars designed to bring peace and order to chaotic societies were just wars because the result of them was to assist the good and to hold the wicked in check. There were those, Solórzano pointed out, who argued that the fierce and savage nature of the Indians meant that they could never be brought to "humane and political ways of living and become accustomed to the laws of Christian discipline" unless they were brought under Spanish control.[33] This being so, God has willed the Spanish conquest of the Americas because of the great good that would accrue to the Indians from the civilizing and missionizing efforts put forth on their behalf. Solórzano cited at this point a contemporary version of what would one day be termed the "White Man's Burden" justification for the conquest of the non-European world. The present inhabitants of the New World, the beneficiaries of Spanish efforts to civilize and convert them, were better off than their ancestors, who dwelled in social and spiritual darkness. The contemporary Indians had acquired "culture and discipline" from the Spanish and so had moved beyond the level of existence of their ancestors.[34] Those who developed this line of argument pointed to the historical example of the peoples whom Alexander the Great's armies had defeated and brought under his control in the course of his conquests. They were much better off than those who had fled the Macedonian's advance. The latter continued to wallow in savagery and uncivilized ways, while the former were led to a better and happier way of life.[35] Solórzano added that Portuguese defenders of the enslavement of Africans made the same argument.

While conquest or enslavement might seem a high price for the benefits that Alexander the Great, Portuguese slavers, or Spanish *conquistadores* brought, Solórzano noted that in Roman law there was a practice that explained the situation neatly. Just as a slave was lightly boxed on the ears and lashed during the ceremony of manumission, so the sufferings of Asians, Africans, and Americans were minimal in comparison to the political and spiritual freedom they obtained as a consequence of coming under Christian domination.[36]

The ultimate example of the long-term social value of conquest was the Roman Empire. The Romans conquered and civilized the barbarian peoples of Europe, a result that pagan and Christian writers praised highly. God Himself blessed their work and Virgil sang its praises:

> Roman, remember by your strength to rule
> Earth's peoples — for your arts are to be these:
> To pacify, to impose the rule of law,
> To spare the conquered, battle down the proud.[37]

Later Christian writers, from Augustine and Aquinas to Solórzano's contemporaries in the sixteenth and seventeenth centuries, repeated this praise.

If the Romans deserved praise for the peace, order, and justice that they brought to the barbarous peoples of the world, how much more important were the blessings that the Spanish conquest would bring to the conquered? The Spanish, after all, brought not only temporal peace and order but eternal salvation as well. Simply in terms of sheer numbers, the Spanish conquest of the Americas brought more peoples to a civilized way of life than any other kingdom had ever done, indeed more than had virtually all the other kingdoms of Europe put together.[38]

One problem remained to be discussed at this juncture. While it was true that many of the inhabitants of the Americas lived at a primitive, uncivilized level, there were also others who lived in organized communities. The Aztecs and the Incas, and some other, unidentified peoples had organized kingdoms, normally a sign of being civilized. Could the argument about the naturally servile status of barbarous peoples be employed to justify the conquest of the kingdoms of Mexico and Peru? Here the argument became not the lack of government, that is, the lack of some kind of *respublica*, but the incapacity of these rulers to govern justly because by nature they were servile. In effect, as Solórzano presented the argument of those who justified the conquest of these organized societies, the barbarous status of the Aztecs and Incas became a matter of an a priori judgment. That is, "because the kings (of the Aztecs and Incas), according to the same teaching of Aristotle, possess the nature of the slave and are in need of the *dominium* and oversight (*gubernatio*) of wiser men . . . ," they should not rule others because "the *imperium* and direction (*moderatio*) of the entire earth ought not to be left to the savage and heedless."[39] The argument here concerned not the manner of life that the inhabitants of the New World followed but the question of their character and self-control. Those who would govern others must be in control of themselves, a position that pagan and Christian writers had long held.[40] Presumably, even though the Aztecs and the Incas possessed the appearance of civilized, orderly societies, their character was that of savage and irrational people who were not in full control of themselves. Only the people in full, rational control of themselves should exercise jurisdiction over others.

The arguments that Solórzano developed in this section of his work were obviously attractive to many defenders of the conquest of the Americas. The example of the Roman Empire, pagan and Christian, was no doubt appealing to Spanish officials and *conquistadors* alike, clothing as it did conquest and pillage in moral garb. He did not yield to this argument, however, and recognized that in the larger legal framework, the Spanish monopoly of the Americas could not rest on such a base, because it would allow any European Christian ruler to lay claim to land in the Americas.

Throughout this chapter, Solórzano wrestled with arguments that centered on the nature of the newly encountered peoples who were in the process of becoming subjects of the Spanish kings. As was the case throughout the *De Indiarum Jure*, Solórzano was obliged to steer a careful course, one that would allow him to reach the conclusion that only the Spanish, operating under papal licence, could legitimately occupy the Americas and subjugate the inhabitants. In this case, demonstrating the humanity of the Indians was essential, because papal jurisdiction extended only to human beings. Those who denied the humanity of the Indians were in effect denying the legitimacy of the Spanish monopoly of the New World, because if the Indians were not human, if they were some kind of subhuman or nonhuman creature, *Inter caetera* would not have authorized the Spanish conquest. Under such circumstances, any European ruler could authorize his subjects to occupy part of the New World and exploit the lands and those who dwelled there as those subjects wished.

On the other hand, Solórzano had to be able to explain how the peoples of the New World, being human, possessing reason, and therefore having *dominium*, could be brought under Spanish, and only Spanish, jurisdiction. This led him to compare the situation of the inhabitants of the Americas with that of various European peoples who had moved from a very primitive state to a fully civilized one. The argument then moved from the question of the anthropological status of the Indians to the question of the historical experience of peoples who, like the Indians, had been fierce and wild, lived in the forests and the countryside, had no rulers and no fixed abodes. Could the Indians be expected to evolve from their primitive way of life to a more civilized one? Looked at in another way, could the inhabitants of the New World be expected to develop in time, and with the assistance of European rulers, to a way of life that was equal to that of Europeans?

Having presented the arguments supporting the view that it was legitimate for the Spanish to conquer the Indians for their own civil and spiritual good because of their primitive, barbarous nature, arguments that he himself could not accept, Solórzano then moved on to consider the objections to this line of reasoning. He began the next chapter of the *De Indiarum Jure* with the assertion that there were many other learned men who denied the legitimacy of the conquest on the grounds that had been alleged in the previous chapter.

Solórzano's argument at this point was historical in nature, providing historical examples of the way in which peoples once defined as barbarous had been able to progress to the ranks of the civilized. Central to this view was the argument that the qualities characteristic of the barbarous way of life, the qualities that caused some observers to conclude that barbarousness was an innate quality that condemned the barbarian to a permanent state of subordination to the civilized, were in fact only superficial characteristics, the products of education and training. That being the case, it was possible for the barbarians to lose those characteristics as they were introduced to the ways of civilized behavior.

Solórzano began the first part of this discussion by denying the opinion of those authors who argued that the right to *dominium* existed among creatures who could legitimately be termed "brute animals" as well as among those who were clearly "rational and intelligent" people. He then asserted that the general opinion among the most authoritative theologians was that only "rational and intelligent creatures" could possess *dominium*.[41] The problem that underlay Solórzano's argument was whether the inhabitants of the New World were barbarians, that is, brutes who were not fully human, in spite of their appearance, rational and intelligent creatures.

The next stage of the argument was to restate the traditional view that all human beings, regardless of their external appearance, possessed *dominium*. Consequently,

> We deny that *dominium* over their possessions can be taken from human beings (*hominibus*), for this cause alone, however barbarous and primitive [they may be], and however deformed by external appearance, bodily condition, or stupidity [they may be].

Admittedly, many of the peoples whom the Spanish had encountered in the New World could "be compared to animals in many ways because of their ferocity and rusticity." Nevertheless, the ferocious way of life that some peoples lead does not justify depriving them of their lands and governments. In spite of appearances,

> since they have some use of reason and some vestige of intellect, there is no doubt that they are to be enumerated among the intelligent creatures and as true human beings, as St. Augustine pointed out.[42]

Finally, there was a brief reference to another statement of St. Augustine that described the differences between Christian Europeans and the barbarous peoples of the world as being only superficial. Augustine had also said that the external deformities of some peoples that had led some to call them monsters would be eliminated on the day of resurrection so that they would be suitable for being counted among the blessed.[43] The point, of course, was that humanity was defined in terms of the capacity for rational behavior, not in terms of external appearance.

The question of the existence of monstrous peoples that Solórzano raised at this point had a long history, one that stretched back to Herodotus. This fifth-century B C historian was "the chief source of the medieval anthropological tradition" upon which Solórzano and his immediate predecessors constructed their anthropology.[44] In the literary tradition, at least, there was a long history of accepting the existence of such creatures and a general consensus that such creatures were not fully human.[45] From the very outset of the Spanish conquest of the Americas, the existence of monstrous peoples was a concern of the discoverers and conquerors. Columbus himself, reporting on his first voyage, observed that he had "so far found no human monstrosities, as many had expected."[46] In making this point, Columbus appears to have been responding to expectations arising from the literary tradition.

In Solórzano's argument the issue of whether such creatures, obviously terrifying to a European, were truly human was of vital concern because, as we have seen, the Spanish claim to the New World rested on papal responsibility for the souls of all men. Did the external appearance of the peoples encountered indicate their lack of rationality and consequently their exemption from papal jurisdiction? Such monsters, after all, had bodies with elements that were similar to those of animals. Some were said to have feet like horses or elephants or teeth like dogs or to be covered with hair and grunt rather than speak. Others were said to live like the animals of the fields, even to the extent of creeping along the ground rather than walking upright.[47] Even though such people would not appear to share a common humanity with Europeans, Solórzano warned against making precipitous judgments about their rationality and therefore about their humanity based only on their physical appearance. Care had to be taken to determine whether they were rational beings, because if they were then it would be possible to lead them to a better state of moral development. Ultimately, if encouraged and taught, such people could gradually be brought to the full use of reason. Citing Simon Maiolo (1520–1597?), he added that "what is more, no stupid natures are born which cannot with skill be cultivated to the greatest standard, and able to reach such fruitfulness that they can be compared to the most talented by their own nature."[48]

The line of argument that Solórzano presented here suggested not only a belief in the existence of a shared humanity between Europeans and non-Europeans, but also a belief in the capacity of all people everywhere to reach the same level of culture and civilization that Europeans possessed. This line of argument rejected any notion of innate European biological, intellectual, or moral superiority over non-European peoples.

In the next stage of Solórzano's rejection of the arguments about the naturally servile status of Indians based on a presumed innate biological or moral inferiority, he developed the notion that history proves that a primitive and savage way of life did not in itself deny to those who followed it legitimate possession of property and government. To present his case, Solórzano drew upon the history of mankind to demonstrate that human beings could and did rise from the most primitive levels of existence to the most sophisticated. Solórzano began this section of his discussion with the biblical picture of the creation of mankind. Adam, the first man, was not only the father of all men, he was also the

> wisest and most eloquent of men, and without doubt did not permit his descendants to wander about like beasts. Rather indeed his son Cain, it is written, built the earthly city.[49]

Thus, the first men lived in organized societies, in *respublicae*. In Solórzano's view, the city was the natural framework for human life from the very beginning. Consequently, he saw Cain's creation of a city in positive terms, although the Book of Genesis linked Cain the murderer of his brother with Cain the founder of a first city, suggesting that the origin of city life lay in criminal behavior.[50] This negative attitude toward the city and government received its fullest expression in St. Augustine's *City of God* and political writings that derived from it.[51] In the Augustinian tradition, government existed as a response to man's fall, to restrain his sinful nature. In the Aristotelian tradition, however, the city was the framework within which men could achieve the highest form of human existence, and government was an instrument for the implementation of this goal.[52]

If the organized community was the natural and best form of human existence, why, then, were there peoples who did not live in such communities? The reason was that some people fell away from this way of life and slid down to a lower level of existence. This came about as human beings became scattered over ever larger territories and wandered about, living more like animals than men. In such a world, men lived not according to the dictates of reason, but for the most part according to physical force. Such people were without knowledge of true religion and lived promiscuously, with the result that men did not even know their own children. In such circumstances, no one had clear title to ownership of anything.[53] This way of life was therefore not the product of some natural or innate defect but the result of "error and ignorance."[54] As a result, these creatures possessed the capacity to rise to a higher level of existence if given the opportunity.

Eventually, among those people who had fallen from an organized way of life emerged "wiser and more prudent" men who provided the leadership necessary to bring the people back from their decadence. These leaders used reason and speech, not force, to persuade their fellows to "become gathered into cities, to be delivered from savagery and wicked behavior to mildness and gentleness, and to be brought to every useful and good thing."[55] This line of reasoning, derived from Cicero's writings, was an attempt to reconcile the Aristotelian argument about the naturalness of life in the city with some late medieval arguments about the origin of organized communities as voluntary acts of the human will.[56] The Ciceronian argument also reinforced the opinion that with the proper leadership and guidance, those who lived primitive lives outside of organized communities could return to the better way of life from which their ancestors had fallen.[57]

The passage from savage to civilized behavior, from living in tiny groups scattered all over the landscape to living in organized communities, was not universal. It occurred in some places and not in others with the result that "even today many peoples are found that seem scarcely [able] to comprehend the use of human reason." According to one of Solórzano's sources, such people do not fit the general definition of the barbarian, however, because barbarians are defined as being those "whose customs are far from rational and who are found to lack the common way of life of men."[58] If the peoples whom Solórzano was describing, people whom he indicated were similar to those who had returned to a civilized way of life, were true barbarians, then "the Greeks, Latins and others, who now live in an organized fashion (*politice*), ought to have been called 'barbarians' when, few in number, they followed a way of life different from innumerable other peoples who, to this day, remain in that state of ancient barbarism."[59]

The barbarian, as Solórzano pointed out, was, in effect, simply someone or some people who were different from the person who used the term. An Athenian might describe someone as a barbarian, but then the Athenian would be a barbarian to a Scythian.[60] Even Plautus "acknowledges the Latins, who are among the more prudent and wiser [of men], by that name [i.e., barbarian] and calls Italy a 'foreign and savage (*Barbariam*) land'."[61]

As in the ancient world, when the stranger, first encountered as a barbarian who subsequently became civilized, that is, who became like unto him who called the stranger a barbarian, was even more true for the peoples who invaded Europe in the declining days of the Roman Empire. "The Germans, as well as the Saxons and the other northern peoples, the Sarmatians, Pannonians, Hungarians, Poles, Suevi, Herules, Russians, Britons, Goths, Alans, and the like," people who now lived in civilized, rational communities, were not many generations earlier living in a savage and primitive fashion. To an observer, such people might have seemed to possess "an inferior nature" such as that then observed in "our Indians or Ethiopians."[62] Numerous ancient writers, including Tacitus, Strabo, and Seneca, had described their barbarian contemporaries in such terms. Yet, in the modern world, these peoples were exemplars of civilized living, having been restored to the organized way of life from which their ancestors had fallen. Here again, Solórzano emphasized that the barbarous exterior of these frighteningly fierce peoples covered potentially civilized human beings who would happily return to an organized way of life if given the opportunity.

In addition to citing ancient pagan authors, Solórzano also cited the observations of several Christian writers who had described the invading barbarians. One, Fortunatus, in a letter to a bishop who had converted some Saxons, set the tone for the way in which Solórzano saw the process through which the pagan peoples of Europe became both civilized and Christianized.

> The rude Saxon people, living as a wild animal lives,
> You having acted as a healer, the wild beast now becomes a holy sheep.

The work of converting these newcomers was not, then, simply a spiritual work, it was a temporal, that is, a civilizing, work as well. The two processes were in fact joined to form a single effort, which would eventually lead to the spiritual and the temporal betterment of these invaders. This process was, however, a long one, as Solórzano suggested in another short description of the primitive life of the Saxons culled from Einhard's life of Charlemagne. As late as the eighth century, the Saxons whom the Franks encountered were still living in a vile, lawless state that was contrary to all the laws of God and nature. What was said of the Saxons in the late Roman and Frankish periods, namely that they were fierce, primitive, and savage, living almost like animals, was also said of the Hungarians living as recently as the mid-eleventh century, according to another writer.[63] In fact, as European Christian societies expanded beyond the boundaries of the Carolingian empire, they continued to encounter societies whose members remained at a primitive level of existence.[64]

To the east of the various Germanic tribes that entered western Europe were other primitive peoples whom the ancients had identified as Scythians. These people too demonstrated a primitive unstable, way of life.[65] Solórzano and his contemporaries continued to apply the term Scythian to various nomadic or semi-nomadic peoples on the fringes of Europe. In his own lifetime, the English royal official and poet Edmund Spenser (1552–1599) classified the Irish as Scythians because they appeared to live as the ancients had reported the Scythians had lived. That is, the Irish, like the Scythians, lived a nomadic existence, one lacking a permanent location and the discipline associated with civilized, settled existence.[66]

Having thus presented several sketches of primitive peoples presumably known to the reader who had an education that included both the ancient classics and at least some introduction to medieval writings, Solórzano then moved on to the point of all this discussion of ancient and medieval primitive peoples:

> Africans, Gauls, and we Spaniards ourselves were formerly said to labor under the burden of barbarity, crudeness and fierceness, as today those Indians whom some people for this reason would go so far as to make slaves [are said to labor].[67]

The implication is obvious. Various peoples, including the ancestors of the very Spanish officials who would enslave the Indians of the New World, had once been considered barbarians and now were clearly civilized. The Indians could be expected to follow the same path if treated properly. It was Cicero, according to Solórzano, who provided the guidelines that colonial officials should follow in their dealings with uncivilized peoples. In a letter to his brother, a newly appointed Roman official, Cicero outlined the proper behavior for an official assigned to govern primitive peoples.

> ... if it falls to your lot to rule over Africans or Spaniards or Gauls, barbarous and monstrous nations, it is your lot to consult your humanity to serve their interests, needs and well-being.[68]

Lest the reader not fully appreciate the similarities among the ancient inhabitants of Spain, Solórzano went on to offer Strabo's (64/63 BC–c. 21 AD) views on the Asturians, Gallicians, and the Basques. The ancient geographer described them as rude and savage and as living in such remote places that they did not meet with other peoples. The result was that they simply did not live as the general run of mankind.[69]

Later writers also attested to the fierce and barbarous nature of those who inhabited Spain. Ammianus Marcellinus (c. 330–after 390), for example, also described the fourth-century Asturians as fierce, undisciplined barbarians. The reputation of the early inhabitants of Spain for uncivilized behavior surfaced in the work of sixteenth- and seventeenth-century writers as well. The Jesuit historian Juan de Mariana (1535–1624), for example, described the ancient inhabitants of Spain in harsh terms.

> The ancient Spaniards were indeed rustic in their customs and without self control, a nature more suitable for animals than for men.[70]

Solórzano also recognized that such descriptions of the ancestors of the Spanish were not popular in all quarters. They clearly offended some of his contemporaries, who no doubt saw such descriptions as a criticism of themselves, not to mention an argument against the status of the Indians as natural slaves. He pointed out that the criticisms made of the ancient Spaniards could be made of other peoples of the time as well. The evils described were not inherent flaws, but the product of circumstances that the Spaniards and others eventually overcame. Furthermore, to assuage his readers' sensitivities Solórzano added that in the final analysis Mariana had said more good things than bad about the ancient inhabitants of Spain.[71]

Having established that the ancestors of sixteenth-century Europeans lived as the Indians appeared to, Solórzano went on to defend the Indians from the charge that they were somehow unfit for self-government. He charged that certain people were disseminating the opinion that

> the Indians were not only barbarians, like the other nations of whom we spoke, but utterly inhuman, stupid and mindless, wandering through the mountains and fields like animals, so that they scarcely seemed worthy of the name of men.

This being the case, such people were, according to the writers to whom Solórzano referred, "totally incapable of learning and keeping the Christian faith." This opinion, he asserted, "is and always was false."[72]

At the same time, it was also quite clear that at least some of the Indians whom the Spanish first encountered in the New World were fierce and savage. Many of these people were indeed killed or mistreated by the invaders precisely because they appeared so frightening to the Spaniards who encountered them. Solórzano suggested, however, that uncivilized behavior of the inhabitants of the Caribbean was a pretext for attacking and despoiling them, not the real cause for such attacks. The consequence of attacking them was to place serious obstacles in the way of converting these people to Christianity, the ultimate goal of the Spanish presence in the Americas.[73]

From Solórzano's perspective, that of a royal bureaucrat, the leaders of the initial Spanish incursions into the Americas were not the best examples of Spanish manhood. They were murderers, pillagers, and looters who used the savage way of life they encountered as camouflage for their own wicked activities.[74] Fortunately for the Indians, the Spanish monarchs intervened on their behalf, asking "pious and religious men" to examine the situation in the Americas and to assist in the development of a suitable policy toward the Indians. What these men pointed out was that even if some of the peoples encountered were primitive and savage, there were also others "who lived in organized societies and were ruled in a civil fashion by their own laws and kings according to their own manner of understanding these things."[75]

The presence of organized societies with laws and identifiable rulers meant that these people were clearly rational and human. They possessed rights that Spanish adventurers sought to take from them, rights that the Spanish monarchs, however, would defend. Furthermore, as the Indians were clearly human and rational, Christian missionaries should be sent in order to preach the Gospel to them because the Indians were clearly capable of adhering to the faith. Furthermore, according to Solórzano, if the Indians received proper instruction from missionaries, the fact that they were indeed clever and many were docile meant that they would learn the new religion quickly.[76] Thus, it was in the interest of the Spanish monarchs to see to the orderly, responsible treatment of the Indians, so that they would become Christians. This would, of course, also mean that the Spanish monarchs should insure that only suitable Europeans enter the New World. The monopoly on access to the New World that Alexander VI granted to the Castilians, if enforced, would presumably guarantee this.[77]

Solórzano did not argue, however, that acquiring the faith would necessitate complete rejection of the Indians' traditional education. He appears to have believed that the Indians had already demonstrated their intellectual capacity by their own cultural development, so that the Christian faith would be added to the "liberal arts" (*artes etiam liberales*) that already formed the basis of their education before the arrival of the Spanish.[78] Here again, his position was that no inherent cultural gulf existed between the inhabitants of the Americas and the Spanish who had conquered them. The Indians were quite capable of evolving to the level of cultural development that the Spanish had reached. Indeed, with the guidance of the Spanish, the Indians would be able to reach that level faster than the ancestors of the Spanish had done, because the conquerors now understood the nature of the process. This knowledge would enable the Spanish to teach the Indians how to avoid mistakes in the process of social evolution.

Although many observers saw the Indians as fierce and savage, others, missionaries like Las Casas and Acosta who had actually dealt with them, asserted that the Indians were docile, intelligent, and fully human, as their experience clearly showed.[79] Furthermore, Solórzano pointed out that leading churchmen, above all Pope Paul III (1534–1549), had long defended the humanity of the Indians. Indeed, Paul III had issued a letter asserting the fundamental humanity of the Indians and condemning those who would deny it, declaring unequivocally that "the Indians are true men."[80]

The letter of Paul III was a response to one from the first bishop of Tlaxcalan, who had written to him about the mistreatment of the Indians by those who asserted the Indians' incapacity for civilized, Christian behavior.[81] The bishop made the point that even if the Indians were as cruel and savage as some individuals had charged, perhaps even man-eaters, "how much the better offering they would be to God if properly converted" to the Christian faith.[82] The bishop also pointed to the fierce and savage way of life of the Spanish to whom the Apostle James had preached.[83] The early Spanish were clearly at least as depraved and savage as the contemporary Indians, yet, under the guidance of St. James, the Spanish had come to the true faith and reformed their way of life. The result was a people renowned for virtue and learning.[84] As the Spanish had once been, the Indians were now, and as the Spanish were now, the Indians would be once the work of conversion was completed.

Having thus made the case for the humanity and the intellectual capacity of the Indians and having emphasized that the Indians were comparable to the ancestors of the Spanish, Solórzano then went on to consider the question in another way. Even if we concede, he wrote, that the Indians "are completely endowed with a dull, barbarous or savage nature," nevertheless "they are true men" and therefore to exclude them from the Christian faith would be a great wrong.[85] The mission of Christ was for all men because they are all the children of God. To those who would deny the humanity of the Indians, Solórzano asserted that "the Indians, however barbarous, are of the same blood as the Greeks and the Romans so they (too) are redeemed."[86] The prophets had declared that "From the ends of the earth we hear songs of praise, of glory to the Righteous One."[87] The inhabitants of the Americas, dwelling as they did in the most distant corners of the earth, were, metaphorically at least, the people of whom the prophet spoke.

The primitive, barbaric way of life that the Indians followed, even the possibility that they might be dull of mind, did not mean that they lacked souls or that they should not be evangelized. After all, Solórzano went on, we know that Christ's apostles preached "to the most remote and the most fierce nations . . . and were not deterred by their savage practices."[88] Even if the peoples whom the Spanish encountered in the far corners of the earth appeared strange or monstrous, Europeans should not discourage missionaries. He pointed out that long ago, St. Augustine argued that the Gospel should be preached to the strangest-seeming men, "even to those headless monsters whose eyes are in their chests," because such men are "ensnared in the error of the Gentiles and for this reason are led into the error of false religion."[89]

Yet again, Solórzano emphasized that a barbarous visage and way of life did not mean a nonhuman or sub-human character. Furthermore, he pointed out that the qualities of the Indians that most distressed the Spanish were not the products of biology but of cultural formation.

> And indeed it is certain that the rustic savagery of this sort or the fierceness of the Indians does not spring from birth or lineage or from the air of their native place. (Such qualities spring from) a depraved education over a long span of time and from the practice, harshness and lack of instruction in their way of life and from the poor quality of the food they consume.

In fact, according to Solórzano, the qualities that the Indians exhibited were those "which we see daily in our rural and agricultural Spanish countrymen," qualities indeed generally found in those "who dwell in the fields and the countryside," an observation that Aristotle himself had made centuries earlier.[90] It was not only the physical environment, according to Solórzano, that had shaped the peoples of the Americas. They were, by nature, intelligent and civil people, but because they worshiped idols they had become dull and uncivilized. Once brought to the true faith, however, the goal of the Spanish presence in the Americas in the first place, the Indians' natural intelligence would flourish.

The qualities that Solórzano identified as typical of rural peoples everywhere, qualities that might lead some observer to conclude that such creatures were not human, were, as far as he was concerned, the product of environment and education, not biology. Therefore, the Spanish should not wage war against the Indians and deprive them of their lives and property, but rather should treat them with gentleness. There is, he argued, "no nation so barbarous, none so stupid, which, over time is educated and instructed correctly, that does not put barbarism away." The fiercest of peoples, if gently treated, "put on humanity and refinement of customs." The evidence for this is the experience of those who have seen "rustic people who have been brought to schools or to court or to famous cities who are transformed into individuals of wondrous cleverness and outstanding talent." The same can be said of "Ethiopians and their children raised in palaces who gain advancement by their talent and being prepared rise to some [position of significance] so that if the color of their skin was different, they could be thought of as being one of us."[91] Solórzano even had an answer for those who argued that the Indians were not only savage and fierce but unintelligent as well. The barbarity and stupidity of the Indians, he believed, had been exaggerated by those who were interested in conquering the New World and despoiling its inhabitants of their property. Some defenders of the conquest had apparently pointed to the terror of the Indians at the sight of Spanish ships, guns, and horses as a sign of their primitive nature. Solórzano did not, however, judge such terror to be a sign of the Indians' primitive or unintelligent nature. Likewise, the Indians' belief that creatures who possessed such things must have come from heaven was not an irrational response. The Indians, after all, had never seen such things before and, as Seneca had pointed out long ago, it was easy to believe that something new, something completely outside of one's normal experience, must have come from heaven.[92] From where else could such a strange and wonderful new thing have come?

What especially astonished the Indians, however, were not the ships or guns but the art of writing. Some defenders of the conquest pointed to the absence of writing among the Indians as a sign of their mental incapacity. Solórzano pointed out, however, that the Mexicans and Peruvians did in fact have systems for recording and transmitting information. The Mexicans, like the Phoenicians described by Lucan, recorded information with images, not words. The Peruvians used knotted strings of several colors to record the deeds of their ancestors and recite them when called upon to do so.[93] Furthermore, the Indians had devices for counting and doing arithmetic, as Joseph Acosta had pointed out. The fact that they did not apparently count above five or ten was not a sign of intellectual incapacity, only the lack of any need to do so.[94] In fact, the inability to count above five or ten or some other small number was also to be found among peoples in Europe. The Albanians who lived on the shores of the Caspian Sea had no need of any number above 100.[95] The ancient Thracians, he added, could not count above four, and another ancient people counted only to five.[96] The thrust of Solórzano's argument was that writing and reckoning were skills that exist only where there is a need for them. Those who live in simple societies may not require these skills in order to live a rational, orderly existence, so that the absence of them does not demonstrate the intellectual inferiority of such people.

Returning again to the awe and amazement with which the Indians reacted to the appearance of the *conquistadores*, Solórzano retold a story from Strabo in conjunction with a story of the Indians. It seems as though, when the Indians first observed Spaniards relaxing and enjoying themselves at a dance, they concluded that the dancers were crazy. Strabo had told a similar story of the ancient inhabitants of Spain, the Vettones, who were amazed at seeing Roman soldiers out walking for pleasure. They thought that such behavior was a sign of madness.[97] Solórzano was underscoring the common humanity of the ancestors of the now-conquering Spaniards with the conquered Indians. Here again, he stressed the theme that as the Indian were now, we had once been, and as we were now, they would one day be.

In similar fashion, Solórzano pointed out that the Indians' fear of natural phenomena was not unusual either and certainly not a sign of mental weakness. Observers had reported that the Indians were terrified when an eclipse occurred, and some defenders of the conquest had argued that this demonstrated the mental weakness or at least the immaturity of the Indians. Tacitus, however, had told a similar story about a group of Roman soldiers, men "to whom the *Imperium* and governance of the whole world belonged." Would anyone suggest that Roman soldiers who became panic-stricken at the onset of an eclipse were somehow not fully human or mature? Not likely.[98]

The crucial issue for Solórzano was not the physical appearance of the Indians or their cultural practices, repellant though they might be. The crucial issue was the demonstrated ability to live in an organized fashion and this, he pointed out again and again, many Indians did. To illustrate this point, Solórzano took some examples from Garcilaso de la Vega's *Royal*

Commentaries of the Incas. He pointed out that critics charged the Indians with having filthy habits, among which was the practice of adorning their bodies in offensive ways. While admitting that there was evidence against many Indian peoples to support this charge, Solórzano pointed out that there were other peoples, such as the Mexicans and the Peruvians, who both adorned themselves and were *politici*, that is, who lived in organized societies. He described the ruler of the Incas as the "*Imperator* of the Peruvians" who had conquered many other nations, thus bringing them under his *imperium*. The use of the terms *imperator* and *imperium* was clearly designed to compare the Incas favorably with the Romans. For Solórzano, one obvious proof of the status of Incan society as political or civil was the story told by Garcilaso de la Vega about the refusal of an Incan ruler to conquer a certain people because they were so filthy and squalid. Presumably, in the eyes of the Incan ruler, the conquest of such a people could only serve to bring his own people down to the level of the conquered. As Solórzano employed the story, it illustrated the Inca's perception of himself and of the people he ruled as superior to those filthy people. Such a judgment underscored Solórzano's argument about the advanced nature of Incan society, in spite of how it appeared to some observers. The Incas were aware of the differences between themselves and these more primitive people, thus demonstrating their capacity to make judgments about levels of social development and their capacity to act according to such judgments. Furthermore, Garcilaso de la Vega's story also indicated that the Incas saw themselves as possessing a civilizing mission, something that the Spanish could surely appreciate. When the Incan ruler decided not to conquer these filthy people, he remarked: "Let us retire, they do not deserve to have us as their masters."[99] This ability reinforced Solórzano's conclusion about their level of social and political development.

Having demonstrated both the filthy nature of some Indian societies and the sensitivity of the Incas about including such peoples in their empire, Solórzano went on to remind his readers that their ancestors lived in a similarly primitive fashion. The ancient Spanish peoples, especially the Iberians and the Cantabrians, lived in a filthy, depraved fashion that horrified foreign observers. They washed themselves in the most filthy water, for example.[100] As for the matter of painting and otherwise adorning their bodies in disgusting fashion, Julius Caesar described the ancient Britons as doing precisely that. In this case, the British painted their bodies blue to instill terror in their enemies. In addition, they shaved their hair in an unusual way and adorned themselves in other ways.[101] Indeed, the practice of adorning the body with paint, pictures, and the like was not unique to the Indians of the New World, it "was common to many other nations."[102] Even the Romans did it, "smearing the bodies of triumphant *imperatores* with red lead."[103]

Solórzano went on to explain why the kings of Aragon did not engage in such practices. When one of the Aragonese kings was informed that he should be decked out in red lead according to the practice of the Romans, he declined. He observed that the custom was suitable for Bacchus only, since he had not only created the custom of the triumph but had discovered the vine as well.[104] The objection to the practice therefore had nothing to do with intellectual or political immaturity or incapacity.

For Solórzano, the examination of the historical record demonstrated that the inhabitants of the New World possessed characteristics similar to those that the ancestors of seventeenth-century Europeans were known to have. The criticisms that the Spanish often made of the Indians' way of life, other observers had previously made about the inhabitants of Spain and other parts of Europe in the distant, and not so distant, past. That being the case, it was not possible to assert that the Indians were permanently sunk in depravity or were biologically or morally inferior to Europeans. At the same time, the fact that the Indians were not permanently handicapped, and were capable of advancing to the civil and religious level of the Spaniards, placed a heavy responsibility on the Spanish as they continued their penetration of the Americas. This led Solórzano to deal with the problem of what the precise nature of the relationship between the Spaniards and the Indians should be. Above all, he had to deal with the argument that the Indians were by nature slaves and thus obliged to live and function under Spanish direction. If the Indians were not natural slaves and if they were, in fact, at a lower level of political, social, and religious development, as the Spanish had once been, then what could possibly justify the conquest of the Americas?

The political consequence of this positive view of the intellectual and moral capacity of the Indians was that the Spanish could not use the behavior of the Indians to justify conquering them and reducing them to slavery. Pointing to the arguments of Sepúlveda and others who defined the Indians, according to Aristotle's definition, as naturally suited for slavery Solórzano argued that they misunderstood the philosopher's argument. In Solórzano's opinion, Aristotle meant that "rude and barbarous men by nature ought to be subjected to wiser men" but that "he did not mean by this that they are true slaves and thus can be despoiled publicly or privately of their liberty and the *dominium* of their goods." What Aristotle did mean was that such people should be placed under the protection of their betters for their own good, "as infants, minors and the permanently insane" are to be protected.[105] Such protection does not, however, mean that such people do not possess goods, property, and the right of self-government. What it does mean, as lawyers have long pointed out, is that such people lose the exercise of such rights as long as they remain minors or insane.[106]

Solórzano stressed that with regard to the Indians and similar people, as with infants, minors, the insane, and others who lack the judgement to exercise their legitimate *dominium*, the guardians must seek the good of those in their charge, not their own selfish ends. The interest of the ward was paramount. The goal of the period of guardianship was to guide these people "to greater wisdom, discipline, justice, and forethought, so that finally with regard to everything else (they would act) as other free, prudent, and civic-minded (*politici*) men would act."[107] Just as the primitive, fierce ancestors of the Spanish had evolved into civilized, Christian people, so too would the Indians.

In the final section of this chapter, Solórzano returned to an issue raised elsewhere: whether the conquest and subjection of the Indians was a necessary and legitimate step in their becoming civilized Christians. In the previous chapter (2.7.66 ff.), he had cited a variety of sources in support of that argument. He now returned to the same authors he had cited in the earlier chapter to demonstrate that their arguments did not necessarily defend the use of force in the process of bringing other peoples to a civilized way of life.[108] Augustine, for example, did not justify the great harm done to peoples whom the Romans had conquered on the grounds that the advantages of Roman government and civilization outweighed the violations of the natural rights that such conquests entailed.[109] In the final analysis, according to Solórzano, citing several chapters of canon law, the end does not justify the means. The desire to civilize and to convert barbarous infidels does not justify violating their rights in the course of a war of conquest.[110] Indeed, Augustine had argued that the Romans would have been even more successful had they sought to civilize their barbarous neighbors by peaceful means.[111]

Before concluding the discussion of the argument that the more civilized had a responsibility to assist the less civilized to reach a "political way of life," that is, a civilized way of life in Aristotle's terms, Solórzano turned to another element of the problem: the nature of the actual inhabitants of the Americas. Who were they and what sort of lives did they actually live?

Were all of the inhabitants of the New World existing at the same level of social life, or were there variations, differences among various peoples that would necessitate a variety of responses by the Spanish to the peoples whom they were encountering. This inevitably led him to the work of the Jesuit missionary Joseph Acosta, who developed a scale against which all human societies can be measured and evaluated in terms of their political and social development.

3. The Mechanics of Political Evolution

Once Solórzano had demonstrated that the Spanish could not legitimately deprive the inhabitants of the New World of their *dominium* on the grounds that they were fierce and savage, he turned to a related issue: the possibility that the Indians should come under Spanish control at least temporarily because the Spanish were wiser and more prudent than the Indians themselves. This argument was rooted in the Aristotelian notion that the less intelligent should be governed by the wiser elements of a society.[1] At the same time, Solórzano avoided condemning the Indians to a state of permanent inferiority by rejecting the Aristotelian notion that some people are naturally suited to slavery or similar forms of unfree status. The Indians could move up the ladder of social and political development under Spanish guidance as the Spanish themselves had passed from a less developed stage to their present state of advanced civilization. Having passed from an uncivilized state to a civilized one and having studied the history of that progression, the Spanish understood how the process operated and could assist the Indians in making the same transformation. As the Romans had once brought the ancestors of the Spanish to a civilized way of life, so now the Spanish would provide the same service for the inhabitants of the Americas.[2]

One might think that Solórzano would have mentioned Sepúlveda and Las Casas at this point because the capacity of the inhabitants of the Americas for civilized existence lay at the heart of their famous confrontation at Valladolid in 1550. Here again, however, Solórzano's hesitation to cite directly the opinion of an author whose work was banned in Spain may have caused him to avoid discussing Sepúlveda's views on the Indians as natural slaves.

To deal with this justification of the conquest of the Americas, Solórzano turned to a consideration of the various kinds of societies that were known to exist. This provided a starting point for a discussion of *dominium* in the Indian societies of the Americas. At the heart of the issue was the question of whether the Indians were fully competent, rational human beings or not. Was the fierce behavior that many Indians exhibited a sign of inherent inferiority or was such behavior simply the product of a primitive environment that, once changed, would lead to a change in the Indians' way of life?

According to Solórzano, the Indians were clearly rational human beings, as Pope Paul III had emphasized in the bull *Sublimis Deus* (1537).[3] While some writers had asserted that the inhabitants of the New World were monstrous creatures who lacked reason, Solórzano pointed out that such was not the case. It was true that many of these people lived in a savage fashion, but this was not the result of intellectual incapacity or some kind of biological inferiority. These people had demonstrated their mental capacity in various ways and "the more true and more certain opinion" about the intellectual capacity of the Indians was the one that defended it.[4] Here again, Solórzano was emphasizing the role of cultural influences in the shaping of people. He pointed out that in comparison with the Spanish and the Portuguese, the inhabitants of the New World were barbarians "not only [because] they had not been illumined by the light of the Gospel but also because they generally shrank from using human ways of life."[5] The implication of this argument was that once introduced to the ways of civilized living, the Indians would accept them and change their practices, thus passing from a savage to a civilized way of life.

Before moving to examining the societies found in the Americas, Solórzano first discussed the wide variety of societies that existed through-out the world. Each of these societies had its own way of life and own ways of doing things.[6] He pointed out that regardless of the variations, however, all the societies found in the new worlds that Europeans had encountered could be fitted into one of three categories that the Jesuit missionary Joseph Acosta (c. 1539–1600) had developed.[7] These categories reflected standards of behavior, activity, and institutional and cultural development, not the moral or intellectual capacity of the people involved, and provided a scale for determining the place of any society along a spectrum of social and political evolution.

The first, and highest, category of non-European society consisted of those people who "do not withdraw much from [the use of] right reason and the practice of the human race but have stable republics, written laws, fortified cities, conspicuous magnificence of wealth, symbols of public office, regular and lucrative trade, a renowned literary tradition, and flour-ishing academies of learning." China, Japan "and many other provinces of the East Indies to which there is no doubt that Asian and European institutions came" are examples of this class of society.[8] This being the case, China and Japan could no more be the objects of European conquest on the grounds that they were not fully developed societies, that is, *respublicae*, than could the kingdoms of Europe. None of the societies that the Spanish encountered in the Americas fitted this classification, however.

The second category consisted of those peoples who "do not know the use of writing and who do not have written laws, or philosophical or civil studies . . ." but who do have "their own established kings or magistrates, a republic, fixed, frequented places where they watch over their polity, military leaders, and order and celebration of their religion, and so they are ruled by a certain [kind of] human reason." This category comprised the Mexicans, the Peruvians, and the Chileans "whose empires, republics, laws and institutions, and their deeds and histories can worthily be admired."[9] What differentiated the first class of society from the second was that the first provided more than stability and order for its members. The political stability and order that societies such as the Chinese and Japanese possessed provided a basis for the development of more sophisticated aspects of human existence. The societies of the second class provided the basic framework for civilized existence, stability, and order, but little more.

The third category of societies consisted of those "who are found living in the wild almost like animals, and have scarcely any human judgment, [existing] without law, without a king, without an agreement among the peoples, without established magistrates and without a republic, [people who] move their location repeatedly or whose fixed locations are more like the caves or holes of animals." Violent peoples, such as the Caribs and others who were bloodthirsty, even eaters of human flesh, fit this category. In addition, some other peoples, though not violent, were in the same category because of the utter simplicity of their lives.[10]

The crucial standard for judging the place of any society within Acosta's categories of development was thus the level of organization that the society had attained. Societies that were orderly and disciplined, where there was what Solórzano defined as a *respublica*, that is, a recognizable form of orderly government, were the equivalent of European kingdoms. In effect, societies everywhere were being judged according to an Aristotelian standard of social order. The inhabitants of such societies possessed *dominium* just as much as did European Christians. Furthermore, Europeans presumably could deal with such societies through their rulers and other officials just as they dealt with one another in Europe. Diplomatic relations, as it were, could exist with such societies.

The fact that such organized societies might engage in behavior that the European would define as barbarous or immoral did not mean that they were not true *respublicae* with true *dominium*. It was the level of political order, not the level of moral behavior, that determined the status of any society. That being the case, the inhabitants of the Americas who belonged to Acosta's second category could not be deprived of their lands or power simply because they were infidels or barbarians.[11] Furthermore, Solórzano argued, by respecting the peoples of the New World, the Spanish would be more likely to them away from barbarous and savage behavior and to win them to Christianity, which was, after all, the ultimate purpose of going to the New World in the first place.[12]

Before moving on to consider the arguments Solórzano presented in support of the opinion that the Spanish had the right, even the obligation, to place the Indians temporarily under their governance, however, it is necessary to consider what he meant by such phrases as "to live in a political fashion" (*vere politicum vivendi modum*) and the terms "republic" (*respublica*), "empire" (*imperium*) and "kingdom" (*regnum*), because by employing these terms he effectively placed the Aztecs and the Incas within a European-based framework for political analysis.[13]

For Solórzano, living in a political fashion meant to live in a society with fixed rules and defined rulers. As Acosta's three-fold classification of societies indicated, political life, life in a polis as Aristotle described it, was orderly, stable, and predictable. Indeed, it was the natural form of life for men because it was a complete one, allowing the individual to develop himself to the fullest. The societies that comprised Acosta's first two categories, the Chinese and the Japanese, the Aztecs and the Incas, all shared these characteristics. The primitive peoples of the third category did not enjoy the stability and order found in the other two classes of society, so such people could not live in a fully human manner.

Solórzano also used the terms "empire" and "kingdom" as synonyms for living in an orderly fashion. Thus, the Mexicans, the Peruvians, and the Chileans had "empires, republics, laws and institutions" the existence of which made them part of the second class of societies. As a result, he could refer to Montezuma, the ruler of the Aztecs, as an emperor, and to the ruler of the Incas as a king. The Aztecs and Incas possessed empires or kingdoms, that is, recognizable political and government units.[14] Furthermore, this classification of the Incas and Aztecs also meant that the Spanish could not legitimately conquer them on the grounds that they were too barbarous, primitive, or undeveloped to govern themselves. Obviously these people did govern themselves in such a way as to satisfy Aristotle and Acosta's definition of the level of political life required of a *respublica*. If this was the case, then on what basis could anyone argue that the Spanish might have the right to govern the Aztecs and Incas, thus depriving them of the exercise of their *dominium*, even if only on a temporary basis?

Solórzano also used the term *imperium* in another way. In addition to meaning a form of government, it could simply mean power or jurisdiction, as it had originally in Latin. In the Roman world, *imperium* had meant the power that officials exercised, above all the power of life and death, over the citizens of the Republic, and it retained this meaning even as it came to mean a particular form of government.[15] As a consequence, Solórzano could refer to the Indians as "living peacefully under the *imperium*" of their kings.[16] Here again, the point was that Aztec, Inca, and other Indian rulers of Acosta's second category exercised the same kind of power as their European counterparts.[17] *Imperium* also had the connotation of ruling over other peoples by force, a usage that applied to the Aztecs and Incas who had conquered their neighbors.[18]

Acosta's three categories provided more, however, than a convenient system for comprehending the numerous societies that Europeans had encountered as they explored the world. They could also be understood as a convenient guide to the stages of political, social, economic, and cultural development as well. In effect, it was possible to understand Acosta's schema as implying that human beings had progressed upward, starting with the simplest, most primitive form of life, passing to true political organization, then moving to the highest form of purely natural society, where commerce and culture flourish.[19] The apex of this development would be the societies of Christian Europe, which possessed all of the qualities found in the most sophisticated societies described by Acosta and the true faith as well.

To some extent, these two interpretations of Acosta's categorization of societies are in conflict, something Acosta himself may not have realized. To the extent that these categories suggest that people evolved politically and socially from primitive to civilized, from living scattered over the country-side to living in an organized society, that is, in a polis, the categories are at odds with the Aristotelian notion that human beings naturally live in organized societies and that those who do not have degenerated from the universal human norm. Seen as an evolutionary schema, Acosta's categories resemble Cicero's conception of organized society as having evolved from primitive disorder through the efforts of a few men skilled in the art of speaking.[20]

It should be noted that Acosta claimed this development only for the natives of America; he did not suggest that it applied to the Old World as well. It may be that he was unwilling to attempt an Old World Application of his theory of development because to do so would involve some contradiction of Biblical tradition. The narratives of Genesis allowed for no stage of primeval savagery. Acosta argued that the descendants of Noah who migrated to America went by land, passing no more than a narrow strait, and that they became savage hunters in the course of their wanderings.[21]

Seen in the light of the Aristotelian model, the peoples of the Americas had fallen away from their original way of life in organized communities, and subsequently some of them regained the civilized way of life through the efforts of eloquent leaders such as Cicero described.

Because it was possible to understand Acosta's schema as providing an outline of the stages through which human societies either had passed as they developed or had passed in the course of returning to a civilized way of life after falling away from it, the schema could then serve as a program for assisting less developed societies to advance more rapidly under the guidance of a government that recognized the right path. Using that standard, European Christian rulers had no right, Solórzano pointed out, to subjugate the societies that comprised Acosta's first class. While it was true that societies such as the Chinese and the Japanese "are to some degree barbarous and diverge from the right way and natural law in many matters . . . they are not to be judged any differently than the Greeks and Romans and the other peoples of Asia and Europe" are judged because "they show potential and some human wisdom and they are found to carry out an organized way of life (*politicam vitam agere*) according to their own understanding."[22] In effect, all that the Chinese, the Japanese, and similar societies needed to complete their socio-political development was to accept the Christian faith that missionaries were already preaching to them. This in turn would indicate to them what social and political practices they should reject.

Turning to the Indians of the New World and applying the same standard, Solórzano argued that the barbarous behavior of the Indians was not in itself sufficient cause for depriving them of their "liberty and the *dominium* of their goods."[23] Furthermore, the Indians were not so "fierce and primitive that if we treat them with patience and pious effort" they would not advance to a more civilized manner of living. Once properly instructed, they would advance to a "Christian and civilized way [*politicis moribus*] of life" as, among others, the ancestors of the Europeans had done.[24]

Solórzano pointed out, on the other hand, that the Indians' way of life left much to be desired. They had rejected "right reason and the customary practice of the human race." In many things, they adhered to practices that were "uncivilized, filthy and inhuman," including "cruel and accursed sacrifices" as well as numerous other kinds of wickedness. Instead of conquering the Indians, however, something that Solórzano's fundamental argument forbade, he proposed that the Spanish monarchs encourage their own subjects "to dwell among the Indians and begin to propagate the faith and as it were create a single republic with those Indians" under Spanish domination. The period of Spanish domination would only be temporary, however, until the Indians, freed of their wicked practices, could be brought to a higher standard of behavior. Then self-rule would be returned to them.[25] Thus, Spanish control would be a period of tutelage from which the Indians would one day emerge.

The justification for the temporary subjugation of the Indians of the second class was simple. The evil practices of their societies, though not a sufficient cause for depriving them of their *dominium*, would inhibit their reception of "the light of the Gospel or a way of life worthy of a free man." Spanish control of individual societies in the New World would not automatically end with the baptism of their members and the formal elimination of practices deemed to be uncivilized, however. Such control would have to continue until it was certain that the newly civilized and Christianized people were disposed to remain firm in their new way of life. How long that would take, Solórzano did not specify.[26]

It is worth noting at this point that Solórzano's argument did not mean that the inhabitants of the New World would have to become entirely Hispanicized before the Spanish government returned the exercise of their *dominium*. Those practices and laws "that are not contrary to the law of nature or the Gospel they can be allowed to exercise freely."[27] This reinforced what he had said earlier about the Indians retaining their own "liberal arts" as well as learning from the Spanish.[28] The Indians and the Spanish were to become a single *respublica*, as he had pointed out earlier, but that would not necessitate eliminating all elements of the traditional cultures of the inhabitants of the Americas, only those parts that were in conflict with natural law or the law of the Gospel.

Summing up this stage of the discussion, Solórzano concluded that the peoples who comprised the second class of society might seem to fit Aristotle's definition of those who are natural slaves. He pointed out that such, nevertheless, was not the case. These people were not natural slaves, did possess *dominium*, and to define them as natural slaves was to adhere to a "very dangerous, indeed false opinion that deserves condemnation."[29] At worst, such people might be deprived of the exercise of their rightful *dominium* temporarily, until they had remedied the defects in their society that kept them from living as human beings should.

On the other hand, the peoples of Acosta's third category, those who had no form of organized society, were in a different situation. These people, "fierce, wild, cannibals, and living without fixed law or a definite king, wandering through the fields like animals," obviously did not dwell in anything like a *respublica*. Consequently, it could be argued that such people might not only be brought under temporary Spanish control, but even be "captured by force, tamed, and reduced to servitude and indeed even be killed if they resist" Spanish efforts to civilize and convert them.[30] As Francisco Suárez argued, such people "can be warred against not to kill them but so that they might be instructed in a human way of life and be ruled justly," an opinion that, Solórzano demonstrated, was found in the work of numerous authors.[31]

The logic of this position entailed a recognition that, in contrast to the peoples of the second class, whose loss of the exercise of *dominium* would be only temporary, the peoples of the third class would come under "a fuller and more absolute domination" while the Spanish worked to civilize and Christianize them. The justification for this arose from the natural order of the world, which mandates that the "lesser intellect (*inferior ratio*) ought to be subject to the stronger," as children obey parents, servants obey their masters, and so on.[32] After all, "according to the natural order, the ignorant are commanded to follow and be dominated while the wise are commanded to lead."[33]

The goal to which the Spanish should aspire was the creation of a "republic composed of Indians and Spaniards," something that has already begun to take shape. Eventually the process would bring the Indians "to Christianity and to a political way of life."[34] Furthermore, in the *respublica* that would develop, Spaniards would not dominate Indians nor would Indians dominate Spaniards. Such a consummate equality lay in the future, however, because all of the Indians, those of the second class as well as those of the third, "appear by far less intelligent and wise than the Spaniards." At the moment, however, the first priority was the teaching of the Gospel. Until that occurred, the Indians of either class would be less wise than the Spanish, so that allowing them to rule the Spanish would be to allow "the foolish to be in higher places than the wised and learned," obviously a violation of the right order of the world, something that the ancient pagans like Homer and Plato knew well.[35] Obviously, if ancient pagans recognized that the wise should rule the less wise, then Christians, who possessed both natural and divine wisdom, had even more right to dominate the Indians, whose level of civilization and whose religious views were inferior to those of the Spanish.

Having presented an argument for at least temporarily depriving societies of Acosta's second and third classes of the exercise of their lawful *dominium* for their own good, Solórzano went on to stress that such a deprivation of a right was not without precedent. After all, it was well-known that "free men who, because of age or defective reason or judgment, were unable to care for themselves, could be cared for and ruled by older and wiser individuals." Furthermore, Solórzano argued that the weaker members of various societies had voluntarily submitted themselves to the "power and guidance (*manu & consilio*) of the wiser and more powerful" members of society. The "exigencies of human existence necessitated this reciprocal relationship" among people.[36] The argument that Solórzano presented here reinforced the traditional notion that societies are hierarchical, not egalitarian, so that the "reciprocal relationship (*mutuam inter homines opem, & societatem*)," the foundation of any society, is not the same as a social contract, that is, an agreement among equals.[37]

The fact that government is based not on the voluntary agreement of equals but on the actual circumstances of human life and exists naturally to advance the common good of all meant that defenders of the conquest of the New World could define that conquest as a legitimate act, on the grounds that the Indians required the assistance of the Spanish if they were to move from Acosta's second class of society to the first or from the third class to the second. So, even though the Indians were "free men and masters of their goods," nevertheless "they were not sufficiently learned to govern themselves appropriately and in a political manner." That is, the Indians continued to engage in practices more suited to a barbarous way of life than a truly civilized one, and they had not yet come to the "humane and civilized" ways. In addition, even though exposed to Christian teachings, the Indians had not yet become Christians. Thus, the Spanish kings had the responsibility for governing these people until they possessed the levels of civilized and Christian behavior that Acosta identified with the first class of non-Christian societies.[38] Again, however, Solórzano stressed that even in this case the role of the Spanish was a temporary one, a necessary intervention by a wiser and stronger society in the development of a younger and weaker one so that the latter would advance more rapidly to the highest levels of human existence. In this argument, there was no doubt expressed about the capacity of the Indians to rise to the same level as the Chinese and the Japanese, not to mention that of the Spanish themselves.[39]

Having outlined a defense of the Spanish conquest of the New World on natural grounds, that is, on the basis of a natural process of socio-political development that the Spanish understood and could, so to speak, speed up to the advantage of the Indians, Solórzano then presented re-ligiously based arguments defending the same opinion. He pointed out that although the relationship between the Spanish and the peoples of the second and third classes of society differed as to the nature and extent of Spanish control over them during the process of social development, in both cases the "precept of charity" bound Christian rulers to assist these peoples in the process of achieving a better way of life.[40] While the ruler of any society in a higher class of development could, presumably, assist the development of a society in a lower category simply on the basis of natural reason, Christian rulers had a special responsibility. Christians, after all, operated not only with the guidance of natural wisdom but also with the "perfect knowledge of the papacy to which the right of ruling and govern-ing souls properly seems to belong."[41]

The existing leaders of such societies were unable to assist in this kind of development because "they were usually cruel and tyrannical . . . and enmeshed in barbarous customs and the darkness of ignorance."[42] Even though the Indians had selected these rulers for themselves, a responsibility of their having *dominium*, the true needs of the society could require the appointment of a ruler who was neither barbarous in his way of life nor ignorant of the proper ends of a society.[43] Because the wicked rulers of these societies had "abused their *dominium*, they deserved to lose it."[44] To grant these wicked rulers the right to govern their people would be as sensible as giving the guardianship of children to a man who was insane or a slave to his passions.[45] No one in his right mind would allow such a thing. Reason and charity agree that the peoples of the New World would need the guidance that only European Christians can provide if they were to advance to the highest levels of human existence.

As for the peoples who constituted the third and lowest class of human existence, Solórzano pointed out that it should come as no surprise to anyone that "the wild and savage Indians who live without a fixed ruler and without fixed laws, those whom we number in the third class, can be warred against, subjugated and deprived absolutely of the governance and jurisdiction over their lands until they become accustomed to a more humane way of life and to formation in Christianity."[46] Implicitly comparing such barbarous people to those who are mentally impaired, Solórzano argued that they could no more be allowed to continue in such a way of life, destructive as it was, than the mentally impaired could be allowed to roam about without restraint.[47] Such people required constraint and strong discipline "until they accept soundness of mind," that is, until they accepted Christian and civilized standards of behavior. Both "the common law of all nations" and the "sacred pages" of the Bible demonstrate that organized, disciplined society is the only way for men to live. Philosophers, theologians, and jurists all agreed on the naturalness of organized society. That being the case, such unsocial men "ought to be restrained by Christian rulers and to be protected and governed," presumably until they have attained the knowledge and habits necessary for dwelling in an organized society like other men.[48] To leave these people to live in an uncivilized fashion would be as wrong as it would be "to leave someone free to harm others." Such unchecked behavior would not be the exercise of true freedom, but rather a violation of true freedom (*imperfectio, & defectus libertatis*).[49] In other words, true human freedom requires discretion and moderation in its exercise.

Indeed, not only would it not be sinful or a violation of the natural rights of those who exist in the lowest category of human society to subjugate them, it would clearly be positive. After all, "all human beings, even if (*quamvis*) they are Jews and infidels, ought to be cherished for humanitarian reasons (*humanitatis ratione fovendi*)" and "be called fellow human beings and our neighbors."[50] This being the case, the Spanish treatment of the Indians, even under some circumstances, their conquest and enslavement, could be justified on the grounds of the barbarous, uncivilized nature of their way of life. Once these people had become settled and civilized, once they had left their barbarous ways behind, once, in other words, they had matured socially and politically, the wars and their consequences would come to an end. Instead, everything would then be done in accordance with the "instruction, gentle governance and liberty of all of the Indians," because the Indians would have risen from an uncivilized to a civilized state of existence.[51]

The argument that all of the advanced societies had passed through various stages of development before reaching their present level meant, of course, that the peoples of the New World, regardless of how politically primitive they might have appeared, could eventually rise to the highest levels of development. At the same time, this line of argument also raised the issue of whether there was a universal standard of behavior that could be applied to every society. Was there a natural law applicable to all men and against whose standards the behavior of all societies could be judged? When the Spanish sought to assist societies of the second and third classes to rise in order to become fully civilized, did they have at their disposal a set of standards to apply to the peoples whom they were assisting? In his discussion of the natural law and what it included, Solórzano sought to answer that question.

4. The Mechanics of Political Evolution — The Natural Law

The concept of natural law applicable to and binding on all people was a staple of medieval legal and philosophical thought.[1] Roman law contained such a definition, making natural law (*ius naturale*) one of the three fundamental divisions of all law. The other divisions were the law of nations (*ius gentium*) and the civil law (*ius civile*). The *Digest* defined natural law as

> that which nature has taught all animals; this law indeed is not peculiar to the human race, but belongs to all animals. . . . From this law springs the union of male and female, which we call matrimony, the procreation and of children and their education.[2]

Furthermore, by the terms of natural law, all people were free. On the other hand, war, slavery, buying and selling, and similar practices belonged to the *ius gentium*, the law of nations, that is, to the common practice of all human societies.[3] It was even possible to place these two kinds of law in a biblical framework, where they could represent two levels of human existence, before and after Adam's fall. Natural law represented an ideal order, one in which there was no war, no slavery, apparently no private property, a world in which people lived at peace, sharing goods and doing no harm to one another. On the other hand, the *ius gentium* represented the world as it actually existed, a world in which people competed with one another for goods, where they waged war and even enslaved one another. Isidore of Seville (c. 560–636), whose *Etymologiae* was one of the fundamental elements of medieval thought, transmitted this understanding of these laws to the Middle Ages.[4] One consequence of this conception of the origin of these two laws was the broad conclusion that by Adam's fall, "man passed out of the state of nature into the state in which the conventional institutions of society," that is, the characteristic elements of the *ius gentium*, are necessary. Thus even slavery could be seen in a positive light, as part of a "disciplinary system by which the sinful tendencies of man may be corrected."[5]

The Roman definition of natural law meant that the law was in some sense part of the natural order and common to all human beings, a notion that in turn appeared in the writings of early Christians. St. Paul, for example, declared that natural law was written on the hearts of all men.[6] The Roman conception of natural law reached the medieval world through the revival of Roman law in the eleventh and twelfth centuries.[7] Subsequently, it entered the canon law tradition when Gratian included the definitions of various kinds of law in *Distinctio I* of his *Decretum*.[8]

Among medieval philosophers and theologians a slightly different definition of natural law developed. Natural law, according to Thomas Aquinas, was only one part of the eternal law that governed the universe. On the one hand, "all things participate in the eternal law . . . as from its impression upon them they have inclinations to their proper acts and ends." To this extent, Aquinas's definition of natural law echoed that of the Roman law tradition. Human beings, however, participated in the eternal law in a unique fashion. They followed that law by way of natural law that he defined as the "participation of the rational creature in the eternal law".[9] Defined this way, natural law included, then, both rationality and instinct.

The legal and the philosophical traditions of natural law clearly had a great deal in common. For the purposes of the present discussion, the most important point of agreement in these two legal traditions was that both asserted the universality of natural law. To the extent that natural law was a matter of instinct, it was something written on the hearts of human beings, all of whom shared it and were, therefore, subject to it. To the extent that natural law was rational participation in the eternal law, all rational creatures possessed the capacity to comprehend it.

The Spanish writers who examined the justice of the conquest of the Americas, whether they were trained as lawyers, philosophers, or theologians, were acquainted with the concepts of natural law and the law of nations. While the existence of natural law was thus recognized in all intellectual circles, the precise content of that law was in dispute, except for the broad statements on marriage, liberty, and the rearing of children mentioned above. This lack of precision about the content of natural law meant that various authors identified a wide, but not identical, range of behavior as violations of it. Some defenders of the Spanish conquest of the Americas had argued that the conquest was indeed justified because the Indians engaged in practices that were contrary to the terms of natural law as the Spanish understood it. Thus, it might be argued that even though the inhabitants of the Americas possessed *dominium*, they could lose the exercise of it through wicked behavior that violated natural law. The Spanish conquest of the New World would then be a period of correction and training for the Indians under the direction of the Spanish government. Natural law would thus provide both guidelines against which the behavior of the Indians could be measured and a set of goals toward which the Spanish would direct them. Underlying all these positions, however, was the assumption that the inhabitants of the New World possessed the capacity to know the universal norms of the natural law. Their failure to live up to them was, therefore, culpable.

Juan de Solórzano Pereira drew upon these various opinions about natural law and the law of nations in the course of discussing the political evolution of the peoples of the Americas. According to Solórzano, echoing Acosta, the fundamental standard for determining the level of sociopolitical development of any society was the existence of a *respublica*, that is, a stable, orderly society with rulers, laws, and institutions; he recognized that others saw matters differently. Other writers had argued that certain practices found in infidel societies — cannibalism, idolatry, and human sacrifice, to name the worst of such practices — would in themselves justify depriving the infidels who engaged in them the exercise of the *dominium* that was legitimately theirs. This brought Solórzano to the question of natural law and law of nations. Did there exist a law against which the behavior of every society could be measured and that would justify the conquest of any society that failed to adhere to the standards of that law? Furthermore, if such a law did exist, could those societies that did adhere to the standards of such a law (or at least claimed to do so) force those societies that did not adhere to it to do so? In other words, could the Spanish justify the conquest of the New World on the grounds that they were simply requiring the Indians to live according to the standards of natural law, standards known to all rational creatures?

The question of the existence of a universally applicable law placed the Indians in an awkward position. On the one hand, the papacy and the Spanish defined the Indians as rational human beings, thus rejecting the argument that the Spanish could conquer them on the grounds that they were like women, children, or slaves, needing to be brought under the guardianship of others. On the other hand, if the Indians were fully mature, rational human beings, and if there was a universal law knowable by all rational human beings, then the failure of the Indians to live according to the standards that such a law set might justify their conquest by the Spanish.

Was it possible, in other words, to deprive people, specifically the inhabitants of the Americas, especially those who comprised Acosta's second class of societies, of their *dominium* because they violated natural law? As the heading of this chapter stated, there were those who argued that

> the Indians might be justly attacked and subjugated because they committed numerous and very wicked sins against the law of nature; they exercised tyranny, they were cannibals and they were devoted in the most horrible fashion to idolatry and to the cruel sacrifices of human beings.[10]

The first point to consider is what Solórzano meant by the *lex naturae*. At one point early in this discussion, he equated it with natural reason, that is, the evils that the Indians committed were "against natural law and reason."[11] Later, in the next chapter where he continued this discussion, Solórzano declared that "the natural law is the light of human reason that God, the author of nature, placed in the minds of men together with nature, for the doing or the not doing of things," a position he attributed to Thomas Aquinas.[12] Such being the case,

> this light has not been denied to the Indians by God, however barbarous they might be, since they are true men and they are not ignorant of those things to which that natural law inclines [men] and what it teaches should be embraced or avoided and also what is not allowed by any [human] custom or regulation.[13]

In support of this argument, Solórzano cited St. Paul, St. Augustine, and John Cassian, all of whom referred to the existence of the natural law among non-Christians. As Augustine said, this law was "written in the hearts of men," Christian and non-Christian alike.[14]

Having proved that natural law was the heritage of all men, the next issue was to identify those practices that violated that law. Solórzano opened the discussion in Chapter 12 of the second book of the *De Indiarum Jure* with a list of violations of natural law that some argued could justify the Spanish conquest of the Americas. These crimes included the fact that

> their princes wickedly and tyrannically domineer over them and most of the Indian peoples sin by means of the fiercest and most foul customs against the law of nature, eating human flesh and, what is worse, being given in wondrous fashion to the wicked cult of idolatry, to false and unnatural images that they construct for themselves, and they are accustomed to immolate and to offer up most cruel and abominable sacrifices and [to engage in] various other [wicked] religious practices.

For doing such wicked things, the Spanish, especially if they were acting under papal warrant, could deprive the Indians of their *dominium*, an opinion Solórzano attributed to Innocent IV and to a number of canonists who followed him.[15]

In fact, however, Innocent IV did not quite say what Solórzano attributed to him. In his commentary on *Quod super his*, Innocent IV did argue that God authorized the pope to punish infidels "who have no law except the law of nature if they violate that law." The only example he gave, however, was the divine punishment of the people of Sodom, who had violated the law of nature by engaging in sexual practices that were forbidden even by the light of natural reason.[16] Innocent IV's commentary did not spell out any other crimes that violated natural law.

Solórzano seems to have derived his list of violations of natural law from Vitoria's *De Indis*, not from Innocent IV. In his first *relectio*, Vitoria had offered the following argument:

> The next title could be either on account of the personal tyranny of the barbarians' masters toward their subjects, or because of their tyrannical and oppressive laws against the innocent, such as human sacrifice practised on innocent men or the killing of condemned criminals for cannibalism.

Vitoria went on to argue that the Spanish could assert that the conquest of the Americas was legitimate because the Spanish were rescuing "the innocent from unjust death," even if the Indians did not ask to be rescued. With this argument he also cited Innocent IV, but only to point out that the pope's opinion was that "sinners against nature may be punished."[17] He did not indicate that Innocent IV had identified any particular sinful acts that would justify such punishment.

Solórzano supported this line of argument with an unusually full series of excerpts and citations from relevant authors. For example, he offered the argument found in some writers that Pope Alexander VI had issued his famous bulls dividing the New World into Castilian and Portuguese spheres because the peoples of the New World "did not observe the natural law and worshipped idols in violation of the natural law."[18] This suggests that he may have believed that these writers had not read the pope's bulls carefully. In fact, they did not justify the Castilian occupation of the Americas on the grounds that the inhabitants of these regions were violators of natural law and were committing various wicked acts that required punishment. Quite the reverse: citing Christopher Columbus's description of the people whom he encountered in the Caribbean, the pope's bull described the people as

> living in peace, and, as reported, going unclothed, and not eating flesh. . . . Moreover . . . these very peoples . . . believe in one God, the Creator in heaven,

and seem sufficiently disposed to embrace the Catholic faith and be trained in good morals.[19]

Having thus inverted the basis on which the papacy awarded responsibility for the New World to the Spanish, Solórzano then moved on to discuss the conquest of the Aztecs and the Incas. Citing the work of several Spanish observers of the conquest, Solórzano pointed out that

> the princes and petty kings (*reguli*) of the Indians . . . in all of the provinces that have been thus far discovered, especially the Mexican and Peruvian regions, which were more politically developed (*quae magis politicae erant*), were undoubtedly tyrants not only because they established their empires on fear and cruelty rather than on rights and laws and on the consent of their subjects but also because in their manner of governing they are unaccustomed to act except by means of fraud, violence and tyranny.[20]

The consequence of this form of perverted government was that the rulers of these peoples treated them "not as men but as animals," burdening them with taxes, labor services, and so on.[21]

Lest the reader fail to appreciate the horrendous conditions under which some inhabitants of the Americas labored and from which the Spanish freed them, Solórzano went on to compare their situation to that of the ancient Israelites. He described the large tombs and other large buildings found in the Incan Empire, the great highways linking the empire that had required the leveling of hills and the filling in of valleys, and the other massive construction projects that dotted the Peruvian landscape. Again following the reasoning of Acosta, Solórzano compared the burden that these efforts placed on the Peruvian people with those that the pharaohs had placed on the ancient Israelites. Just as "in ancient times, the pyramids and mausoleums of the Egyptian kings" were built with "bricks extracted from the people of Israel" by the tyrannical power of the pharaoh, so too had the rulers of the Incas loaded their people with unconscionable burdens.[22]

It is interesting to note at this point that Solórzano did not take the obvious route to condemn the pharaohs, that is, to cite the Book of Genesis. Instead, he cited several ancient pagan authors, Josephus, Strabo, Herodotus, Pliny, Diodorus Siculus, and, "above all, Aristotle," as well as contemporary writers. The point he sought to make here was that royal tyranny was a violation of natural law, not of divine law, so that the divine punishment of the pharaoh resulted from his tyrannical treatment of the Israelites, a violation of natural law, and was not the consequence of some violation of divine law. As Solórzano pointed out, to a non-Christian such as Aristotle, the pyramids had been built by tyrannical rulers anxious to keep their subjects so busy that they could not plot against them.[23]

By using the term "tyrant" to describe the rulers of the Incas and the Egyptians, Solórzano was paving the way for a discussion of the traditional distinction between the tyrant and the king. The tyrant was a wicked ruler who exploited his people for his own private interests, while the king was "he who rules justly, seeking rather the convenience of his subjects than his own personal interest." The ancient authors, he added, long ago noted that "tyranny was the greatest sin and, as it were, included the seedbed of cruelty and all the injuries done to men, and all evils."[24] At the end of this discussion, Solórzano presented the argument that "kings who do not know God, that is infidels, are tyrants rather than kings" because of the manner in which they rule, that is, because they exploit their subjects.[25] Whether he realized it or not, Solórzano's argument at this point could have been used to deny the existence of legitimate *dominium* in infidel societies. Furthermore, this identification of nonbelief with tyranny would mean that the rulers of infidel societies were tyrants even though they could not possibly have known the "true" religion.

Thus, natural reason demonstrated that the tyrannical ruler was the greatest of all evils. That being the case, there were those who argued that the conquest of the Americas was justified if the rulers were clearly tyrants. As far as Solórzano was concerned, there was certainly much evidence to demonstrate the tyrannical nature of Inca government. For example, the Incan rulers, "the aforementioned tyrants over the Indians, rarely grew old in their empires, or transmitted them to their sons and nephews," suggesting that the rulers killed one another off rather than developing a plan for peaceful succession to the throne.[26] This, in turn, meant that this society lacked one of the fundamental ends for which government was established, stability and order.

The situation in Peru was so violent and tyrannical that "the Peruvian Indians admitted that it was by the just judgment of God that they were conquered (*sub jugum missos*) by a small number of Spaniards because He wished to punish the tyrannical and fratricidal Atahualpa the Inca in this way." As a result, the Peruvians called the Spaniards "*Viracochas*, signifying by that name a people sent from heaven."[27] This being the case, it could be argued that the conquest of Peru was legitimate simply because the people accepted the conquering Spanish troops as their deliverers, not as their oppressors, thus consenting to Spanish overlordship. Again, Solórzano was echoing the argument that Vitoria had made about the possibility of the Indians freely accepting the Spanish as their rulers.[28]

Having dealt with tyranny, defined as the root of all evils in the political order, Solórzano moved to consider other violations of the natural law that defenders of the conquest of the Americas could advance. "Many writers," he pointed out, had criticized the Indians for their "universal laziness, stupidity, ingratitude, cruelty, nakedness, drunkenness, polygamy, for their promiscuous desires that they exploited at the expense of their mothers and sisters, and for many other wicked activities to which nearly all of the Indians were devoted."[29] To illustrate this point, Solórzano pointed out that "Montezuma, the Mexican Emperor, had numerous wives, of whom he had 150 pregnant at any given time."[30] Other infidel rulers similarly exploited scores, even hundreds, of wives in similar fashion, producing numerous offspring.[31] Solórzano then went on to describe a variety of sexual practices in which the Indians engaged that, in his opinion, clearly violated natural law.

The next evidence of the wickedness of the inhabitants of the New World was the practice of cannibalism, a practice, Solórzano pointed out, that numerous observers, beginning with Columbus, had documented.[32] Evidence of cannibalism existed in Mexico and Peru, as well as in other parts of the New World.[33]

Finally, Solórzano examined the practice of human sacrifice in the New World. In Mexico and in Peru human sacrifice was practiced on a large scale, according to Spanish observers.[34] Even the introduction of Christianity did not wipe the practice out, as royal ordinances directed against it demonstrated.[35] While the Spanish were revolted by the idea of human sacrifice generally, they were especially horrified by the practice of sacrificing children. Solórzano pointed out that "these sacrifices are recognized as being contrary to the precepts of natural law, which precepts desire that men assist one another [and] that children be begotten and educated by their parents, not slaughtered by them."[36] Furthermore, these acts were forbidden not only to Christians but to all human beings because they violate natural law, not divine or ecclesiastical law.[37] Again, Solórzano cited numerous ancient pagan writers who condemned human sacrifice, thus demonstrating that it clearly violated natural law because it violated the natural reason that all humans possess.[38]

The fifth argument that Solórzano offered in support of the assertion that the Indians' violations of natural law could justify their conquest was that the Indians worshipped idols, and idolatry was a violation of natural law. The sin consisted in "offering to false and filthy idols the honor that men ought to show to the one true God."[39] Solórzano did not explain why idolatry itself was a violation of natural law; one would think that knowledge of the one true God could not possibly exist within a society where the Gospel had not been preached. Those who argued that idolatry violated natural law appear to have taken the position that the evils associated with idolatry, human sacrifice in particular, were its consequence, and justified punishing those who worshipped idols.[40]

Later in the discussion, Solórzano identified the beings that the Indians' idols represented. They were not divine beings but instead represented

> that very dangerous demon, always the enemy of the human race, who blinded the barbarians with these and other errors and mocked them with ambiguous oracles, so that he not only usurped for himself the divine honors and even the ceremonies by which God is worshipped, so that he might emulate Him.[41]

This being the case, the conquest of the Americas could be justified on the grounds that the Spanish were protecting the Indians against their most dangerous enemy, the spirit of evil who was leading them to eternal damnation.

The obvious difficulty with the argument that idolatry would justify the Indians' conquest by the Spanish was that it was a violation of natural law only in Christian eyes. All of the sources that Solórzano cited in this stage of the discussion were either from the Bible or from the writings of Christian philosophers, theologians, missionaries, and so on. Those who employed this argument could and did point to the punishments that God inflicted on the Jews when they turned away from worshipping Him and to the gods of other peoples.[42] This situation was not identical with that of the infidels of the New World, of course, since the ancient Jews knew the true God and had knowingly turned away from worshipping Him. Further on, Solórzano presented some writers' argument that even ignorance was no defense in the case of idolatry.[43]

In the next chapter of the *De Indiarum Jure*, Solórzano continued examining the argument that the Spanish could legitimately conquer the Indians and other idolators who violated natural law. He restated the argument that the Indians clearly violated natural law not only because of their idolatry but because of various sexual perversions as well.[44] This being the case, the Spanish monarchs had the right, so some would argue, to "wage war against the Indians in order to stop them from engaging in these wicked practices and to force them to observe the natural law."[45] The Spanish could not do this on their own initiative, however, but only "by the authority of the Pope who has jurisdiction over all infidels in this case in his capacity as universal vicar of Christ," as a long line of medieval canonists and popes from Innocent IV to the present had decreed.[46] He pointed out that more recently Pope Pius V (1566–1572) had issued a decree re-affirming the responsibility of Christians to insure that the Indians heeded the dictates of natural law. He argued that if the Spanish rulers of the Americas did not do so, they would be encouraging Indian converts and Spaniards living among the Indians to engage in these evil practices.[47] Indeed, these evils were so dangerous that any Christian prince who learned of such practices among those over whom he had jurisdiction should strive to eliminate them even without papal licence.[48]

Furthermore, Solórzano pointed out, citing Peter of Aragon (c. 1544–c. 1592), that under the circumstances, if the Spanish did not intervene in the Americas to protect people whose "*respublica* was turning to idolatrous worship or within which injuries were being inflicted on innocent people," then it would be the Spanish who were violating natural law. After all, "the natural law commanded" assistance of people in such straits by those who were in a position to do so.[49] Here again, the lack of a fixed definition of the contents of natural law meant that all kinds of activity could be included. Further on in this discussion, Solórzano added that "men, driven either by humanity alone or by reason of natural relationship, ought to direct the practices of other men to the good, punishing the great evils and wicked deeds, the injuries and oppressions that they suffer under the yoke of tyrannical rulers."[50] Thus the Spanish, no less than the infidels who inhabited the New World, were subject to the terms of natural law.

As the preceding argument led to the conclusion that natural law required those who could to protect those being harmed by the actions of others, Solórzano then presented the argument that "it is licit to wage war against the infidels, restraining and punishing them, since by the practice of idolatry great harm is done to God."[51] Here, of course, the citations in support of this position came only from Biblical and Christian sources, idolatry not being a crime clearly knowable by human reason alone. Among the proofs Solórzano adduced in this section was the argument of Orosius (fl. 410) and St. Augustine that the collapse of Rome was the consequence of the survival of idolatrous practices even after the official Christianization of the Empire.[52] The nearest that Solórzano could come to providing evidence that idolatry was knowable as a grave sin even to non-Christians was the argument that the occasional unexplained collapse of idols in the ancient pagan world signified even to pagans the coming end of idolatry and the arrival of the true religion.[53]

As Solórzano recognized, the obvious objection to the argument that idolatry and related sins concerning the worship of other than the true God could justify the conquest of the Americas was that the Indians were simply unaware of His existence, because the Gospel had never been preached to them before the Spanish came to the New World. He reiterated a point made earlier in these discussions, namely that

> since the law of nature is the light of human reason that God, the author of nature together with nature, inserted in the minds of men for guiding them about what to do or not to do . . . it can not be believed that regardless of how barbaric the Indians may be, since they are true human beings, this light was denied to them by God and thus be ignorant of those things to which that nature inclines men.[54]

The basic tenets of this law known to all men were "to worship God, to seek the good, to avoid evil, not to do to another that which you do not wish to be done to you, and other things of a similar nature." The consequence of this argument was that the Indians could not legitimately claim to be "invincibly ignorant" of this law as a defense against Spanish conquest.[55] Even the ancient pagans, Epicurus, Cicero, and Aristotle, to mention but a few of Solórzano's citations at this point, recognized the existence of "a fundamental principle of all things, greater than everything else that existed and on which everything depends and is directed, by which all men are led by the light of nature alone."[56] Thus even infidels, as long as they were truly human, could not claim "to be exempted [from conquest by the Spanish] on the grounds that they did not know that idolatry was a crime, since none are unaware of the existence of the one true God."[57]

The theme of the arguments that Solórzano presented at this point was that natural law required the Spanish to punish those who violated it. Furthermore, the fundamental terms of that law were known to all rational creatures by virtue of their humanity. Ignorance of natural law was no defense against punishment for violating it. Thus, the Spanish conquerors would be justified in seizing control of the New World because they were punishing violations of natural law known to everyone. At the same time, the purpose of the conquest was not simply conquest and punishment, but also to improve the lives of the Indians by freeing them from evil rulers in this world and from eternal damnation in the next.

Having presented the arguments supporting the right, even the obligation, of the Spanish to subjugate the Indians in order to reform them and their way of life, Solórzano then provided a series of counterarguments in the next chapter. In this section of the *De Indiarum Jure*, Solórzano did not deny that the Indians were violating natural law, nor did he accept their ignorance of that law as a defense against conquest. Instead, focusing on the ultimate goal of reforming the Indians and their way of life, he presented the argument that such reform should take place only as the result of peaceful entry into the New World. In other words, while accepting the ultimate goal, he was arguing for a different means of achieving it.

In this phase of the overall argument about the legitimacy of the conquest of the Americas, Solórzano pointed out that there were numerous learned men who had argued that

> war can not be waged against infidels who are not subject to Christian rulers, even with papal authorization, regardless of whether they are bound under the imperium of tyrants, are the slaves of idols and commit the worst, most abominable crimes against natural law and reason.[58]

This was so even if the people committing these crimes received warnings from the Christians about the evil nature of their activities. Even if these people refused to reform, the Christians had no right to intervene militarily, according to this line of argument. The proponents of this position argued that "those wars are just and legitimate which are defensive, punitive, or for the purpose of avenging a wrong, that is, wars which ward off injuries and harm to ourselves" or are waged for similar reasons.[59] The crimes that the infidels committed against natural law, heinous though they might have been, were not injuries done to Christians or to anyone subject to Christian rulers.[60] Even the pope could not authorize the conquest of infidels who were clearly violating the terms of natural law, because he had no jurisdiction over them.[61] Finally, this line of argument ran, "just as an individual citizen does not have the power to punish another citizen no matter how wicked he was, so similarly one respublica can not acquire a right to another respublica not subject to it because of the fact that in that other respublica the most wicked evils are committed."[62] The defenders of the absolute autonomy of infidel societies from military interference stressed that even the argument that the conquest of the infidels was for their own eternal good was specious. To conquer another people for their own good was to act "under the pretext of charity or piety," rather than legitimately.[63] Furthermore, even papal authorization was not sufficient, because such a war would be an improper involvement of the Church in mundane matters, as Bernard of Clairvaux had argued in a letter to Pope Eugenius III.[64] Thus, there was no legitimate basis for invading infidel lands.[65]

In the second stage of this chapter, Solórzano presented a line of argument that sounds ironic, if not clearly sarcastic. After listing the usual crimes against natural law, he pointed out that some saw these as crimes against God Himself. This being the case, Christians could legitimately act to defend the divine majesty. Solórzano responded with the observation that "God, if He so wished, was easily capable of defending Himself against such injuries and punishing these wicked men for their evil deeds."[66]

The larger significance of this line of argument was that since God could directly punish those who offended Him because, as He says, "vengeance is mine" (Deut. 32:35), no man had the right to act on His behalf in order to avenge wrongs done to Him. Even the pope's power to act in God's name as Christ's vicar was clearly a limited power: "The power conceded did not include power over those who had not received the sacrament of baptism . . . but over those who had submitted themselves to the Christian faith."[67] Thus any claim to possession of the Americas based on the assertion that the conqueror was only avenging wrongs done to God was unacceptable.

Solórzano then observed that Thomas Aquinas had argued that the Christian Church should not tolerate the religious practices of infidels. Some unidentified writers had apparently employed this argument to justify the punishment of the inhabitants of the New World for practicing idolatry and other behavior that was at odds with Christian belief. Solórzano responded that Aquinas was arguing for the approach that Christian rulers should take concerning practices of their non-Christian subjects. That is, a Christian monarch could restrain his non-Christian subjects from practicing those aspects of their religion that were in some way harmful to Christians. Such a ruler had no power over infidels who were not subject to him.[68] Thus, Aquinas's argument could not then be applied to the situation that existed in the Americas.

Furthermore, Solórzano added, Christian rulers should take care to tolerate the practices of infidels where possible, if only to make it easier to bring them to the true faith. He pointed to the advice that John Chrysostom (c. 347–407) and Augustine had given to their fellow Christians about participating in social life with infidels. To avoid the company of infidels in daily life would mean the loss of opportunities to convert them.[69] Here again, Solórzano was emphasizing the need for peaceful approaches to non-Christians.

The next point that Solórzano raised in this chapter was associated with Innocent IV's opinion that since "the infidels are ruled only by the law of nature and thus if they commit a crime against that law, they can be

punished by the pope and by Christian princes [acting] under his authority." Innocent IV went on to add that "this being so, we ought to agree
without any exception that they can not only be punished and warred
against not only because of their sins against nature . . . but also because of
other sins which they committed against the natural law." The list of crimes
that would fit this circumstance included "theft, fornication, adultery, mur-
der and in general any similar sins, since all these sins are contrary to natural
law or natural reason and thus are against natural law."[70]

To take this approach to violations of natural law was "absurd," however, because it would not only mean that the pope would have to order
Christian rulers to attack infidel societies in order to correct their violations
of natural law, but that he would also be constantly ordering attacks on
Christian kingdoms "since in every region there are numerous sinners" who
deserve correction. The result would be political instability, since the pope
"would be able to change kingdoms on a daily basis."[71] Furthermore,
Solórzano pointed out, many theologians took the position that ignorance
of natural law was excusable in the less mature or less intelligent. While
these writers did recognize that all people should recognize the general
principle of "not doing to others what you do not want others to do to
yourself," they argued that knowledge of the specific terms of natural law
was too much to expect from those who by birth, age, or education, had not
been instructed in its particulars.[72] Furthermore, Solórzano again pointed
out that the ultimate responsibility of Christians toward infidels was to
insure the successful preaching of the Gospel, not simply to punish violations of natural law that the infidels were committing. "Christ, after all, did
not come to judge the world but to save it."[73]

Turning to another line of argument, Solórzano noted that even the
most heinous crimes attributed to the Indians would not justify their
conquest by Christians. After all, all of the crimes attributed to the Indians
were committed by other peoples known to and admired by European
Christians in the seventeenth century.[74] The ancient Israelites, the world-
conquering Romans, the wisest philosophers of antiquity, all of these
people had engaged in various practices that violated natural law.[75] Even
more immediate ancestors of contemporary Europeans engaged in wicked
practices such as cannibalism. The Britons and the Poles, for example, were
charged with eating human flesh, just as the inhabitants of various newly
discovered parts of the world were accused of this practice.[76]

Even if the rulers of the Indians were engaging in serious violations of
natural law, waging a war against them might well mean the death of far

more people than the actions of the rulers caused.[77] Prudence alone would thus seem to dictate caution in advocating the use of force to eliminate evil behavior in infidel societies. In addition, Solórzano argued that "the Church ought to tolerate the religious rites of pagans, even those not subject to us, in order to avoid greater harm and scandal."[78]

Turning to the specific crime of cannibalism, Solórzano suggested that even that crime, such an obvious evil to Christians, might not seem so to people cut off from the mainstream of legal thinking on such matters. Furthermore, human sacrifice might also not seem to be as evil as Christians perceived it. After all, in the past "it was in use in almost every nation, not only barbarous ones but also in those that were known for their greater learning and wisdom."[79] Solórzano then went on to list numerous peoples who engaged in human sacrifice, a list ranging from the ancient Carthaginians, Romans, and Israelites to the various barbarian tribes that entered Europe in the declining days of the Roman Empire.[80] Even the ancestors of the Spanish engaged in the practice.[81] This being the case, the seventeenth-century Spanish were wise to hesitate before condemning the inhabitants of the Americas for their practice of offering human sacrifices to their gods.

Even the practice of idolatry by the Indians might not have justified the Spanish conquest of the New World. Each ancient society had its own gods, strange though they might be. The Hebrews, God's own people, occasionally fell to worshiping false gods.[82] Closer to home, the ancestors of the Spanish had also worshiped idols.[83] Turning to the other great religious crime, blasphemy, often judged a legitimate basis for attacking infidel societies, Solórzano noted that blasphemy, like idolatry, was a great sin against God but was something that God Himself could punish whenever He wished.[84]

The final segment of this chapter concerned the argument that the Bible provided numerous examples of the ancient Israelites waging war legitimately against infidels because they engaged in idolatry.[85] Solórzano countered that "the people of Israel never occupied the lands of the Canaanites, Amorites, and other people on their own authority" because these people were infidels or violators of natural law. They did so "by the special and explicit command and grant of God who promised them those lands for their homeland."[86] Here again, Solórzano stressed that generally speaking, no people have the right to correct other societies regardless of the evil practices of those societies. This line of argument also emphasized that men should not assume the role of God in their relations with other societies.

In the next chapter of the *De Indiarum Jure* (2.15), Solórzano summarized the main arguments found in the three chapters that had dealt with the problem of violations of natural law by infidels. The conclusion of this chapter was that in the final analysis, the treatment of infidels by Christians was always subject to the goal of conversion. At the same time, a distinction had to be made between infidels who were already subject to Christian rulers and those who were not. The infidel subjects of Christian rulers, all authorities agreed, could be required to give up their idolatrous practices and those actions that were clearly violations of the natural law.[87] As for those infidels who were not subject to Christian rulers, if they sinned against natural law, Solórzano accepted the position of Innocent IV, who had stated that if infidels refused to change their evil ways even after Christians had instructed them, then the pope could authorize Christian rulers to punish them for these violations.[88]

As for the argument that God can punish those who harm Him by engaging in idolatry and other violations of natural law, Solórzano pointed out that the fact that God was capable of avenging wrongs done to Him did not necessarily mean that Christians had no right to do so as well. What it did mean was that the Church had no direct power over the infidel; they were *extra ecclesiam*.[89] Solórzano also suggested that when St. Paul argued that infidels were of no concern to Christians in matters of sin, all that he meant was that the Christians lacked the power to do anything to stop the infidels from doing evil but not the right to do so.[90]

Thus, the Church did have the right to punish infidels who violated natural law by employing the services of Christian rulers who would act under papal direction.[91] The presumption was that the Spanish would not use force against the Indians until after the Spanish had peacefully instructed them in the errors of their ways.[92]

Finally, Solórzano dealt with the argument that the use of force against the Indians would interfere with the process of converting them to Christianity. In such a situation, to punish them for activities they had engaged in previously would seem excessively harsh. They should be led to the baptismal font in the most gentle and peaceful manner. On the other hand, if the Indians, after being instructed in the right way of living and accepting the Christian faith continued to violate natural law and remained mired in their old evil ways, then the Spanish could legitimately punish them.[93] In effect, by becoming Christians and agreeing to change their ways, the Indians would have placed themselves within the Church and under the jurisdiction of the Spanish. In such a situation, the Indians could legitimately expect punishment from Church and secular authorities if they returned to their earlier, sinful practices.

Solórzano's extensive discussion of the place of natural law in relations between Christians and non-Christians was central to the *De Indiarum Jure*. In the first place, he established the existence of a natural law binding all people and accessible to all through the use of the reason that everyone possesses. The existence of natural law placed the Indians of the New World in an awkward position. On the one hand, their essential humanity and the legitimacy of the *dominium* they possessed were recognized. On the other hand, being rational creatures, they should have known the terms of natural law in at least its broad outlines, thus leaving themselves open to judgment by Christians.

The fact that Christian Europeans had come to understand natural law not only in broad terms but in detail as well meant that Europeans could evaluate other societies according to their degree of adherence to natural law. It was not sufficient for an infidel society to have established an orderly, stable form of community, something akin to Aristotle's polis. The Aztecs, the Incas, and the other stable societies who formed Acosta's second class of societies had done that, but it was not sufficient to exempt them from being judged according to the terms of natural law. These societies had not eliminated a variety of practices that kept their members in a barbarous way of life that taught them evil practices instead of virtuous ones. The Spanish, with their knowledge of the virtuous way of life, could instruct the Indians in how to raise themselves up from their primitive level of existence to a more fully human one.

Solórzano and his contemporaries expressed no doubt about the capacity of the Indians to rise to the more humane level of existence that would come from adherence to the terms of natural law. In fact, if his words are to be taken at face value, he would seem to believe that once having heard the teaching of the Europeans about the behavior proper to human beings, the Indians of the second class of society would readily accept the proffered way of life. He was certainly optimistic, it would seem, regarding the ease with which the Indians of the second class of society would pass to the higher stages of civilization.

At the same time, it is also worth noting that Solórzano did not suggest that each and every Christian ruler could or should take upon himself the responsibility for bringing the benefits of a more advanced way of living to the infidels whom they and their subjects encountered. It was not to the advantage of the Spanish to encourage any and all comers to seek out and to civilize the inhabitants of the newly discovered lands. The Spanish monarchs were certainly not interested in having competitors in the task of civilizing the inhabitants of the New World. As a result, Solórzano could accept the notion that the infidels were subject to the terms of natural law only if the task of informing them of its terms and coercing them, if necessary, into accepting these terms derived from some higher authority, from some official who would insure that the work would be done in an orderly fashion. The result was that for Solórzano, obtaining papal licence to engage in such work was essential. In effect, Solórzano's arguments led up to the assertion that the process of civilizing and converting the infidels could take place legitimately only if papal approval was obtained in advance. Papal responsibility for the spiritual well-being of all people was thus the apex of a program of international order.

5. A Legitimate Claim to the Indies — The Theory of Papal Power

Having demonstrated that claims to possession of the New World based on the mental or moral incapacity of the Indians were invalid because the Indians were fully human and rational, Juan de Solórzano Pereira moved on to discuss the one just basis upon which the Spanish claim to the New World could rest. In the twenty-second chapter of the second book of the *De Indiarum Jure*, Solórzano began the discussion of what he termed "The tenth and most efficacious title [to the New World], that which is derived from the donation and grant of the Roman Pontiff."[1] Even though the thrust of Solórzano's argument up to this point had been leading the reader to a discussion of the role of the papacy in the acquisition and possession of the New World, nevertheless it is rather surprising to see that role stated so bluntly. Why, especially by the early seventeenth century, when the Reformation had taken its toll on the papacy, would a Castilian royal official still insist that legitimate possession of the New World required papal authorization?

Part of the answer to that question lies in the way Solórzano structured his entire treatise. All along, he had rested his position on Pope Innocent IV's discussion of the relationship between the Church and the infidels. Once Solórzano had defended the essential humanity of the Indians and had concluded that they would follow the path that the European Christians had followed to a civilized, Christian way of life once they received the proper guidance, the only possible justification for Spanish possession of the New World was to insure the religious conversion of the Indians. In terms of the arguments that he had supported, there was no legitimate military, economic, or political basis for justifying the conquest. The Indians possessed a natural right to *dominium* in property and governance and they posed no military threat to Europeans. Innocent IV had made it clear that such people, even though infidels and sunk in spiritual darkness, could not be subjected to Christian rulers by force unless the pope deemed it necessary for their salvation. In effect, the only legitimate basis for seizing control of the lands of infidels would be the refusal of the Indians to allow peaceful missionaries to enter and to preach.

Furthermore, the historical record constrained Solórzano to rest his case for Spanish possession of the New World on papal authorization because, as he demonstrated in this and succeeding chapters, Christian rulers had long been accustomed to justify the acquisition of land on such authorization.[2] Indeed, his previous historical argument would seem to demonstrate that only by means of a papal grant could Christian rulers acquire the lands of infidels. For a Catholic ruler to claim the right to attack an infidel kingdom on the basis of its ruler lacking true *dominium* because he was an infidel would leave the Christian ruler open to the charge of accepting the Donatist heresy. Given the terms of his argument, not to mention his desire to defend the Spanish monopoly of the Americas, Solórzano had to rest possession of the Americas on the title that Ferdinand and Isabella received from Pope Alexander in the bull *Inter caetera* of 1493. This could be the only legitimate basis for Spanish possession of the Americas. It was by this bull that the pope

> granted, conceded and assigned with full right to Ferdinand and Isabella and their heirs and successors all the islands and mainlands that were discovered toward the west and the south and that may be subsequently discovered and that were not found actually in the possession of any other Christian prince at the time.[3]

Solórzano was well aware that there were many critics, even in Catholic circles, of the theory that the papacy could legitimize European possession of the newly discovered lands. Within a few years of the publication of *Inter caetera*, Henry VII (1485–1509) of England, simply ignoring Alexander VI's bull, unhesitatingly authorized John Cabot to sail westward on a voyage of discovery.[4] In 1541, the French king, Francis I (1515–1547), when told that the New World belonged to the Spanish and the Portuguese by virtue of papal grant, retorted that "the sun shone for him as for others, and he would like very much to see Adam's will to learn how he divided up the world!"[5] The objection of these Catholic kings to papal intervention in the work of discovery and acquisition of new lands was rooted in the traditional medieval conflict between Church and State. From the perspective of some Catholic rulers, Alexander VI's unilateral allocation of jurisdiction over all the peoples of the New World to Castile and Portugal was simply another papal intervention into matters that properly belonged to secular rulers.[6]

If the papal claims on which *Inter caetera* rested were unacceptable to Catholic kings, it is easy to see how little attention Protestant rulers would pay them. The papal claim to legitimize or to condemn European seizure of land in the New World was central to the contemporary debate about the nature and extent of papal power, which was, in turn, was at the heart of the Reformation debate about the nature of the Christian Church. To Protestants, the Roman pontiff symbolized all that was wrong with Catholic Christianity. The papacy had created a legalistic, clerically dominated Church that had deviated fundamentally from the faith of Christ and His apostles.[7] Thus, for Alexander VI to claim the right to restrict the newly discovered lands to the Castilians and Portuguese alone was simply another example of papal hubris, an assertion of a power that was in contrast with the teachings of Jesus.[8] A representative of Henry VII's Protestant granddaughter, Elizabeth I (1558–1603), bluntly told Spain's ambassador that "the Pope had no right to partition the world and to give and take kingdoms to whomsoever he pleased."[9] The English Queen had none of the qualms that might have affected Henry VII as he set about defying Alexander VI's bulls.

Therefore, in order to defend the legitimacy of Castile's possession of the Americas, Solórzano had to first defend the legitimacy of the authority on which Spanish possession of the Americas rested. This involved presenting at least the outlines of the current debate about the powers of the papacy. Consequently, at the outset of Chapter 22 Solórzano raised the issue of whether papal donation was the most just basis upon which Spanish title to the New World could rest. Solórzano began his discussion with a question: Did Alexander VI's donation give the Spanish a just title to the Americas? The answer would depend on

> whether the Supreme Pontiff, the Vicar of Christ on earth, is over all men and rules over all things and can dispose of the kingdoms and lands of the faithful [and of infidels — 1629 ed.] not only in spiritual matters but in temporal matters as well.[10]

Stated this way, Solórzano was presenting the conquest of the Americas in terms of the debate about papal power that stretched back to the investiture controversy of the eleventh and twelfth centuries. If the claims to power that the medieval papacy had made were in fact invalid, the legitimacy of the Spanish conquest of the Americas would be in serious doubt. Part of the problem concerned the nature of the papal claims. As Solórzano presented the case, the popes claimed supreme authority in both spiritual and temporal affairs. He offered the counter argument.

In the first place, there are indeed some who think that the Supreme Pontiff by divine law has absolutely no temporal power and jurisdiction, and cannot in any way command the secular rulers of the faithful and much less command the rulers of the infidels, not to mention to deprive them of their kingdoms and lordships, even if they commit some sin that deserves this [punishment] or some other penalties.[11]

The defenders of this position, among whom Solórzano listed John Calvin (1509–1564) "and other sectarian authors of this time," would restrict papal power to the spiritual realm alone, if they recognized its existence at all. In doing so, they reinterpreted a famous biblical passage used by defenders of papal power to explain the origin of that power. Defenders of papal power had always pointed to the two swords that St. Peter possessed (Luke, 22:38) as demonstrating that Peter and his successors held jurisdiction in both temporal and spiritual matters.[12] Commentators on this image generally concluded that the pope had the power to act directly in spiritual matters as possessor of the spiritual sword. In temporal matters, however, though the pope possessed the sword, he could not exercise it himself; he had to call upon Christian secular rulers to exercise it. Calvin and the other Protestant writers to whom Solórzano had pointed in this connection interpreted the two swords differently. Rather than seeing them as representing spiritual and temporal powers, they understood one sword as signifying "ecclesiastical or spiritual power" and the other as signifying "knowledge or discretion."[13] Thus the power associated with the symbol of the swords was restricted to the spiritual realm, giving the pope no power in the direction of the temporal order, only the right to advise and to guide secular rulers.

To counter this Protestant position, Solórzano pointed out that the denial of papal jurisdiction in temporal affairs was a heretical opinion, one that the Church had condemned long ago. Drawing upon Robert Bellarmine's (1542–1621) defense of papal power, he cited three canon law texts in support of his argument. Careful examination of the canonical sources he cited, however, does not fully support his argument. The first two sources, canons drawn from the *Decretum*, dealt with papal power in spiritual and ecclesiastical matters, not temporal ones.[14]

The third source Solórzano cited at this point seems to be a curious choice, given the document's reputation. He cited Boniface VIII's (1294–1303) famous defense of papal power, the bull *Unam sanctam*, issued in 1302 during the pope's bitter struggle with Philip IV of France. *Unam sanctam* was the most complete statement of papal power ever published. It was, in fact, a summary of the major points made during the medieval

church-state conflict. In this document, the pope stressed the papal possession of the two swords and has often been understood to have claimed
direct papal power in both spiritual and temporal matters.[15] At this point in
the argument, Solórzano would seem to be defending the most extreme
papal claims to power in temporal matters against the Protestants, who
would deny the existence of any papal right, however limited, to intervene
in secular affairs.[16] By citing *Unam sanctam*, Solórzano was identifying
himself, and the Castilian position, with the papacy against its current
enemies.

At the same time, Solórzano appears to have had some doubts about
this particular line of argument, so, to buttress it against the Protestants, he
offered another explanation for papal power in temporal affairs, the Donation of Constantine.[17] The Donation of Constantine was said to be the
granting of the western half of the Roman Empire by the Emperor Constantine (307–337) to Pope Sylvester (314–335) in the early fourth century.[18] This grant provided a theoretical basis for the papacy to claim
jurisdiction over all of western Europe on a secular basis, not a spiritual
one. As Solórzano used the Donation, it served as a counter to the Protestant argument that Christ did not give temporal jurisdiction to Peter and
his successors. Even if one granted legitimacy to Calvin's argument about
the nature of the second sword, that it signified only knowledge, the
Donation of Constantine would justify direct papal involvement in temporal matters, because it traced papal jurisdiction in temporals to a secular
source.

Solórzano then went on to point out that there were still other positions on the nature and extent of papal power in regard to temporal affairs.
For example, there were those who agreed that the pope possessed both
swords but then asserted that he could exercise direct power in temporal
matters only in the Papal State, because only there was he both a spiritual
and a temporal ruler.[19] Elsewhere, in the Holy Roman Empire or in the
other kingdoms of Europe, the pope had no jurisdiction in temporal
matters, so this argument went, because rulers there did not derive their
offices from the pope.[20] In fact, according to the proponents of this argument, secular rulers derived their power from God, just as the pope derives
his.[21]

While Solórzano presented a number of citations in connection with
this particular argument, two are especially interesting. The first was the *De
Monarchia*, Dante's famous defense of the independence of the Holy Roman Empire from papal interference in its internal affairs.[22] This particular

essay was on the *Index of Forbidden Books*, a commentary on the Counter-Reformation papacy's view of its contents.[23] The second citation of interest was the opinion of Antonio de Rosellis that "he was a heretic who asserted that the Roman Pontiff had and has temporal power from God and gives it to the emperor."[24] What makes this citation interesting was not the statement itself, but the author. Rosellis was a fifteenth-century lawyer and advisor to Pope Eugenius IV (1431–1437) who wrote a legal opinion about the legitimacy of the Portuguese conquest of the Canary Islands, a commentary that rested on the same canonistic foundations as the *De Indiarum Jure*, that is, on Innocent IV's theory of universal papal jurisdiction.[25]

Having set out the theoretical framework of the discussion, Solórzano went on to provide a historical basis for discussing the right of the papacy to claim jurisdiction in temporal matters. He began this section with a reference to the fact that the Emperor Louis IV (1314–1347), the Bavarian, had issued a decree stating that it was treasonous (*Majestatis reatum*) to say that the person elected by the German princes to the office of Holy Roman Emperor was "not the true emperor until he was crowned" by the pope.[26] This was the position which Pope Innocent III had stated in his bull *Venerabilem* (1202) and which had remained the papacy's position.[27] Indeed, according to the argument that Solórzano presented, several hundred years earlier the true situation was quite the reverse. Instead of the emperor depending upon the pope for the powers of his office, the newly elected pope required imperial approval before his coronation. Solórzano correctly pointed out that the *Decretum* contained a statement to the effect that a papal decree issued by Pope Adrian I (772–795) granted to the Emperor Charlemagne (768–814) "the right and power of electing the Roman Pontiff and determining who should occupy the apostolic see."[28] Seen in these terms, the papal claim to interfere in temporal matters was not only false, it was an inversion of the true relationship between the papacy and the empire and, by implication, between the papacy and the secular order in general.

The most vehement response to papal claims to oversee temporal matters was that of the French king, Philip IV (1285–1314), to whom Boniface VIII had addressed the bull *Unam sanctam*. According to Solórzano, the struggle concerned the king's claim that he could appoint individuals to ecclesiastical offices, prebends and benefices, without first seeking papal approval. Philip claimed this by royal right (*Regio jure*). The pope asserted that the king was subject to him in spiritual and temporal matters, a claim that led the king to order the burning of the papal letter that contained those assertions, a flat rejection of any assumed papal right to intervene in temporal affairs.[29]

Solórzano then went on to point out that numerous French scholars had written in defense of the king's position. These authors argued that each king swore at his coronation to defend "the rights and the statutes of the ancient Gallican Church." These "rights and statutes" included the right of appointment to all ecclesiastical offices, at least as Solórzano understood them. He next cited another French scholar who denied that the pope could, under any circumstances, "give the kingdom of France to anyone else or remove its king or dispose of it in any way."[30]

The arguments asserting the independence of the Gallican Church from papal oversight had a long history, but a history that was not quite as long as some French scholars claimed. Although some scholars claimed great antiquity for the origins of the Gallican Church, in fact the true age of the formulation of these ideas was the fourteenth and fifteenth centuries, during the contest between the papacy and the supporters of Church councils. The conciliarists wanted to limit the powers of the pope and make him responsible to the council that was seen as the representative of the entire Church.[31]

However, as Solórzano pointed out, the papacy's theologians and canon lawyers had long rejected the pretended powers of the Gallican Church and its claim to exemption from papal jurisdiction. The defenders of the papal position argued that the pope, as Peter's successor and possessor of the keys to the kingdom, had "not only spiritual, but indeed temporal domination and jurisdiction over the entire world. . . ." In general, the pope did not exercise jurisdiction in temporal matters, but when necessary he could do so.[32] Solórzano was careful to add that secular power originates in God, so that "every kingdom and empire proceeds immediately from God but mediately, and as from a second cause, from the Church and its Vicar" who can transfer and otherwise order about all secular rulers.[33] As another of Solórzano's sources declared, "The Supreme Pontiff is called the Lord of the whole world and is the Supreme Prince, having all plenitude of power. . . ."[34] The pope could even, should he wish, transfer the Holy Roman Empire from the Germans to the Spanish.[35]

Although Solórzano went on to cite many more examples of the arguments in support of papal jurisdiction over secular rulers, there is no need to cite them all; the point is quite clear, even if made in a redundant fashion. Having thus presented these arguments, he then returned to rejection of the specific arguments that had been made in support of princely exemption from papal jurisdiction. Following Bartolus (1314–1357), he stated that those who "deny to the Pope the power of the temporal sword and its exercise or [who say] that possession of the imperial title does not depend upon ecclesiastical approval are heretics."[36] As a consequence, he pointed out, Church officials had condemned Dante, Philip IV, and Louis the Bavarian for such views. [37]

As for Louis the Bavarian's assertion that his power came directly from God and that he possessed the powers of the imperial office even before the pope crowned him, Solórzano pointed out that Louis was a great persecutor of the Church and, therefore, a man whose views on the nature of papal-imperial relations could not be taken seriously.[38] Furthermore, those who held this limited view of the pope's powers were clearly adherents of John Huss (c. 1369–1415), whose heretical ideas the Council of Constance (1414–1417) had condemned.[39] Solórzano did not specify to which of the various opinions of John Huss he was referring here, but most likely he meant Huss's rejection of the belief that Christ Himself established the papacy. If Christ had not created the papacy, then the pope would have to base the powers he claimed nonscripturally, and Louis the Bavarian and other secular rulers would be quite justified in rejecting any papal claim to power over them.

In Solórzano's opinion, although *Unam sanctam* was specifically directed at the pretensions of Philip IV, the bull in fact had a much wider audience. It was designed not simply to inform Philip of the nature of papal-royal relations, but to inform all Christian rulers of their place in the hierarchy of powers.[40]

The condemnations of Dante, Louis the Bavarian, and Philip IV were, so to speak, one side of the papal relationship with secular rulers. There were other, very concrete illustrations of the nature of the proper and positive relationship between the pope and secular rulers. For example, the sixteenth-century successors of Louis the Bavarian, the Dukes of Bavaria, were, unlike their condemned ancestor, known to be among the most zealous defenders of the rights of the Church, second only to the imperial house of Austria in such matters.[41] Furthermore, there existed in the Lateran palace a fresco illustrating the right relationship between pope and emperor. In it, the Emperor Lothair (1125–1137) prostrate like a vassal at the feet of Pope Innocent II (1130–1143), accepts the imperial crown as a fief from the pope.[42] These two references illustrate the behavior of righteous emperors, men quite unlike Louis the Bavarian. The good emperors were zealous in the defense of the Church and recognized that their power came from the pope.

In the case of France, Solórzano had opposed the heretical Philip the Fair, the contemporary figure of Henry IV (1589–1610). Unlike his famous ancestor, Henry IV returned from the pit of heresy into which he had fallen. He heeded the words of condemnation that emanated from Rome and turned from those writers who argued that the pope had no right to condemn a ruler or to sentence him to deprivation of his kingdom. Henry IV saw the light, "recognized that the pope's power was greater than his own," and submitted to the pope in 1595.[43] This is the course of action that Philip the Fair should have followed, but did not.

Solórzano obviously selected these examples with contemporary circumstances in mind. The good Christian ruler was obedient to the pope and recognized that his kingdom, though ultimately derived from God, came through the Church. Thus, Henry IV's submission demonstrated that secular rulers recognized their subordination to the pope in both spiritual and temporal matters, at least according to Solórzano. He added several more citations to materials that, in his opinion, provided additional "examples of kings and emperors who have exhibited the greatest reverence and obedience to the Apostolic Roman See in spiritual and in temporal matters."[44] The overall aim here was to defend papal jurisdiction with historical as well as scriptural evidence. The historical examples of secular rulers of the highest rank submitting themselves and their kingdoms to papal judgment were concrete evidence of the historical relationship between secular rulers and popes, a relationship that had been challenged over time but never successfully overturned. To suggest that popes had no jurisdiction over kings was to stand convicted of heresy. If rulers such as Henry IV were indeed the model of proper royal relations with the papacy, then any contemporary French monarch who refused to accept the papal award of the New World to Ferdinand and Isabella and their heirs would be acting contrary to the good example of Henry IV and in accord with the bad example of Philip the Fair.[45]

A major weakness in this line of argument was historical in nature. The history of papal-imperial relations that the *Decretum* outlined included situations, as mentioned previously, in which the pope had subordinated himself to secular rulers. Had not Charlemagne received the power to elect the pope? Was not the pope in historical fact subject to the Frankish king's jurisdiction, and not the reverse? Solórzano's answer to this was to distinguish between the papacy's possession of jurisdiction and its exercise in particular situations. As he saw things, the situation described in canon law reflected the fact that the eighth-century papacy found itself under great pressure from the Lombards who had invaded Italy. The pope sought Charlemagne's assistance and "gave to him the power to elect the Roman Pontiff and to set the Apostolic See in order."[46] This did not, however, mean that the pope was surrendering the papacy's independence permanently to Charlemagne and his successors. It was done as a temporary measure to save the papacy from disaster.[47] Referring his reader to another canon, *In memoriam* (D.19, c.3), Solórzano pointed out that Charlemagne had in fact honored the Roman Church as the head of the entire Christian Church.[48]

Solórzano went on to add that Charlemagne's successor, Louis the Pious, surrendered this power of electing the pope back to the Church once the condition of the Church had improved.[49] Here again, Solórzano was placing additional emphasis on the temporary and emergency nature of Charlemagne's role in the selection of the pope. Yet again, the righteous Christian ruler publicly recognized the papal headship of the Church and piously returned to the pope powers that he had briefly exercised in the name of the Church.

One might think that at this point, having explained Charlemagne's possession of the right to select the pope in such a way as to deny its significance in the contemporary world, Solórzano would have moved on to another argument. Instead, he returned again to the story of Charlemagne's right to select the pope. This time, however, rather than explaining it away, he denied the authenticity of the documents. Citing a number of contemporary authorities, including the renowned ecclesiastical historian Caesar Baronius and Robert Bellarmine, Solórzano specifically denied the authenticity of the canons *Adrianus* and *In synodo* (D.63, cc.22, 23) that described papal subordination to the emperor. According to Solórzano, the only historian who accepted these texts was a monk named Sigebert (d. 1112), who "in his histories written in the year 1112, 342 years after the death of Charlemagne, very deceitfully and fraudulently created this fable and wove it into his writings on behalf of the schismatic emperor Henry [IV] whose views he eagerly supported."[50] Sigebert's goal was to provide a legal basis, however fragile, on which Henry IV (1056–1106) could base his opposition to Pope Gregory VII (1073–1085). When Gratian came to compile the *Decretum* in the mid-twelfth century, he carelessly incorporated this story about Charlemagne's right to select the pope without examining it closely. As a result, Gratian "provided an opportunity for others to believe to be true what had been affirmed as mendaciously as possible by Sigebert."

Solórzano went on to point out that elsewhere in the *Decretum*, Gratian included decrees of Charlemagne that guaranteed the free election of the pope and of the other bishops as well.[51] This canon, not the others, represented the correct way for an emperor to behave, as far as Solórzano was concerned. After all, from the perspective of Solórzano and the monarchs he served, it would have been dangerous to accept the argument that the Holy Roman Emperor could appoint the pope, because if that was the case, a pope, at the behest of an emperor, could end Spain's monopoly in the Americas. It was to the advantage of the Spanish that the pope was, in theory at least, free of imperial or other secular pressure, so that he could act in the best interests of the peoples of the Americas. In this case, as Solórzano saw things, the best interests of the peoples of the New World coincided rather nicely with those of the Spanish monarchs.

Once Solórzano had completed his refutation of the argument that at one time the emperor could appoint the pope, he moved on to discuss a more moderate view of papal power than that which he had offered previously. This moderate or, rather, timid view about papal power was held by those who, Solórzano felt, wanted to avoid arguments on this topic.[52] Their position was in fact a very traditional one. On the one hand, the moderate position "affirms that there is no doubt that the Supreme Pontiff holds the two swords and the fullest spiritual and temporal power over all kings and emperors and secular princes." On the other hand, the pope had the right to exercise the spiritual power directly, but the temporal sword was, as it were, sheathed, meaning that the pope granted its exercise to secular rulers rather than exercise it himself. Not only should the pope not exercise the temporal sword directly, "he ought not meddle or impose himself [in secular affairs] except for a great and serious reason."[53]

Those who supported the view that the pope should not exercise the temporal sword directly did not deny to the pope the power to order secular rulers to punish those who rebelled against the Church. This meant that Christian rulers who had become heretics, schismatics, and apostates should fear not only papal spiritual fulminations, but also physical punishment by loyal Christian rulers operating at papal request against them.[54]

In spite of previously judging this opinion about the indirect power of the pope in secular affairs as timid, Solórzano then went on to point out that it was shared by many significant canonists, including Innocent IV, who was not usually described as timid.[55] Furthermore, he pointed out that another writer defined this position on papal power in temporal matters as the *communis opinio* of those who followed the teachings of Thomas Aquinas.[56] Many of those who discussed the legitimacy of the Spanish conquest of the Americas, Vitoria and Las Casas among them, followed the opinions of Innocent IV and Aquinas. In using the arguments of Innocent IV, "the light of the law . . . who knew the laws better than anyone else," and Aquinas, Solórzano was in effect saying that the greatest legal and philosophical minds of the Middle Ages adhered to the moderate position on papal power, thus granting it almost insurmountable authority.[57]

The result of this teaching was the development in the early-modern world of the theory of indirect papal power in temporal matters, a teaching Solórzano identified with Robert Bellarmine. The theory did not separate the secular order from spiritual oversight. It only identified a sphere within which the secular power could ordinarily operate without papal interference. At the same time, the operations of the secular order were subordinate to spiritual ends as the lesser good is subordinate to the higher.[58]

Lest this discussion of Bellarmine's theory of indirect papal power in temporal affairs seem to undermine the power of the pope, Solórzano followed it with a strong restatement of the papacy's ultimate power over secular rulers, lest there be any confusion. The "temporal power is indeed distinct from the spiritual power," with the consequence that "kings and secular princes are not subject to the Roman Pontiff in temporal matters," a fact that kings underscored when they stated that they "rule by the grace of God alone."[59] Solórzano then added that this meant that the pope did not possess "direct and ordinary power in temporal affairs" but he did possess "supreme, overarching, indirect power [in temporal matters] which, as we have said, is joined with the spiritual power and, as we read, when necessary (*causa existente*) he can subject to himself secular rulers and their kingdoms and their empires."[60]

The next stage of the argument emphasized that the theory of indirect papal power in temporal matters was not new or original with Cardinal Bellarmine. This theory was rooted in the medieval canonistic tradition, reaching back to Innocent III, who had asserted that, while the pope had no regular jurisdiction over secular rulers, he did possess jurisdiction over rulers who had no superior in secular matters. Thus, he refused to act in a case involving the legitimization of a noble's illegitimate child, because the noble was a vassal of the king of France, and the matter properly belonged to the king's court, not to the pope's.[61] Had the situation involved, for example, the king of France, a ruler who had no superior in temporal matters, then the process of legitimization would have belonged to the papal court. Finally, he pointed once again to Boniface VIII's *Unam sanctam* as evidence of the pope's overriding jurisdiction in temporal affairs.

Having made a general, theoretical statement about the nature of papal power, Solórzano, as was his practice, then went on to emphasize that the historical record demonstrated that numerous popes had censured secular rulers. Popes had "not only issued spiritual censures against emperors, kings and other secular rulers, they also drew the material sword and deprived them of their kingdoms and empires or the administration of and jurisdiction over them [i.e., their kingdoms and empires]."[62] Here again, to demonstrate his point Solórzano referred to several chapters of the canon law traditionally cited in debates about the nature and extent of papal power.

Solórzano then went on to mention briefly a few specific cases from both the distant and more recent past, cases that he no doubt expected his audience would recall, in which a pope took forceful action against a secular ruler. He pointed to Pope Gregory VII's (1073–1085) famous quarrel with Emperor Henry IV (1056–1106) that eventually led to the emperor's deposition and subsequent reconciliation at Canossa.[63] The next case to which Solórzano referred was a much more recent one involving the Kingdom of Navarre. Pope Julius II (1503–1513) "declared King John of Navarre and his wife to be heretics and deprived them of their kingdom." As a result, Navarre passed into the hands of Ferdinand of Aragon.[64] In 1569, Pope Pius V (1566–1572) issued the bull *Regnans in excelsis*, ordering the deposition of Elizabeth of England on the grounds that she was a heretic. This bull authorized Catholic rulers to declare war against her and to occupy her kingdom. Subsequently, in 1588, Pope Sixtus V (1585–1590) invested Philip II (1556–1598) of Spain with the throne of England.[65] Solórzano, however, discreetly avoided mentioning the fate of the Spanish Armada Philip sent to achieve the pope's aims in England. Solórzano ended this chapter of the *De Indiarum Jure* with a restatement of the importance of subjecting secular authority to ecclesiastical oversight. Here again he cited Bellarmine, underscoring the importance of the notion of the papacy's indirect power in secular matters.

It might seem surprising at first glance that Solórzano insisted on the medieval papal dualistic notion of power or on Bellarmine's contemporary restatement of that theory in his conception of indirect papal power in temporal affairs. One might think that he and his masters would have preferred to stress the direct grant of secular power to the king from God without any papal intervention. The brief discussion of Ferdinand's acquisition of Navarre, however, provided the key to understanding Solórzano's position. The Spanish monarchs were important beneficiaries of papal largesse. Indeed, as the next chapter of the *De Indiarum jure* was to demonstrate, the legitimacy of the Spanish possession of the New World rested on precisely this theory of papal power. The good secular ruler, acting as the pope's agent, supporting the work of the Church, would not only contribute to fulfilling the Church's mission, he would also benefit in a material fashion as well.

Solórzano not only provided his readers with a description of the right sort of relationship that should exist between popes and secular rulers, he also gave examples of rulers who did not act correctly with regard to the Church. He was careful, of course, to point out the bad examples of a German emperor, a French king, and an English Queen. And he omitted any discussion of medieval papal criticism of those Spanish rulers whose treatment of their Muslim subjects was deemed too tolerant.[66] Solórzano's Spanish kings were paragons of royal virtue, fully deserving of the benefits that the papacy had conferred upon them. Thus, when Pope Alexander VI came to issue the bull *Inter caetera* in 1493, he was acting within his proper sphere of jurisdiction and employing the services of the most virtuous of Christian kings in the spiritual work of converting the New World to Christianity.

6. A Legitimate Claim to the Indies — Papal Jurisdiction over the Infidels

Once Solórzano had demonstrated that the pope did possess jurisdiction over the temporal affairs of Christians under some circumstances, he then went on to consider the jurisdiction of the pope over those who did not belong to the Church. This was, of course, the crux of the entire *De Indiarum Jure*. He began with the observation that in the course of the argument thus far he had dismissed as "absurd and condemned" the assertions that the pope possessed no jurisdiction in temporal matters or that his jurisdiction in temporal matters was restricted to the Papal States, where the pope was obviously a secular ruler as well as a spiritual one.[1]

On the other hand, there were two other schools of thought that would attribute to the pope at least some jurisdiction in secular affairs. The first consisted of those who asserted that "under the rubric of that absolute and universal power, which they establish in his person, clearly nothing seems to be excluded [from papal jurisdiction]." Then there was the school whose members saw in the pope only a power that was "indirect or supreme and zealous for spiritual [ends]." If this latter argument was accepted, then the pope would have no basis for depriving infidel rulers of their thrones and for granting their kingdoms to Christian rulers "under the guise of religion (*sub praetextu Religionis*)."[2] That being the case, Solórzano thought it best to consider these arguments at some length.

As the foundation of this part of the argument, Solórzano referred his reader back to the earlier discussion of Innocent IV's theory of the right of all people, Christian and infidel alike, to possess *dominium*.[3] He asserted that Innocent IV's argument denied to the pope any authority over the lands of infidels or any power to remove infidel rulers. In support of this opinion Solórzano cited a number of late-medieval and sixteenth-century lawyers and theologians, including Francis Vitoria, indicating that Innocent IV's opinion was clearly that of the leading thinkers in the Church.[4] There was, however, one exception to this rule that Solórzano admitted. This was the argument, again rooted in Innocent IV's commentary on *Quod super his*, that the pope did have the right to insure that the Gospel was preached to infidels. This did not, however, grant him any temporal or spiritual jurisdiction over them.[5] Solórzano concluded this segment of the discussion with an opinion he attributed to Ambrosius Catharinus in a commentary on St. Paul's Epistle to the Romans. This commentator, said Solórzano, "dared to write that they were excessively simple-minded or worshippers of the Pope who say that to him *de jure* belongs all lordship of the whole world, even in temporals."[6]

The issue of papal power over those who were not members of the Church came to a head in Alexander VI's *Inter caetera*. Solórzano presented the issue this way. By the terms of the bull, the Castilians

> by virtue of his [concession] . . . were not able to acquire full and absolute *Imperium* in the lands of the barbarians, but only a certain right [*jus*] to lead them to the Catholic faith and orthodox customs by means of suitable ministers of the Gospel, to protect those led to the faith, to punish apostates and troublemakers.[7]

Here Solórzano reached the heart of the matter. Christian Europeans had no general right to invade and conquer the New World. He certainly did not deny them the right to go there and, presumably, to engage in trade with the inhabitants, perhaps even to settle there. What Europeans could not do was to impose their will upon others simply because the others were infidels, even if the infidels engaged in horrible practices that violated natural law. Even the pope did not have that kind of authority, and if he did not have it, surely he could not give it to anyone else. The most that the pope could do was to give Christian rulers a limited right in an infidel society, a right contingent upon the work of bringing the inhabitants to a civilized and Christianized way of life.

Solórzano then proceeded to present statements from a number of authors, usually, but not always, Spanish, who agreed with this position. Joseph Acosta, for example, criticized those who sought to invent a legal basis for the conquest of the Americas: "It is not necessary to invent false titles [to justify the conquest]; for with respect to the Indians, in regard to our Spanish kings, they are competent only by right of care and spiritual administration, so that the Indians are not to be driven off from their goods and lordship, unless they are found to be doing harm to the faith and being a danger to themselves."[8] Other Spanish writers had pointed out that since the pope was not the *Dominus mundi*, the lord of the world in Roman law, he did not possess the lands of infidels and could not, therefore, give them away. The bull *Inter caetera* had not been issued to the Spanish monarchs "for the destruction and despoliation of the Indians but only so that they might remove the impediments which the barbarian nations set up against the preaching of the Gospel."[9]

At this stage of the discussion Solórzano advanced yet another, but slightly different, argument for papal involvement in determining which Christian secular rulers could legitimately dominate infidel societies. Here again he cited Robert Bellarmine, the proponent of papal indirect power in temporals who had argued that Alexander VI's *Inter caetera* could not be used to demonstrate the existence of papal power in secular affairs and over infidels. There were those, he admitted, who argued that when "Alexander VI had divided the recently discovered world between the kings of Spain and Portugal . . ." he demonstrated the existence of such papal power. Bellarmine responded that the pope issued this bull for the protection of the missionaries and their potential converts. In addition, however, Alexander VI acted as he did "so that he might prevent conflicts and wars among the Christian princes who wished to engage in business in those new lands."[10]

The notion of the pope as the ultimate judge of conflicts among Christian rulers was of course not new. As with many of the other ideas that Solórzano advanced, the medieval papacy and the lawyers who served it had developed this one four centuries earlier. Various thirteenth-century popes had insisted that the papal court was the appropriate place for settling disputes between Christian rulers. Innocent III (1198–1216) had been especially active in this area, seeking, for example, to settle the quarrel between John of England (1199–1216) and Philip II (1179–1223) of France that eventually led to the English loss of Normandy.[11] Solórzano could also have pointed to the more recent examples of popes allocating spheres of responsibility for missionary activity between the Portuguese and the Castilians as both kingdoms pushed out into the Atlantic. Solórzano's positive view of Bellarmine's argument here suggests that he too saw the pope at the head of human society, settling conflicts that would otherwise disrupt the good order of Christian society as a whole. As Christian missionaries fulfilled their task of preaching to all people and as infidel societies became Christian, the pope would become the ultimate judge of all human beings and all nations everywhere.

At the same time, Solórzano also recognized that there was a great deal of opposition, even among Catholics, to the argument for papal power, whether direct or indirect, in temporal matters. Obviously those who did not accept the Catholic faith would reject any such papal claim. He pointed out that Protestant heretics were writing outrageous books containing arguments that ridiculed the papal claim to award the New World to the king of Castile or to anyone else.[12] He even labeled as a heretic Girolamo de Benzoni (1517–1570), an Italian Catholic who had spent many years in the Americas and whose chronicle of his travels in the New World, the *Historia del Mondo Nuovo* (Venice, 1565), was highly critical of the Spanish treatment of the Indians. Benzoni's work provided the text to Theodore de Bry's engravings that described the Spanish treatment of the Indians in brutal detail. As a consequence, his work, although translated into several languages, was not translated into Spanish, being viewed, reasonably enough, as anti-Spanish.[13]

Solórzano drew from Benzoni's work some other examples of non-Catholic critics of the papal claim to universal jurisdiction. For example, the Italian traveler told of the king of the Peruvians, one Atabalibam, who, when informed by a Spaniard that the pope had awarded his kingdom to the King of Spain, responded: "The pope is remarkably foolish and impudent to have handed [it] over to him so easily because he bestows freely [that which belongs] to another." According to Solórzano, "the heretic," that is, Benzoni, added at the end of this story the question "By what right can the pope give away these [kingdoms] in which he never had any right?"[14]

Elsewhere in his book, Benzoni referred to presumably orthodox Catholics who did not recognize the pope's claim to determine who could possess which parts of the New World. He discussed the French expedition to Florida in 1562, part of an attempt by Huguenots to establish a presence in the New World under French auspices.[15] The French attempt at settlement was obviously in direct opposition to the bull of Alexander VI, since they had made the settlement without asking the permission of the Spanish monarch. According to Benzoni, as quoted by Solórzano, "the Spanish had no right to those very extensive lands in the west, neither islands nor the provinces of the Indian continent unless perhaps under the umbrella of a papal donation (*nisi forte umbratili Pontificis donatione*) of those places that are not his."[16] The implication of the Italian traveler's work, however, was clearly that the pope could not lawfully make such a grant.

The final author whom Solórzano discussed at this point was the (to him) anonymous writer of a tract entitled the *Mare Liberum*. The unknown author was, as mentioned earlier, Hugo Grotius.[17] Solórzano indicated that he learned of this work by way of Freitas's book. What he learned was that the unknown author "wrote shamelessly in disdain for that donation [i.e.,

Alexander VI's] and for the Roman Church." Furthermore, this writer "denied absolutely in chapters 3 and 4 that it [the Church] had any power over the land or goods of infidels. . . ." Solórzano's response to this assertion by the unknown author was to breath a sigh of relief because "all copies of this book were properly ordered eliminated in the catalog of forbidden books" issued by Cardinal Sandoval in 1612.[18]

In the next stage of the argument, Solórzano proceeded to deny to the pope direct jurisdiction over infidels, following the arguments that writers such as Vitoria and Bellarmine, among others, had advanced.[19] The biblical injunction to "Feed My sheep," used to demonstrate papal jurisdiction over all people, applied only to those who were within the Church. The infidels were, by definition, not members of this community of faith.[20] With regard to nonbelievers, Christ's injunction to His Apostles was to "go teach all peoples and baptize them." This language did not authorize the use of force against infidels or their conquest. The words simply announced the divine mission to all men. They did not authorize the seizure of the goods and other possessions that infidels had because such *dominium* "belongs to them by natural law and by the common law of nations" and thus they cannot be deprived of it simply because they are not Christians.[21]

To this argument, Solórzano added arguments from Thomas Aquinas and his followers to the same effect. These included the assertion that the pope has spiritual power over Christians and judges them according to Christian laws, but that he has no such jurisdiction over infidels, only the responsibility for insuring that the Gospel is preached to them.[22] Likewise, centuries earlier, St. Paul had denied that the Church had any jurisdiction over infidels and pagans.[23] More recently, Pope Eugenius IV (1431–1447) had described baptism as the door leading to membership in Christ and His Church. To this, Solórzano added the observation of St. Jerome (c. 345–c. 420) that "foreigners, Jews, heretics, and gentiles are outside the Church," that is, outside the door.[24] Being outside the door of the house of the Lord, in other words, outside His church, meant that all these peoples were not subject to the jurisdiction of the Lord's vicar, the pope.

At first glance, these arguments would seem to place Solórzano in the same camp as the King of the Peruvians, Benzoni, Grotius, and others who denied the pope any jurisdiction, temporal or spiritual, over infidels. The next stage of the argument developed the same theme even further. Clearly the pope, the vicar of Christ, could possess and exercise no more power than Christ possessed and exercised.[25] Clearly, in His capacity as a man, Christ "was not the king of the whole world and did not possess or exercise temporal jurisdiction or domination over it as seems clearly demonstrated."[26] Solórzano then went on to list several traditional biblical citations used to demonstrate that Christ explicitly denied possessing and exercising any temporal authority.[27] Not only was Christ not the Lord of the temporal world, He and His apostles "possessed virtually nothing" (*paucarum rerum dominium habuisse*).[28] After listing numerous additional authorities on this topic, ranging from Thomas Aquinas to more recent writers such as Vitoria and Bellarmine, Solórzano concluded this section of his argument with the firm conclusion that "neither by right of inheritance nor by right of conquest or by right of election was Christ the temporal lord of the world in his human capacity."[29]

The key to Solórzano's argument at this point was obviously the attention that he paid to Christ in His human capacity. As Christ was, theologically, both God and man, there remained His divine capacity to consider and with that the relationship of His vicar to that capacity. The theologians with whom Solórzano dealt in this section of the argument "following the middle way, indeed denied that Christ in His human capacity possessed a temporal kingdom." What Christ did possess, however, was "another kingdom, a distinguished kingdom, one of a higher order, granted to Him by God over all created things fully and absolutely from the gift of union by means of which He was established as head of men and angels. . . ."[30] Not all of those powers that Christ possessed passed to His vicar, however. Clearly, for example, Christ could institute sacraments, but the pope could not; Christ could perform miracles but not the pope.[31] There were, then, clear-cut limits to the powers that the pope could exercise in his capacity as Christ's vicar.

In the next stage of the argument, Solórzano raised the point about the powers attached to the papal vicariate in a different way. Even if "we grant that the aforementioned power and general domination over temporal kingdoms was transferred to the Roman Pontiffs as the Vicars of Christ," nevertheless, they should not exercise that power, since Christ had not exercised it. Christ made no effort to remove "non-believers, tyrants or sinners" from exercising their right to possess goods and to rule their people, and so the pope should not.[32] The implication here, of course, was that the right to property and lordship was a natural right, one that even Christ in His divine capacity did not, or even could not, override. Even a sinner has a natural right to property or to public office. Here Solórzano provided the traditional arguments for Christ's rejection of the use of temporal power, including the story of Christ telling Peter to put up his sword (John 18:11). This story was conflated with the scene in the Gospel of Luke in which Christ, being told that his followers possess two swords, says that two swords were enough (Luke 22:38). The standard interpretation of these words, an interpretation that Bernard of Clairvaux proposed, was that the swords represented the two powers, spiritual and temporal. The Church, represented by St. Peter, possessed the two swords, but could exercise only the spiritual one.[33] Christ's kingdom was not of this world and so no secular ruler should have to fear losing his office on the orders of Christ or His Vicar. On the other hand, the good Christian ruler would recognize that his power, the temporal sword, was to be employed in the service of the Church.

In the fifth and last stage of this part of the argument, Solórzano turned it back to Christian society. It now being clear that the pope had no jurisdiction over infidel rulers by virtue of being Christ's vicar, the question might be raised as to the basis of his jurisdiction, if any, over Christian rulers. Did the division between spiritual and temporal jurisdiction apply to Christian society as well? Here, lest any Christian monarch who heard these arguments jump to the conclusion that he was as free from ecclesiastical oversight as his infidel counterparts were, Solórzano stated that indeed Christian rulers were subject to ecclesiastical jurisdiction. Furthermore, although in Christian society the spiritual and the temporal powers were clearly distinct, the pope possessed the power to remove rulers from office under certain circumstances.[34]

At this point, Solórzano brought together a series of traditional references from canon law to explain the relationship between the spiritual and the temporal spheres of jurisdiction. These included Pope Gelasius I's (492–496) famous observation in a letter to the Emperor Anastasius I (491–518): "There are two forces, August Emperor, by which this world is ruled, the sacred authority of the popes and the royal power."[35] The traditional interpretation of that observation was that papal jurisdiction was of a higher order than royal or temporal because the pope ruled on the basis of *auctoritas*, a term that implied moral superiority, while secular rulers ruled on the basis of *potestas*, that is, force. Among the other citations that Solórzano offered was a letter written by Pope Innocent III, *Solitae*, in which he compared the papal power to the sun and the royal power to the moon. The point of the images was that as the sun and the moon are distinct, so ecclesiastical and secular powers are distinct, but as the sun is the greater of the two and the source of the moon's light, so the ecclesiastical power is greater than the secular and the ultimate source of secular power.[36]

Solórzano, however, rejected the argument that the pope had only indirect power in the secular sphere, because it seemed to undermine the power of the pope. In his opinion, "the more true and more common opinion [is that] which establishes in the Roman Pontiff the power and authority of the two swords, that is the spiritual and the temporal authority and power, not only as an indirect authority and power but direct." As a consequence, the pope possessed "supreme domination and jurisdiction over all kingdoms and provinces [whether in the hands of] the faithful or of infidels when a just cause requires it."[37] Solórzano concluded this section of his argument with a reference to a list of citations in the previous chapter that supported this view of papal power, demonstrating that this line of argument was indeed the mainstream of legal, philosophical, and theological thinking on the issue of papal power.

What, then, did this line of argument have to do with the Spanish acquisition of the Americas? In fact, Solórzano pointed out, to some canon lawyers the argument that the pope possessed the two swords had everything to do with the legitimate presence of the Spanish in the New World. He began with a discussion of Hostiensis's argument that "after the birth of Christ all *dominium* and *imperium* was transferred to the Roman Pontiff and resides in him as in the vicar of Christ the true king." This being the case, the pope "is able to give by his own right the kingdoms of infidels to whomever he wishes and to compel them [infidels] to recognize the authority of the Roman See."[38] This would mean that the infidel inhabitants of the New World had no legitimate right to possess property and to govern. As sixteenth-century writers applied this theory, "the Supreme Pontiff could not only grant [to Christians] the kingdoms of infidels that were formerly in the hands of Christians, but even the lands and islands recently discovered and which were held and occupied by other peoples and often this was done by the pope."[39]

Here again, Solórzano supported the argument with citations from a number of authors who had written on the topic in these terms. One writer went so far as to say that "Jews and other infidels can be despoiled of their goods by papal authority and hold them only as *peculium*," that is, as a slave in Roman law could own something subject to the will of his master.[40] Thus, the *dominium* of infidels would be legally precarious, that is, dependent upon the willingness of Christians to recognize it and not based on a natural right that Christians were obliged to respect.

This line of argument did not, however, mean that any Christian ruler could on his own initiative invade and conquer an infidel kingdom. This could only be done with papal permission, the unique papal power that underlay Alexander VI's *Inter caetera*.[41] Other commentators who discussed papal power had gone as far as describing the pope as "the sole and supreme monarch of the world and, as a consequence, they extended his jurisdiction to the infidels."[42] One supporter of this view of papal power described the relationship between the pope and secular rulers as similar to that of workmen who function under the direction of an architect and who do as he directs.[43]

Solórzano then went on to provide a number of extreme statements of papal power drawn from a long list of writers. One of these described the pope as "God living on earth."[44] Another related that "whoever speaks falsely of the pope has committed a sacrilege just as if he had spoken falsely of God."[45] These extreme opinions about the pope and his powers, Solórzano recognized, had not gone unchallenged. He pointed out that "although there were many authors of the opinion that in Christ, as man, no temporal kingdom nor *dominium* existed . . . the more true, however, and more common opinion seems to be that of those who say that all creation was made subject to Christ and governed by Christ not in his capacity as God but in his capacity as man."[46] Those who hold this opinion argue that Christ, "from the moment of His conception, by the gift of God the Father and by virtue of the hypostatic union, possessed absolute and universal rule (*monarchia*) of the entire world in both spirituals and temporals."[47] The fact that Christ possessed this absolute rule did not, however, deprive human beings of their natural right to property and lordship, which, after all, "God had granted to them." Besides, Christ had become man not to rule but to serve mankind as the Gospels pointed out.[48] In other words, Christ possessed ultimate power over all people, but did not exercise it.

In the third stage of this argument, Solórzano went on to consider the implications of the dual nature of Christ for the papal role in temporal affairs. He presented the argument that Christ "wished to share this kingdom, or temporal *dominium*, that he possessed with the Church and the pope who represents Him."[49] As Duns Scotus (c. 1266–1308) had pointed out, "the pope is Vicar of Christ not only in so far as He was Head of the Church but also in so far as He was Lord of the entire world and so he can give orders about the condition and goods of men."[50]

This power that Christ granted to St. Peter and his successors was obviously to be used with care. It was not to be used to obtain human domination or for some other evil or mundane end. Christ gave "universal power to Peter and his successors in order to direct men to the joy of eternal life and so to that ultimate end, he had also to subject all secular powers, to which it belongs to direct men to virtue and temporal happiness which serve as a means to acquiring eternal life." Indeed, if Christ had not granted power over temporal affairs to the Pope, "the *Respublica Ecclesiae* would seem less than perfectly established and directed. . . ." Consequently, there is "one [*Respublica Ecclesiae*] and there is one prince and lord of all.[51]

Having emphasized the role of the great theologians of the Church in developing the conception of supreme papal power, Solórzano went on to point out that there was also a great deal of biblical and legal support for this opinion as well.[52] These sources also emphasized that this papal power extended to jurisdiction over infidels as well.[53] First, Solórzano cited Thomas Aquinas and the scholastics who cited the prophesy of Jeremiah: "See, I have set you this day over nations and over kingdoms, to pluck up and to break down, to destroy and to overthrow, to build and to plant. . . ." Previously, Solórzano had observed that this quotation was generally taken to refer to the powers that Christ had given to His Church.[54] At this point in the argument, however, he noted that this power was not restricted to members of the Church. It extended to infidels as well, since Christ's power extended over both believers and nonbelievers.[55]

Having demonstrated that the foremost scholastic philosopher and the foremost theologian had taken this strong opinion on the powers of the pope, Solórzano then went on to demonstrate that the leading legal minds had taken the same position. In the decretal *Solitae* (X.1.33.6), for example, Innocent III had brought together the prophesy of Jeremiah and the tradition of interpretation it engendered along with Christ's statement that "whatever you bind on earth shall be bound in heaven," to demonstrate the power of the pope over believers and nonbelievers alike.[56] In addition to these biblical supports for the claim that the pope had jurisdiction over all people, Solórzano pointed to Innocent III's argument that "in arduous and difficult matters," the priests ought to be consulted, whether spiritual or temporal affairs are involved.[57]

Here again, Solórzano turned to *Unam sanctam* because this bull presented in abbreviated fashion virtually every major papal statement about the superiority of the spiritual power over the temporal that appeared in canon law.[58] Solórzano did not include the entire text of the bull in the *De Indiarum Jure*, but the material he did include, approximately the last half of the text, stressed the points that he had already made about papal power. The excerpt from *Unam Sanctam* began with Boniface's discussion of the two swords and the superiority of the spiritual sword over the temporal.

The excerpt also included the prophecy of Jeremiah and the statement about binding and loosing that Innocent III had cited. Solórzano ended the excerpt with the famous concluding lines of the bull: "We declare, state, define, and pronounce that every human being must be subject to the Roman Pontiff if they wish to be saved."[59] Solórzano was well aware that some years after Boniface VIII's death, Pope Clement V (1305–1314) issued a letter, *Meruit*, that some have seen as weakening or even revoking the bull. In fact, according to Solórzano, Clement V could not have "revoked or weakened" his predecessor's statement because those statements were "eternal and immutable."[60]

Having demonstrated the general superiority of the spiritual power over the secular, Solórzano then went on to consider what was obviously the most important consequence of this superiority in the context of the *De Indiarum Jure*, the nature of the just war. In an obvious allusion to the dual nature of Christ and its implications for papal power, Solórzano began his argument with the statement that learned men agree that "those wars are judged to be just that are carried on by the command or authority of God." So too they agree that "wars also ought to be judged as just which are ordered proclaimed by His Vicar against the infidels for the increase of religion or for other just causes."[61] Christians can legitimately keep the property and lordships they seize from infidels under such circumstances.[62] The power and authority that the papacy possessed over infidels and their possessions was, as Solórzano saw it, simply an extension of the power that the pope possessed over Christians. The pope possessed the authority "over the lands and islands of infidels, pagans and heretics."

At this point in the argument, however, Solórzano disagreed with Las Casas, whose views he had generally accepted. According to Solórzano, Las Casas did not agree with the common scholarly opinion that the pope had general jurisdiction over the lands of infidels. Las Casas would restrict such papal jurisdiction to those lands that had been occupied by Christians until they were conquered in an unjust war. This would apply, for example, to the reconquest of Spain from the Muslims. Furthermore, Las Casas would make a distinction between "Saracens, heretics and other enemies of the faith on the one hand and those who were simply infidels on the other."[63] In support of this argument by Las Casas, Solórzano raised the problem of giving away that which one did not actually possess, the point that the King of the Peruvians, as Solórzano identified him, had suggested. It would seem to be "a rash and imprudent piece of advice" to suggest dividing up someone else's property before actually winning it.[64]

The more serious answer to Las Casas's distinction between enemies of the faith and peaceful infidels was that the mainstream of canonistic and theological thought defended the papal claim to universal jurisdiction in temporal affairs over Christians and nonChristians alike.[65] Even if infidels, strictly speaking, did not belong to "the flock of Christ and of the Church . . . it is more true that they belong under the Church's care and direction."[66] Here again, Solórzano cited what he identified as a letter written by Innocent III, the decretal *Licet* (2.2.10), to support the argument that papal authority extended to "Saracens, gentiles and schismatics."[67] Furthermore, as Solórzano saw matters, the phrase "Feed My sheep," central to the whole concept of papal office, meant "to rule and govern them."[68] Thus the pope, as Christ's vicar, as the substitute shepherd of the flock, was responsible to the owner of the sheep for the well-being of all the folds, not simply the one that comprised the Christian Church.

Solórzano erred in attributing the theory that asserted papal jurisdiction over infidels to Innocent III's decretal *Licet*. He was, in fact, not citing the decretal itself but Innocent IV's subsequent commentary on *Licet*.[69] The conflation of the theories of these two thirteenth-century popes illustrated an important point in the development of the theory of papal jurisdiction over infidels. Innocent IV, who developed the general theory of universal papal jurisdiction, had in fact done so in commentaries on decretals of Innocent III. Innocent III had previously developed the theory and the practice of papal power to its highest point within the context of Christian European society. Innocent IV took it one step further, to those outside of the Church, making papal power universal, not simply restricted to Europe or to Christian society alone.

Moving to the next argument against any attempt to limit the pope's jurisdiction in secular matters, Solórzano pointed out that, while it was true that Christ refused to involve Himself in secular affairs, this refusal "proceeded from his free choice rather than from a lack of power." Christ acted in this way out of "contempt for temporal matters and because He resolved to live a humble life." Furthermore, according to Solórzano, Christ did mix in temporal affairs, as when He ordered the unclean spirits out of a possessed man (Matthew 8.28) or when he drove the vendors from the temple (Matthew 21.12).[70]

Even one of the most famous examples of Christ's unwillingness to enmesh Himself in secular affairs, the case in which he was asked to resolve a dispute about an inheritance (Luke 12:13), did not prove, according to Solórzano, that Christ lacked the power to judge temporal affairs. All it meant was that Christ had more important things to do. It did not mean that He lacked the power to settle the dispute if He had chosen to do so.[71]

Solórzano next responded to the argument that while Christ as God did possess universal jurisdiction in temporals (*dominium & imperium temporale*), only those qualities that He possessed in His human capacity passed to Peter and his successors. While Solórzano agreed that some of Christ's powers did not pass to Peter, jurisdiction over temporal affairs did because "it was necessary for the direction of the Church."[72]

Solórzano then went on to discuss the double nature of Christ's kingship that was transmitted to Peter and to his successors as vicar of Christ. In the first place, Christ was a king through His descent from King David. He was also a king in His capacity as God. In addition, Christ was also the high priest. The result is that the pope, His vicar, possessed two kinds of royal power and the supreme priestly power as well.[73] The fact that Christ rarely, if ever, used these royal powers did not, of course, mean that He, or His vicar, did not possess them. What it did mean is that the pope should follow Christ's example and not use his legitimate power in temporal matters.

Another writer analyzed Christ's supreme royal jurisdiction differently, building on the fact that Christ was both God and Man. This writer distinguished between Christ's *dominium* before and after his crucifixion. Before His death, Christ refused to involve Himself in temporal matters, such as judging between heirs, out of humility. His role at this point was as the humble sacrificial figure who was to offer Himself up to redeem mankind. Once Christ died and rose again, however, the situation was quite different. Then He possessed all power "in heaven and on earth."[74] According to Solórzano, it was this latter power that Christ intended when designating Peter to be His vicar. In order to make this argument, however, Solórzano and those in the tradition he followed had to conflate two scenes from the Gospel of Matthew.

> Whence it follows that when, after the resurrection, He gave the power of the keys and the responsibility for the flock to Peter, as it says in Matthew, the last chapter and ch. 16, we ought to measure the power of His vicar according to the power of God and grant to him supreme and universal jurisdiction in spirituals and in temporals all over the world when he judges what is useful for the common good of the Church.[75]

Strictly speaking, the last chapter of Matthew that Solórzano cited here did not contain any reference to the transmission of power. In it, a scene that takes place after His crucifixion, death, and resurrection, Christ did say that all power was His, but the grant of the keys with their powers had come before Christ's passion and death. Using the distinction previously made, it would appear that the pope did not obtain Christ's universal *dominium*, because the grant of the keys came before Christ had asserted His universal jurisdiction. Nevertheless, for Solórzano and those whom he cited in support of this position, the two scenes refer to the same, universal, *dominium*.

In similar fashion, Solórzano was able to reinterpret another famous line from the Gospels that would seem to have demonstrated that Christ had no temporal *dominium* to grant to the pope. Facing Pilate, Christ had said that His kingdom was not of this world. (John 18:36, 37) While this would seem to mean that Christ was not in possession of any temporal power, Solórzano took the position that Christ simply meant that at the moment at which He said this to Pilate, standing before him for judgment, readying Himself for death on the cross, He chose freely not to exercise His rightful *dominium*. At the resurrection, however, Christ would assume all his rightful power and become the true king of the world.[76]

The final stage of this argument dealt with the legal tradition in which the relationship between the spiritual and the temporal powers had long been subject to debate. Solórzano pointed out that in the legal tradition, there were statements by popes indicating that they did not possess any power in temporal affairs, that the two powers were separate and distinct. On the other hand, it was also clear that there was a hierarchy of powers, the spiritual obviously being the higher, and these two powers ought to assist one another in the achievement of their respective ends.[77] The roles of the respective powers should not be confused, however, and one should not interfere improperly in the other's realm.

As an example of this theory, Solórzano pointed out that the pope was, as Bartolus said, the "ordinary judge of all men of the whole world."[78] At the same time, however, what is decided routinely "by secular judges may not be appealed to the pope because they are not subject to his temporal jurisdiction." The clear distinction between the powers is thus retained. In situations where "an injustice perpetrated by an emperor or king or some other secular ruler who recognizes no superior in temporal matters is notorious, and in difficult situations and cases" the pope could hear appeals, because there was no one else to hear them. Here again, Solórzano was taking the *via media* that Innocent III had defined long before.[79] While the totality of power existed in the pope as the vicar of Christ, he did not exercise that power except under very unusual circumstances.

At this point, Solórzano brought up once more Bernard of Clairvaux's letter of advice to Pope Eugenius III (1145–1153) to illustrate how another document generally used as an argument against papal involvement in temporal affairs could in fact be used to demonstrate the reverse. Bernard had stated that the pope had "jurisdiction in criminal matters but not in matters involving temporal possessions, and these lowest and mundane matters ought to be left to the kings and princes of the world." Presumably, Bernard made a distinction between criminal and property matters, because criminal behavior contains a moral aspect lacking in matters simply involving possession of land and goods. Solórzano went on to say that in making this distinction, Bernard did not deny that the pope could intervene in matters involving temporal possessions "when necessity, a spiritual purpose or some other just cause demanded it." As Bernard saw matters, for the pope to mix in mundane matters was to lower himself from the high plane that he occupied and to busy himself with unimportant and trivial activities instead of the more important activities that fell within the purview of his spiritual office.[80] Nevertheless, in Solórzano's view, the pope could intervene in such matters when necessary.

Turning next to the image of the two swords, Solórzano pointed out that this image clearly described the relationship between the spiritual and the temporal powers. Christ's command to Peter, "Put your sword back in its sheathe," indicated that Peter possessed both swords, but did not exercise both of them. On a day-to-day basis the secular rulers employed the temporal sword.[81] Again using a statement of Innocent III, a letter to the emperor at Constantinople, to make the point, Solórzano stressed that although there was a clear-cut distinction between the two powers, this did not mean that "the one jurisdiction was not subordinate to the other and that the temporal jurisdiction was not dependent upon the spiritual."[82] In fact, like the moon, which derives its light from the sun, the temporal power derived its power from the Church.[83]

Solórzano concluded this chapter of the *De Indiarum Jure* with a firm reassertion of the papal claim to judge all matters, even feudal ones, if the matter involved was a serious one. Again citing a letter of Innocent III (*Novit*), he pointed out that the pope refused to interfere in the ordinary hierarchy of feudal courts. It was Innocent III's position that papal intervention in the temporal order, except in cases where the pope was also the secular ruler or feudal overlord, was improper, but not forbidden.[84]

The theoretical position that Solórzano took on the issue of papal power was in line with that of Innocent III. This dualist position asserted the existence of two distinct spheres of jurisdiction, spiritual and temporal. Both of these were designed by God for a particular end. At the same time, they were related in a hierarchic fashion. The higher, that is the spiritual, power was directed toward the higher end of humanity and had a controlling jurisdiction over the temporal power. In this realm the pope acted without any interference from the representatives of the temporal order. On the other hand, while the pope, generally speaking, did not intervene in the jurisdictions of secular rulers, he had the right to intervene if the actions of a secular ruler were endangering the ends of the spiritual power. This was the position that Innocent III had articulated in a number of important decretal letters, many of which Solórzano cited in the course of this stage of his argument and which became the *communis opinio* of the medieval canon lawyers upon whom Solórzano drew.

Solórzano held the dualist position in opposition to the so-called hierocratic position, that is, the theory that the pope possessed both powers, spiritual and temporal, and could exercise both of them. This position would deny any autonomy to the secular power.[85] Canon lawyers rarely defended the other logical position, namely that the pope's power was purely spiritual in nature and had no role in the temporal order. Indeed, the papacy condemned the work of Marsilius of Padua for asserting that position in his *Defensor pacis*.[86]

For Solórzano, the dualist position was the *communis opinio* of the canonists, and therefore the position that he would be inclined to take on the issue of papal power. At the same time, it was also a position that, as the next chapter will demonstrate, was quite compatible with the interests of the Spanish kings in the New World. The dualist position required the cooperation of the papacy and secular rulers in order to achieve the two ends of humanity, the spiritual and the temporal. This was an advantage to the Spanish, who could rest their claims to the Americas on the ground that they were assisting the papacy in achieving the spiritual well-being of the Indians. The possession of a papal charter, so to speak, for their role in the Americas emphasized the ultimately spiritual end that they had in mind when they entered and conquered the New World. Furthermore, the Spanish favored orderly expansion into the New World, by which they meant on terms that gave them a monopoly over the Americas. If all European princes would recognize the power of the pope to authorize Christian rulers to acquire control of specific regions in the New World, it would end the possibility of wars among the various European nations that were interested in acquiring overseas possessions.[87] On the other hand, if the

Spanish denied the dualist position, they would have denied the right of Alexander VI to award the East Indies to the Portuguese and the West Indies to the Castilians. This in turn would legitimize French and English activities in the New World that would ultimately compete with those of the Spanish. Solórzano's defense of papal power and his heavy reliance on the statements of Innocent III with regard to the nature of that power were a necessary support for the Spanish control of the Americas.

7. A Legitimate Claim to the Indies — The History of Papal-Royal Relations

If Solórzano had simply restated the traditional theoretical arguments about the nature and extent of papal power, then the *De Indiarum Jure* would not have marked a significant advance in the debate about the legitimacy of the Spanish conquest of the Americas. What distinguished his work from that of many others is that he did not rest his argument on purely theoretical arguments, legal, theological, or philosophical. Perhaps because he was a lawyer, Solórzano also emphasized the historical evidence, that is, concrete historical situations or precedents, to support his argument. From a lawyer's perspective, the historical record provided evidence of customary practice over a long period of time. It illustrated the centuries of experience that the papacy shared with secular rulers in the process of achieving the ends for which each was established. For medieval lawyers, historical experience, imbedded in customary law, was of great significance in everyday legal practice. Even though during the thirteenth century Spanish kings had adopted Roman law with its conception of the ruler as legislator, Spanish legal practice nevertheless continued to include a great deal of older legal practices that had become part of the customary practice of various regions.[1]

Having previously rejected a variety of bases upon which the Spanish conquest of the Americas might rest and having spelled out in great detail the power of the pope in temporal affairs, Solórzano next moved to examine Alexander VI's bull *Inter caetera* at some length. The opening paragraphs of Book 2, Chapter 24, restated many of the themes that Solórzano had already developed. Indeed, this chapter could in fact be read in isolation and still give the reader the full flavor of the previous discussion of papal power.

Solórzano opened this chapter with a restatement of his position on the temporal power of the pope. He argued that the consensus of Catholic thinkers was that the pope "has, at the least, control, jurisdiction, and temporal power over all princes, whether believers or infidels in as far as a supernatural end would seem to require it." As a result, the pope could deprive all rulers, Christian and non-Christian alike, of their *imperium* if the need arose.[2] Solórzano pointed out that the pope could not, however, act arbitrarily in such matters, but only in accordance with the common good. In support of this position, Solórzano gave few citations, having already given the basic argument and citations elsewhere. The citations that he did choose to present here, however, underscored his overall approach to the issues that the discovery of the New World raised. The first was Seraphinus de Freitas's defense of the Portuguese claim to a monopoly of the trade routes to the East Indies. The second was a reference to the work of the famous fourteenth-century Roman lawyer Baldus de Ubaldis (c. 1327–1400), in which he cited three bulls of Innocent III.[3] This particular mixture of citations reinforced the main theme of the *De Indiarum Jure*; that is, Solórzano rejected the approach to international relations that Grotius represented and reasserted the medieval papal-canonistic view of the world and the papacy's role in it.

For Solórzano, the only basis upon which the pope could act in temporal affairs, even to the point of removing a secular ruler from office, was a spiritual one. Neither natural law nor the law of nations provided any basis for such papal action.[4] The basis for it had been spelled out in Innocent IV's commentary on *Quod super his* almost four centuries earlier.[5] Having thus reminded his reader of the bases of discussion, Solórzano then moved to the issue at hand. Las Casas, Bellarmine, and others, according to Solórzano, held the opinion that "no one of sound mind ought to doubt that the Pope and no one else except him has the power to deprive emperors, kings and other great princes of their empires, kingdoms and principalities."[6] Furthermore, this temporary exercise of the material sword, that is, secular power, should not proceed simply from the pope's personal judgment of a situation but only with the advice of learned and prudent men.[7] Again, the emphasis was upon papal exercise of temporal jurisdiction in a particular case for the spiritual well-being of a particular people. Well-being in such circumstances consisted of the acquisition of virtue, the goal that all people should desire.[8]

In Solórzano's opinion, Alexander VI was completely within his rights to commit "to our Catholic kings of Spain . . . the responsibility for converting these people to the faith." This was not all that was included in Alexander's grant, however. The pope also granted to Ferdinand and Isabella "full and supreme *dominium* and jurisdiction" over the peoples of the New World as well.[9]

Solórzano noted at this point that some would argue that the fierce and primitive nature of the inhabitants of the New World, living as they did far from civilization, would in itself justify their conquest.[10] Nevertheless, as he had demonstrated earlier, arguments supporting the conquest of the New World by the Spanish on the grounds of the primitive, savage nature of the Indians were not sufficient.[11] The most secure title, indeed the only legitimate one, derived from papal grant. As a consequence, Ferdinand and Isabella, being pious Christians, anxious to deal with the inhabitants of the New World in a lawful way, "requested of the Roman See the donation or confirmation of the New World recently discovered by the effort of Columbus at their behest (*a se*) so that they might be enabled to occupy and possess more safely and securely the already discovered lands and those yet to be discovered." Solórzano added that "many learned men of that time believed that such a concession was in no way necessary to the justice of this conquest."[12] Nevertheless, being spiritually minded, Ferdinand and Isabella sought the advice and permission of the pope in what was clearly a matter of grave importance, precisely the kind of situation where, according to the canonists, papal guidance ought to be sought. Specifically, they were acting as good Christian rulers, as the rulers of Portugal and Castile had been acting for a century when dealing with the Atlantic islands off of Africa and with the west coast of Africa: aware of the rights of the inhabitants of these lands and islands, yet anxious to find a legitimate basis upon which to operate there. This behavior was not simply pious, but a prudent recognition of long-standing legal and political tradition as well, a calculated combination of piety and expediency.

Turning to the papal role in *Inter caetera*, Solórzano claimed that when the pope received word of Columbus's first voyage, he was overjoyed because "he realized the vast expansion of the Church and of the Christian faith" that this discovery would cause. After discussion with his cardinals and with their support, Alexander VI granted the newly discovered lands to the Castilians and the Portuguese. The papal grant gave to the Spanish monarchs "all the islands and mainland territory to the west and south up until now discovered by their effort and at their expense and all such lands that will be discovered in the future." The pope then demarcated the lands he had assigned to the Castilians from those assigned to the Portuguese. All of this was done as an exercise "of the plenitude of papal power."[13] In order for his readers to appreciate what precisely the pope had granted, Solórzano then included the texts of several bulls that Alexander VI had issued in response to the Castilian request for authorization to take control of the newly discovered lands. What he did not include was the text of the first version of *Inter caetera*. This bull, dated May 3, 1493, had granted to the Castilians the right to occupy the newly discovered lands and any others that were to be found later as long as no other Christian ruler possessed them at that time. This version of the bull did not include the famous line of demarcation that divided responsibility for sending missionaries to the newly discovered lands between the Castilians and the Portuguese.[14]

What Solórzano did place in the *De Indiarum Jure* was the second version of the bull, the one dated May 4, 1493. This bull contained the line of demarcation drawn from pole to pole 100 leagues west of the Azores and Cape Verde Islands, granting the newly discovered lands west and south of the line to the Castilians. The lands to the east of the line were reserved to Portugal. In effect, this protected the lands the Portuguese had already obtained along the west coast of Africa.[15] He also included *Eximiae devotionis*, May 3, 1493, and *Dudum Siquidem*, September 26, 1493.[16] These bulls further clarified the division of the newly discovered lands between Castile and Portugal. Finally, Solórzano also mentioned the final phase of the struggle over the line of demarcation, which ended with the redrawing of the line 370 leagues west of the Cape Verde Islands by the terms of the Treaty of Tordesillas in the summer of 1494.[17]

Solórzano's history of the relationship between the Spanish monarchs and Alexander VI stressed the way in which the good Christian ruler reacted when faced with a new and serious situation. He should do as Ferdinand and Isabella did, seek papal guidance as to the proper course of action, and act only with papal authorization. The picture that Solórzano provided indicated that Ferdinand and Isabella recognized that the peoples of the New World, however primitive, possessed rights that could not be infringed upon by European Christian rulers acting on their own initiative, even if some of their learned subjects thought otherwise.

At the same time, Solórzano must also have known that his history of the events surrounding the issuance of *Inter caetera* was not completely accurate. It is difficult to believe that he was unaware of the fact that in keeping with the practice of petitioners to the papal court, Ferdinand and Isabella had instructed the Castilian chancery to draw up a petition that, in effect, provided the text for the desired bull. If the pope chose to grant the petition, the papal chancery would then draw up the necessary letter in proper form, incorporating the substance of the petitioner's request. Furthermore, there existed a formula for such a letter, as the papal chancery had been issuing similar bulls for a century to the rulers of Castile and Portugal.

For Solórzano, these papal bulls demonstrated that because the pope "possessed full and complete *dominium* and jurisdiction over the lands of the New World and over the infidels who dwelled there" he could award these lands and people "to the Catholic Kings on the condition and with the responsibility that they demonstrate great zeal for preaching, spreading, and preserving the faith and the Christian religion among these people."[18] The proof that the pope had acted correctly in granting these lands to the Spanish was that now the Indians were no longer idolators and "enjoy perpetual civil peace."[19] Here again, the Spanish conquest of the New World was justified for two reasons, namely the spiritual guidance of the Indians and their temporal or civil good as well.

Solórzano also recognized that there were those who denied that the pope actually possessed the kind of power that Alexander VI claimed in issuing these bulls. Cardinal Bellarmine, for example, initially argued that the pope could only authorize the Spanish rulers to send missionaries to the New World. He could not, according to Bellarmine, deprive these people of their right to rule themselves. Subsequently, however, when he finally obtained a copy of the bull and read it carefully, he agreed that Alexander VI had the right to act as he did.[20]

In addition to the legality of the papal grants contained in *Inter caetera*, there was also Alexander VI's spiritual and moral qualities to consider. Protestant writers such as Martin Luther (1483–1546) and John Calvin, along with anti-papal Catholics such as Francisco Guiccardini (1483–1540), criticized the bulls on the grounds that Alexander VI was a wicked man. In response, Catholic writers such as Thomas Bozius (1548–1610) pointed out good qualities that Alexander VI possessed. Furthermore, Bozius argued that the Protestants were not capable of bringing the inhabitants of the New World to the baptismal font.[21] From the Catholic perspective, the missionary efforts being made in all parts of the New World demonstrated the Church's adherence to Christ's injunction about preaching His word to all people everywhere. In one sense, this missionary activity was evidence of the Roman Church's authenticity. On the other hand, Protestant writers sometimes expressed horror at the picture of Catholic missionaries baptizing thousands of infidels who would then adhere to a false version of Christianity, and so be damned.[22]

Having presented Alexander's bulls granting the Americas to the rulers of Castile and having given a brief defense of the papal power on which the pope based his grant, Solórzano went on to explain that there was a long history of such papal grants, a history known to the pope and his curia.

Alexander VI was clearly not the first nor the only pope to exercise the jurisdiction that *Inter caetera* asserted belonged to the pope. Numerous other popes had exercised the same power over a long span of time and numerous European rulers, not only the kings of Castile and Portugal, benefited from it.[23]

The example of papal jurisdiction over secular rulers that Solórzano chose to begin his history of this kind of papal power was, at first glance, a curious one. He began this section of the *De Indiarum Jure* with a discussion of Pope Adrian IV's (1154–1159) bull *Laudabiliter*.[24] It authorized Henry II of England (1154–1189) to occupy Ireland in order to bring the native Irish back to the faith from which they had lapsed in recent centuries. In effect, the pope deprived the native Irish rulers of their lawful *dominium* in order to achieve a higher spiritual goal. Solórzano argued that this bull was based on virtually the same premises as *Inter caetera*. Furthermore, this authorization to gain control of Ireland had created a feudal relationship between the papacy and the kings of England.[25]

The Irish situation was, of course, not identical with that in the New World, which Solórzano realized. The Irish, as *Laudabiliter* portrayed them, were Christians, even if bad ones. No one would deny the pope's right to restore proper ecclesiastical discipline to a Christian people who had gone astray, although some might quarrel with the transfer of the government of Ireland from the native rulers to Henry II. Solórzano began with this example of papal power no doubt because it fitted his argument unusually well. He might have reached all the way back to the early Church to find the roots of the power that Alexander VI claimed in *Inter caetera*. Luis Weckmann has argued, for example, that the roots of Alexander's bull lay in the Donation of Constantine, specifically the papal claim to possess jurisdiction over all islands found in the Donation.[26] Solórzano did not, however, place the origin of *Inter caetera* in the Donation for a number of reasons. Probably the most important was that he would have been resting the Spanish claim to the New World on a power exercised by the pope but ultimately derived from a secular authority. Such a derivation might have meant that the same secular authority could, at some point, seek to reclaim the power granted to the papacy. This in turn might mean the loss of Spanish title to the New World.[27]

By selecting *Laudabiliter* as the starting point of a history of papal grants of other kingdoms to secular rulers, Solórzano was resting the Spanish title to the Americas on the practice of the papacy in the wake of the Investiture Controversy of the eleventh and twelfth centuries. Earlier, he had defended the power claimed by the papacy both within the Church and over those outside of it, power that was defined and achieved only in the course of the Investiture Controversy. It was the papal victory over the claims of the Holy Roman Emperors in this period that laid the foundations of the great age of the papacy. Innocent III, Innocent IV, and Boniface VIII, all of whom Solórzano had cited in the course of dealing with the theory of papal power, had acted within the context that their eleventh- and twelfth-century predecessors had created.

Furthermore, *Laudabiliter* did share some important elements with *Inter caetera*. In the first place, it was the product of a royal request that the papacy approve a course of action. Adrian IV had issued it in response to a request from Henry II, a secular ruler outlining the religious situation that led to the promulgation of the bull designed to correct it.[28]

Laudabiliter began with a statement of the papal mission to all people and of the role of the Christian ruler in fulfilling that mission. Henry II wanted to "enlarge the boundaries of the Church," to preach "the truth of the Christian religion to a rude and ignorant people," and to "root out the growths of vice from the field of the Lord." He had applied to the pope for authorization to do these things because "Ireland and all islands on which Christ the sun of righteousness has shone, and which have accepted the doctrines of the Christian faith, belong to the jurisdiction of the blessed Peter and the holy Roman Church." Henry II agreed to pay Peter's Pence, a charge of one penny levied on each hearth, in return for permission to enter Ireland and, in effect, to bring the Irish Church into conformity with the ecclesiastical reforms that the Investiture Controversy had generated.[29]

Adrian IV's letter also presented many of the fundamental claims about papal power that *Inter caetera* was to incorporate three centuries later. The most important of these claims was that the Church had a mission to all people everywhere. In this particular case, the people involved, the Irish, were at least nominally Christian, even if their relationship to the Church was in disarray. They had lapsed from the practice of the faith and they were not adhering to the standards that the Church reform movement had established. The pope suggested that he expected the English entrance into Ireland would be peaceful and expressed the hope that "the people of that land shall receive you [Henry II] with honour and revere you as their lord. . . ."[30] At the same time, he was making it quite clear that he possessed the right to transfer the rule of Ireland from native rulers to Henry II in order to achieve the overriding goal, the salvation of the souls of the Irish.

The fact that the Irish were at least nominally Christian did not make

Laudabiliter significantly different from *Inter caetera*, although the latter dealt with infidels, not lapsed Christians. The theory of papal power that Solórzano was defending clearly defined it as universal, not restricted to the Christian world, at least not since Innocent IV had explicitly extended the pope's jurisdiction to infidels. The basic premises on which the pope's power was based were the same, whether the application concerned Christians who were clearly within the Church, schismatics and heretics who were rejecting some aspects of the Church, Jews and Muslims who shared something with the Church, or infidels who had never heard of Christianity until missionaries appeared to instruct them.

In addition to stressing the place of *Laudabiliter* in the history of the papacy's theory of its universal jurisdiction, Solórzano also employed *Laudabiliter* to make an interesting and ironic point about the Protestant English king's possession of Ireland in the seventeenth century. Solórzano's contemporary, King Charles I of England (1625–1649), included among his titles that of King of Ireland. This title, first employed by Henry VIII, had evolved from the title Lord of Ireland that Henry II's youngest son, John (1199–1216) bore before ascending the throne of England.[31] That title in turn was derived from the English occupation of Ireland that had begun in 1170. If the English could claim Ireland on the basis of a papal grant, how could the English logically criticize the Spanish for occupying the Americas on the same basis?

Having discussed *Laudabiliter* and using it as the starting point for demonstrating the longstanding relationship between the papacy and secular rulers in the work of dealing with people who dwelled on the fringes of Europe, Solórzano then moved to a discussion of papal bulls more closely connected to *Inter caetera*. He began this section of his discussion with the bulls connected to the Portuguese drive down along the west coast of Africa that Henry the Navigator (1394–1460) had initiated in the early-fifteenth century. Referring the reader back to the earlier discussion of the Portuguese prince's role in the work of discovery, Solórzano pointed out that it was Prince Henry whose efforts gained for Portugal new lands "in perpetuity." He also cited several popes who had issued letters guaranteeing Portuguese control over the newly discovered lands. These included: Martin V (1417–1431), Eugenius IV (1431–1447), Nicholas V (1447–1455), Calixtus III (1455–1458), and Sixtus IV (1471–1484).[32]

These fifteenth-century papal bulls recognized the efforts of the Portuguese who had been expanding in Africa since the time of John I (1385–1433), the father of Henry the Navigator. In the earlier section of the *De*

Indiarum Jure, Solórzano had provided a brief history of the Portuguese in the East Indies as part of the background to *Inter caetera*. He now turned to the content of some of the papal bulls involved, specifically Calixtus III's bull *Inter caetera*, March 1456, to illustrate papal power over infidels and their lands.[33] This bull, sent to Alfonso V (1438–1481), consisted of two parts, a copy of Nicholas V's bull *Romanus Pontifex* of January 8, 1455, and the granting of new concessions to the Portuguese.

Solórzano did not excerpt all of *Romanus Pontifex* and he did not include any of Calixtus's bull, except for some introductory material. The point he wished to make was that from as early as 1420, five years after the Portuguese captured Ceuta in North Africa and made it their permanent base for further voyages down the west coast of Africa, Portuguese rulers had been obtaining papal permission to retain those lands that they "had discovered and subjugated by their virtue and warlike efforts."[34] The stated motives for this activity of the Portuguese included the desire to assist Christians in the East whom the Muslims were oppressing and to spread the Gospel of Christ. In order to insure that the Portuguese were properly rewarded for their efforts in this work and also to supervise Christian contacts with these infidels lest they acquire the navigational and military skills of the Europeans and thus be enabled to resist the Portuguese more successfully, Nicholas V ordered that no one sail to these regions for any purposes without the permission of the Portuguese monarch.[35]

The ultimate reward that the Portuguese would reap for these efforts was the acquisition of the lands and goods "of these enemies of Christ" and their reduction to slavery.[36] Here Nicholas V was working on the assumption that those whom the Portuguese would encounter as they progressed on their voyages of exploration along the coast of Africa were enemies of Christians, most probably Muslims.

In a brief discussion of the significance of Nicholas's bull, Solórzano stressed that the papal grant to the Portuguese included complete jurisdiction over the newly discovered lands so that no one, not "even emperors and kings," could enter them without Portuguese permission. Those who did violate this papal grant would be subject to ecclesiastical punishments, including excommunication and interdict.[37] In stressing this point, Solórzano was setting out the foundation of his conception of world order. The pope should authorize those Christian rulers who were willing to invest time and money in seeking out the peoples of the frontier to develop a monopoly of trade and other benefits that would arise from such contacts. He would also seem to be suggesting that the pope should not grant such licences and authorizations until a ruler had demonstrated his involvement in such activities. There seems to be no suggestion that the pope should offer such monopolies to entice Christian rulers to expand contacts with the infidels. Monopolies were to be the reward of exploration, not a motivation for it.[38]

Solórzano then stressed that Ferdinand and Isabella remained quite conscious of the need to justify the conquest of the Americas in accordance with the terms that the papacy and the canon lawyers had established over several centuries, even after receiving *Inter caetera*. Thus, in 1513, using the advice of learned men, which was a characteristic of good Christian rulers, the Spanish monarchs had arranged for the composition of a document that, when read to infidels whom Spanish explorers encountered, would explain why the Spanish had come and how the newly encountered peoples should respond.[39] This was, of course, the *Requerimiento*, which stated the reasons for the arrival of the Spanish and what they intended to do. No attack was to be made against the inhabitants until the *Requerimiento* had been read to them, although there was no obligation to learn the local language first so that the hearers would be able to understand the words being shouted at them. At this point, Solórzano included a copy of the *Requerimiento* in Spanish, the original of which the Emperor Charles V had sent to Francisco Pizarro (1476–1541) in 1533 during the conquest of Peru. In fact, this was a comparatively late use of this document. Cortés, for example, had employed it earlier in his conquest of Mexico.[40] Solórzano gave no reason for including this particular copy of the *Requerimiento* in his treatise, but there are two obvious possibilities. In the first place, he himself had served in the *audiencia* in Peru and may have been inclined to underscore the legitimacy of the conquest of the particular region in which he had served. In the second place, the introduction to the text states that a copy of the *Requerimiento* was sent to Pizarro along with orders to conquer Peru.[41] Solórzano seems anxious to demonstrate that the conquest of Peru had proceeded as the legal theorists, following the papal authorization of such endeavors, had admonished it should be done. That is, Pizarro acted not on his own but under the express command of Charles V who, in his capacity as Charles I of Castile, possessed papal authority for ordering the conquest of Peru. This authority in turn was derived from a long line of papal letters reaching back to Calixtus III and even Adrian IV.

The *Requerimiento* explained to the Indians who the Spanish were and why they had come to the New World and contained a summary of basic Christian doctrine designed to justify what the Spanish were doing. It began with a statement that the Spanish represented the rulers of Castile and Leon, famous as "subduers of the barbarous nations."[42] The text went on to point out that although all people were descended from a single set of parents, presumably making all human beings members of a single family, they had gone in various ways and created a multitude of societies. To bring men back into a kind of familial harmony, God made St. Peter "Lord and Superior of all the men in the world, that all should obey him, and that he should be the head of the whole human race." As a consequence, the entire world was the "kingdom and jurisdiction" of St. Peter. Men of St. Peter's own time "took him for Lord, King, and Superior of the universe" and had continued to regard Peter's successor, the Pope, in the same way.

The Pope, as "Lord of the World," granted the New World to Ferdinand and Isabella and to their heirs, making them "kings and lords of these islands and land of Terrafirme." Some of those whom the Spanish had informed of this donation accepted Spanish overlordship without question and accepted the clergy sent to teach them about the Christian faith. The Peruvians, it was argued, should follow the good example of these people and accept the Spanish at once. Should they do this, then the Spanish would leave the people in possession of their lands and goods "free without servitude." Failure to respond positively to the *Requerimiento* would, however, have very harsh consequences for the Peruvians.[43] The Spanish would then be justified in waging war against them, subjugating them to "the yoke and obedience of the Church" and of Charles of Castile. They might even be made slaves as a consequence of refusing to accept the terms of the *Requerimiento* as read to them.

Solórzano did not analyze the text of the *Requerimiento* in any detail, even though much of what it stated was at odds with his own arguments. For example, thus far in his argument Solórzano had defended the right of the inhabitants of the New World to *dominium*. Being legally possessed of property and lordship, the Indians could not be deprived of it except under specific circumstances. The theme of the *Requerimiento* appears to be that the pope had awarded the New World to the Spanish without any consideration of the actual circumstances that existed in it. In fact, had the Indians refused to admit peaceful missionaries? If not, then to deprive them of their *dominium* would be a violation of Innocent IV's views on infidel *dominium* and an acceptance of Hostiensis's opinion that with the Incarnation, all *dominium* was transferred to Christians, a view that elsewhere Solórzano rejected as being out of step with the *communis opinio* of the canon lawyers, and even possibly heretical.

Furthermore, the history of papal power that the *Requerimiento* provided was obviously at odds with the history of the Church that Solórzano knew. Solórzano must have been amused at the statement in the *Requerimiento* that Christ gave to St. Peter "the world for his kingdom and jurisdiction," and that "men who lived in that time obeyed . . . St. Peter and took him for Lord, King, and Superior of the universe."[44] Even the notion that the Spanish monarchs received the lordship of the New World from the pope as a grant or donation was somewhat misleading. After all, the Castilians and the Portuguese negotiated the line of demarcation between the East and the West Indies and then sought papal approval for it. Furthermore, the papal grant was based on the papal responsibility to insure the conversion of the inhabitants of the New World. The *Requerimiento* would appear to assume that the hearers would not accept missionaries peacefully. Acceptance of Castilian lordship, not religious conversion, was its chief message to the infidels.

Not only did Solórzano choose not to deal with the contents of the *Requerimiento* in any detail, neither did he pay any attention to the fact that in practice, the text was simply read to, or, more precisely, shouted at, Indians in a language they did not know. The reading of the *Requerimiento* became a legal ritual rather than a serious attempt at initiating the conversion of the Indians. Indeed, it can even be argued that the purpose of reading the *Requerimiento* had more to do with protecting the Castilians from a charge of heresy, that is, of accepting the Hostiensian position on post-Incarnation *dominium* among infidels, than with the actual conversion of infidels.[45] That is, by reading the *Requerimiento* the Spanish could say to critics of the conquest that they had first sought peaceful entry but, having read the document that outlined their reasons for being in the Americas and then being refused admittance, they could legitimately attack the indigenous population. One could even imagine a Spanish official arguing that the failure of the Indians to listen to and then to respond to the message of the *Requerimiento* in rational, that is, accepting, fashion would demonstrate their lack of rational capacity and therefore their nonhuman or subhuman status.

Rather than analyzing the *Requerimiento*, however, Solórzano went on to defend it and the consequences that flowed from it. The first point that he made, one stemming from Roman law, was that "if someone has legitimate possession as a consequence of a judicial decision," a subsequent judicial decision "by a legitimate and competent judge is sufficient for taking away true *dominium* and transferring it to someone else."[46] In support of this opinion, Solórzano cited a number of opinions linked to a case that he found similar to the situation in the Americas regarding the right of the papacy to transfer *dominium* from one ruler to another. The case was that of the Kingdom of Navarre, which Pope Julius II (1503–1513) had awarded to Ferdinand of Aragon in 1512.[47] Palacios Rubios, the presumed author of the *Requerimiento* and author of a major defense of the Castilian acquisition of the New World, had written a treatise defending the acquisition of Navarre as well, a treatise that Solórzano cited at this point.[48] The point that Palacios Rubios supported was that we "ought to admit that . . . [the Supreme Pontiff] is the supreme and competent judge of all men, believers and infidels in spirituals and also in temporals, where a just cause requires it," as the previous arguments have demonstrated.[49]

This discussion of papal power Solórzano then supported with a number of citations from theologians and canonists who described papal power in the most enthusiastic terms. The theme of these citations was that in grave and serious matters, the pope was the individual best qualified to judge what ought to be done. The pope, or a secular ruler in situations where it was proper, had discretion to find a solution for a new situation. In such cases, where there was no particular legal precedent to apply, the pope, acting according to the general principles of the law, could make a ruling that everyone should accept.[50] Some writers even went so far as to argue that any opinion that emphasized papal power was to be preferred to an opinion that did not support papal power.[51] Another writer argued that papal decisions should always "be presumed to be just and legitimately and canonically issued."[52] After all, the pope is the "fountain of justice," and in him "resides the fullness of perfection and wisdom."[53] Thus, even if the entire world opposed a papal decision, a good Catholic would adhere to the papal position. Solórzano summed up this section of his argument in the following way:

> what the pope approves or reproves, everyone is bound to approve or reprove and he who is not with the pope is against Christ and who is not of Christ is of Anti-Christ and he sins greatly who attacks the Church that he ought to defend.[54]

In effect, this would mean that those who opposed the papal decision to award the New World to the Castilians and the Portuguese were heretics.

According to these standards, the division of the Indies between the two Iberian kingdoms was a just and reasonable decision. The Church, after all, was the "tutor and guardian of justice," and so was "unable to do anything contrary to justice."[55] When Alexander VI, with the advice of his counsellors, determined that Castile and Portugal should share responsibility for the peoples of the Indies, he was clearly acting within the proper framework for making such a decision, and other Christian rulers should not attempt to defy that ruling.

Toward the end of this chapter, Solórzano raised another argument that had some historical relevance. Even granting the supreme power of the pope that enabled him to decide in all kinds of situations that required the most sophisticated thought, did the pope have the right to make such decisions without consultation with anyone? Could, or did, Alexander VI issue *Inter caetera* without any consultation with his cardinals and with other learned men?[56] As Solórzano pointed out, the pope possessed the *plenitudo potestatis*, the fullness of papal power, and he could exercise that power. He was also required, however, to consult with the cardinals, something that "divine law, natural law, and the law of nations" demonstrated.[57] Solórzano also pointed out that at one time the popes took an oath that they would consult with the cardinals in serious matters.[58]

The division of the newly discovered regions between the Castilians and the Portuguese was clearly a serious matter, one that would have required consultation with the cardinals and other members of the papal court. Some critics of *Inter caetera* had apparently suggested that the bull was invalid because it did not contain an explicit statement that Alexander VI had consulted the cardinals and others before making his decision.[59] Solórzano pointed out that, in fact, many bulls made no mention of consultation, although the pope had obviously sought assistance in making the decision contained in it.[60] Although the pope did consult with various individuals during the process of making his determination, the bull was issued over his name alone, not over a list of contributors to the decision.[61] Ultimately, the bull was a product of the *plenitudo potestatis* that belonged to the pope alone, not to a committee consisting of the pope, the cardinals, and the learned men who attended the papal court.

The theme of this chapter of the *De Indiarum Jure* was that the power of the pope to apportion responsibility for the inhabitants of the newly discovered Indies between the Castilians and the Portuguese was rooted in historical precedent as well as in legal and theological theory. Solórzano was anxious to demonstrate that the powers asserted in *Inter caetera* were not new, that popes had claimed and indeed exercised such powers over a long span of time. Furthermore, he was arguing that the legitimacy of this power was rooted in two series of precedents. The first dealt with papal bulls that preceded *Inter caetera*. Solórzano wanted to insure that his readers were aware of just how long the papacy had been involved in the selection of secular rulers, clearly a major involvement in secular affairs. The second dealt with the way in which a pope made decisions in grave matters.

It was Solórzano's position that the papacy had not only claimed the right to remove secular rulers from office and to award their lands to other rulers, but that popes from the twelfth century onward had actually exercised this power, and secular rulers had acceded to it.[62] Rather curiously, while he recognized that there were critics of the theory of papal power that would allow the pope to remove secular rulers, he did not seem to have been interested in finding examples of secular rulers who denied the pope's right to intervene in their affairs. One result of this approach was that European rulers, as Solórzano described them, did not seem to have objected to such papal activity. The Irish rulers, for example, who presumably lost some power when Henry II entered Ireland under the terms of *Laudabiliter*, were not cited as having objected to Adrian IV's bull.[63] Solórzano did not even discuss Philip IV's forceful rejection of Boniface VIII's claims contained in *Unam sanctam*. Solórzano saw the history of papal intervention in secular affairs only from the perspective of the papacy, that is, in terms of the working out of the papal theory of power in specific historical situations. The history therefore did not provide the basis upon which the theory was constructed; rather, the history illustrated the papal application of the theory.

In the latter part of this chapter, when Solórzano moved back to the realm of theory and away from historical illustrations of its application, he felt obliged to justify the quality of judgment involved in making decisions such as that contained in *Inter caetera*. One might have expected him to assert that some kind of divine guidance assisted the pope in making such momentous decisions. He did not. Instead, Solórzano described the pope as consulting with the cardinals and with the learned men employed at the papal court. He was describing, in effect, the church governance structure that had emerged in the wake of the Investiture Controversy. The structure of governance described here was something that not only Protestant reformers criticized, but a number of Catholics had as well. Along with its legal underpinnings, the canon law, this structure formed the head of the institutional Church. The pope was not isolated from the institutional structure, he was part of it, its peak, its capstone, but still part of the structure. The historical tradition was that he made decisions after consultation with the cardinals and others and in keeping with the legal principles upon which the Church was constructed. The pope thus acted in accordance with spiritual principles, employing rational analysis of circumstances in order to apply these principles in individual cases.[64]

Solórzano's lines of argument in the 24th chapter of the second book of the *De Indiarum Jure* set the stage for the 25th and final chapter. In this chapter, after a careful, rational analysis of the circumstances involved, he would explain to his reader how the papal power to transfer rulership from one prince to another was used to award the Americas to the Castilian ruler.

8. Order and Harmony Among Nations

The structure of the *De Indiarum Jure* led almost inevitably to the theme that characterized the last four chapters of the second book. If God had not directly authorized the Castilian monarchs to undertake the conquest of the Americas, if the inhabitants of the New World possessed *dominium* in land and governance, and if the moral failings of the Indians did not necessitate or justify their conquest, what arguments remained that would legitimize the Spanish conquest and occupation of the New World? These chapters provided such a basis. They present the argument that there was a natural order of the world that could be learned and put into place. In effect, the final chapters of the *De Indiarum Jure* deal with the question of world order, specifically Christian world order, and how it might be achieved.

The notion that there was a natural order of the world was rooted in the medieval intellectual tradition. The scholastic tradition assumed that all knowledge could be fitted into a hierarchical schema. Peter Abelard (1079–c. 1142) launched this work of recovering the learning of the past, dealing with problems of provenance and meaning, correcting errors, and then reconciling what seemed to be contradictions among the various materials. The belief that all knowledge could be thus ordered and arranged underlay the great philosophical and theological *summae* that culminated in Aquinas's *Summa theologica*. In the canonistic tradition, Gratian's great volume of canon law, the *Decretum*, known as the *Concordance of Discordant Canons*, provided the same service. The *Decretum* was to bring harmony from dissonance, as Stephan Kuttner has described it, that is, to reconcile all of the materials that, in an inchoate fashion, formed the canon law.[1]

The desire to bring order out of chaos in the intellectual sphere led easily to a desire on the part of the same intellectuals to see the political order in the same terms. Seeing European Christian society as a congeries of competing political units, many writers on political issues considered the possibility of a universal Christian order that would unify the Christian states into some form of hierarchical structure. The essence of this approach to Christian society was described through the often-used image of bees and the hive. In *On Kingship*, a discussion of the ruler's responsibilities written for the King of Cyprus, Thomas Aquinas stated the analogy this way: "Among bees there is one king bee, and in the whole universe there is One God, Maker and Ruler of all things."[2] While Aquinas was using the analogy at this point in order to explain why monarchy was the best form of government, the same argument could also be made concerning the human race as a whole, and it was. In the *De Monarchia*, for example, Dante used a similar argument to explain why the Holy Roman emperor should rule the entire human race.[3] Even in the later Middle Ages, as the real power of the Holy Roman Empire declined steadily, there continued to be those who supported the formation of some kind of universal Christian society. In the middle of the fifteenth century, the celebrated humanist Aeneas Sylvius, subsequently Pope Pius II (1458–1464), defended the universal jurisdiction of the emperor in a treatise on the Empire.[4]

The discovery of the New World had renewed interest in the question of a peaceful political order. This time, however, the issue was considered not simply in terms of Christian Europe but in terms of the entire world. Was it possible to define and enforce a set of standards of international behavior that would operate throughout the world? If such was the case, should or could there be a universal government and, if so, who should head it? Francis Vitoria had raised these questions in his *De Indis* when he had discussed whether the pope or the Holy Roman emperor was in some way the *dominus mundi*, the Lord of the World, a phrase in the *Corpus iuris civilis* that described the Roman emperor.[5]

Solórzano considered these questions in the last four chapters of the second book of the *De Indiarum Jure*. In Chapter 21 he examined the argument that the emperor, indeed the Lord of the World, could consequently authorize the conquest of the New World by designated Christian rulers. In chapters 22–25, he dealt with the argument that the pope could grant the newly discovered lands to Christian rulers of his own choice. The result was that, far from being merely a discussion of the moral failings of the infidels or of the responsibility of the papacy for the spiritual well-being of the infidels, the *De Indiarum Jure* became a discussion of world order and the means by which it might be achieved.

Part I — The Emperor as *Dominus Mundi*

In Chapter 21 of the second book of the *De Indiarum Jure*, Solórzano discussed the imperial claim to universal jurisdiction and its relation to the

Spanish possession of the New World. He began with the statement that some scholars had asserted that Spanish possession of the Americas rested on the *auctoritas* and *potestas* of the Roman emperor. This particular choice of words was striking because they were traditionally employed in discussions of the relationship between the spiritual *auctoritas* and the secular *potestas*, the two powers that cooperated in the direction of the world. *Auctoritas* referred to the moral authority that the Church possessed because of its interest in the highest goal, the salvation of all people, and because of the source of this authority, God Himself. On the other hand, secular rulers possessed only physical force, that is, *potestas*, because they were responsible only for the peace and order of secular communities, a lesser goal than that of eternal salvation. In a rightly ordered world, these two powers would work together to achieve their common ends, the security of people in this world and their salvation in the next. The goal of earthly peace and order was subordinated to the higher goal of salvation. The secular rulers would govern in such a way as to make the Church's goal more achievable. Kings, emperors, and other secular officials would carry out their duties under the general supervision of the pope, that is, the secular *potestas* would operate under the direction of the papal *auctoritas*.[6]

There were, of course, those who had defended the autonomy of the secular government, but when they appeared on the scene, they faced an already existing and thoroughly articulated papal world view. Those trained in Roman law, for example, defended the emperor's universal role. The great medieval debate about the nature of the spheres of jurisdiction that properly belonged to the emperor and to the pope, the crux of the conflict between church and state, was very much a debate among lawyers representing two legal systems.[7] Although extremists on both sides could and did articulate positions that would reduce either the spiritual or the temporal sphere of jurisdiction to absolute subjection to the other, the main thrust of the debate was about where to draw the line between the two jurisdictions. As independent kingdoms emerged, their leaders also insisted that papal jurisdiction was limited. At the same time, the *communis opinio* of those engaged in this debate was that the spiritual and the temporal authorities must work together. The governance of Christian peoples was a joint endeavor, because the ultimate goal all people sought, eternal salvation, required the establishment of orderly societies on earth within which they could prepare themselves for their eternal destiny.

The nature of the imperial power was not simply a matter of antiquarian interest for Solórzano and the other Spanish writers who dealt with the argument that Spanish possession of the New World rested on an imperial grant. The most glorious phase of the conquest of the Americas had come during the reign of Charles I of Castile, Aragon, and the other Spanish kingdoms (1516–1556), who was also Charles V (1519–1555) of the Holy Roman Empire. It was easy to overlook the fact that Charles occupied these various thrones on the basis of a personal union. That is, the thrones were not united institutionally or structurally. What linked these kingdoms was the person of the ruler who occupied them. At his death, they could be bequeathed to one or more heirs, as Charles divided the Habsburg holdings between his brother Ferdinand and his son Philip in a series of abdications in 1555 and 1556.[8]

The fact that the king of Aragon and the king of Castile was also the Holy Roman emperor during the greatest period of Spanish expansion in the New World, the period that saw the conquest of the Aztec and the Incan empires, made it possible to see the conquest in terms of an imperial claim to universal jurisdiction. The argument could be made that the conquest of the New World took place under imperial auspices. As Solórzano well knew, however, this line of argument raised a series of problems for the Spanish. In the first place, Charles became Holy Roman emperor only in 1519, well after Columbus had reached the New World. Furthermore, Hernán Cortés, the conqueror of Mexico, had also begun his expedition before Charles became king of Germany and emperor-elect. Although Solórzano did not mention the fact, it would appear that Cortés may have been the first to link the conquest of the New World with the Roman Empire when he wrote to Charles offering him an empire in Mexico to go with his empire in Germany.[9]

In addition, Charles V had divided his possessions in such a way as to grant the imperial title to his brother Ferdinand I (1558–1564) and Spain and its overseas possessions to his son, Philip II (1556–1598). The result was that imperial power again became clearly distinct from Spanish power. Furthermore, Spanish lawyers had long asserted that Spain itself was not subject to imperial jurisdiction, because the Empire had not defended the Spanish from conquest by the Muslims; as early as the thirteenth century, a Spanish canon lawyer had argued that Spain was no longer subject to imperial jurisdiction because the emperor had not protected Spain from the eighth-century Muslim invasion and the Spanish had subsequently begun the work of reconquering their lost lands without imperial help.[10] To argue now that Spanish possession of the New World stemmed from imperial grant would fly in the face of a long Spanish tradition of denying any form of subordination to imperial power.

For Solórzano, the key to dealing with the possible imperial origin of the Spanish claim to the Americas was to recognize that Charles of Habsburg ruled a number of kingdoms and principalities, but that he ruled them individually, not collectively. That is, while Charles was in Castile, he was Charles I of Castile, when he was in Aragon he was Charles I of Aragon, and when he was in Germany, he was Charles V of Germany and the Holy Roman Empire. Multiple office-holding was a common occurrence in medieval and early modern kingdoms at all levels of both secular and ecclesiastical government, so lawyers were accustomed to distinguishing among the various capacities in which an individual could act. For the purpose of legal analysis, the holder of several offices could be considered as several persons.[11]

Having defined the terms of the problem, Solórzano then moved on to discuss the arguments in favor of the emperor as the source of legitimate Spanish possession of the New World. He pointed out that the *communis opinio* of the imperial lawyers was that "the Roman Emperor had unlimited jurisdiction in temporal matters (*in temporalibus omnia posse*) and had been granted overlordship and jurisdiction over the entire world by God Himself," just as God had granted power in spiritual matters to the pope.[12] In the final analysis, each form of power involved in human existence, spiritual and temporal, came directly from God to a single figure who then acted on His behalf.[13] The result was a conception of a Christian society in which there were two parallel hierarchies of power. The subordination of the temporal power to the spiritual was implicitly rejected in favor of the pairing of equals. When applied to the question at hand, the basis upon which the conquest of the New World could legitimately rest, Solórzano concluded that this conception of the two powers would suggest that even if the pope could claim power over the lands of infidels, the emperor had an even better claim, since his power specifically concerned temporal affairs.[14]

Solórzano then went on to consider the argument that from the beginning of imperial power, the rulers of the Roman people took the position that they possessed imperial jurisdiction over the entire world.[15] Roman law used the phrase *dominus mundi*, Lord of the World, to describe the emperor. In another place, the Roman law included a statement from the Emperor Justinian (527–565) that the "jurisdiction of his empire extends from east to west and north to south."[16] As Solórzano pointed out, however, this grandiose conception of the Roman Empire as possessing a universal jurisdiction was based on equating the city of Rome with the entire world.[17] To the Roman, Rome was the world, that is, the civilized world, the only world worth possessing. Polybius had asserted something similar when he wrote: "The Romans conquered not some part of the world but almost the entire world," by which he obviously meant virtually all of the known world that was worth conquering.[18]

It was not only the pagan Romans who identified Roman imperial rule with universal jurisdiction, however, according to Solórzano. The canon law also contained a number of statements supporting the opinion that the empire possessed universal jurisdiction. For example, the *Decretum* included St. Jerome's restatement of the Roman cliché that, as there "is one head among the bees," there is also but "one emperor [and] one judge in a province." Solórzano then noted that the glossators added that in consequence of there being but a single ruler of the world, "all kings ought to be crowned by the emperor" as a sign of their subordination to him.[19] In reality, of course, this was not the case. Nevertheless, according to this interpretation of the principle that the emperor was the *dominus mundi*, there would be an orderly world if all rulers subordinated themselves to imperial oversight. Furthermore, even the New Testament supported the universal claims of the Roman Empire, according to the proponents of this opinion. When, for example, Christ pointed out that there were things that belonged to Caesar and things that belonged to God, He was in effect upholding the Roman claim to universal jurisdiction.[20]

On the other hand, Solórzano pointed out in the next stage of this argument, while Rome did possess universal jurisdiction under Augustus and the other pagan emperors, subsequent events led to the shrinking of such a claim. For example, the emperor Constantine gave the city of Rome to the Church and removed the seat of the Empire to Constantinople. Thus the Donation of Constantine gave the western regions of the Roman Empire to the papacy and the Church, reducing the territory subject to the Roman emperor and effectively eliminating the basis for any claim to universal jurisdiction by the emperors. Furthermore, in either 800 or 801, the pope crowned Charlemagne, king of the Franks, as emperor, thus transferring the seat of the Empire from Constantinople back to the West (*a Graecis ad Gallos transierit*). Subsequently, in the tenth century, after the extinction of the Carolingian family, the papacy again transferred the Empire, this time from the Franks to the Germans in the person of Conrad, King of the Germans.[21] Nevertheless, even though the Roman Empire has become only a vestige of its former self, the image of a world subject to Roman domination remained in the political and legal vocabularies.[22]

Solórzano ended this stage of the discussion by pointing out that some say "almost all the peoples who obey Holy Mother, the Church of Rome, are also members of the Roman people or empire. Thus, if any deny that the emperor is the Lord of the World," they reject the very words of the Gospel. At the same time, citing a contemporary author, Solórzano offered the opinion that "if the emperor is not the Lord of the World, at least he should be recognized as the overseer (*moderator*) of the whole world." In other words, even if the emperor no longer possessed coercive imperial power over the world, he should be recognized as the ruler to whom all conflicts between lesser rulers should be presented for resolution. The supporters of this universal imperial jurisdiction found support for it in "either the divine or the natural law, or even in the [civil] laws and the canons."[23] The loss of real imperial power over the lands that the Roman Empire once possessed did not prevent legal theorists and other defenders of imperial power from continuing to assert a universal role for the emperors at least *de iure*. Underlying that continuing notion of imperial power was, no doubt, the memory of the Roman Empire as providing peace and stability over the entire Mediterranean world at the time of Christ, a condition that had made the spread of Christianity possible.[24]

In the next stage of the discussion, Solórzano considered one of the most important consequences of the claim that the emperor was, in theory at least, Lord of the World. If the emperor did possess such power, then defenders of the conquest of the New World could argue that he possessed the power to deprive the infidels of their lands and jurisdiction.[25] Solórzano cited a number of canon lawyers in defense of this position, including Hostiensis, who had commented that "the emperor was lord of everything, everywhere."[26] Further along in the same discussion, Solórzano cited commentators on the Roman law who argued that the emperor possessed universal jurisdiction and that he was "the natural lord of the entire world," with the power "to divide up and to unite lands and those things which pertain to them."[27]

Having presented arguments about universal imperial jurisdiction that he admitted were well developed and defended, Solórzano then went on to present the other side. The "more true and safer opinion is that of those who deny that the Roman Emperor can have any right (*jus*) in the lands and provinces of the infidels, and especially [in the lands] of those barbarians discovered by the Spanish." The reason for this was that the "Roman Caesars neither possessed [those regions], nor did they even know of their existence."[28] In effect, the jurisdiction of the Roman Empire was limited, not universal, and so the emperor could not possibly have given the New World to Christian rulers, as some had alleged.

The crucial issue in dealing with the imperial claim to universal jurisdiction was the source of imperial power. Did "the emperor derive his temporal power directly from God, or he did derive it from the spiritual power which the Pope exercises?", a question that Solórzano proposed to discuss fully in the following chapters of the *De Indiarum Jure*. This question was an old one and it had been at the heart of the medieval debate about the relationship between the pope and the emperor. At this point, for purposes of debate, Solórzano recognized the emperor's power as having come from the people in some way.[29]

The more immediate question for Solórzano concerned the relationship of the emperor to people who were not formally subject to him. Even if the emperor did not derive his power from the pope, but obtained it directly from God, and even if the spiritual and the temporal powers were separate and distinct, this would not necessarily lead to the conclusion that the emperor had universal jurisdiction.[30]

Having set the terms of this stage of the argument in this quite traditional fashion, Solórzano went on to discuss the nature and extent of imperial jurisdiction. He began with the traditional image of the two swords representing the two fundamental kinds of power, the spiritual and the temporal. This image could suggest that the two powers were co-equals, so that the spiritual power as exercised by the Church was universal in scope, so too the secular power in the guise of the empire must also be universal in extent.[31] To this idea, Solórzano responded with the arguments of various Spanish writers. They argued that any imperial claim to universal jurisdiction based on some kind of parity with the Church was invalid "because the ecclesiastical power exercised by one man throughout the entire Christian world was derived not from the consent of the people who belonged to the Church and by political units but was instead granted directly by God to Peter and his successors." On the other hand, "all temporal power, even the supreme temporal power, belonged to the people and thus kings and princes obtained [their power] from the people." The people being the source of all secular power, the fact that all the people of the earth had never come together to select one individual as its ruler meant that the Roman emperor could not claim universal jurisdiction. Thus the emperor did not posses a universal jurisdiction in temporals comparable to the papal universal jurisdiction in spirituals.[32] Indeed, Solórzano went on to conclude this section of the chapter with the opinion that Aristotle and St. Augustine agreed that, while a single ruler in a city was a natural condition, "an empire over many people was not thus and kingdoms were customarily [governed] more peacefully by a king since each one of the kingdoms was enclosed within the boundaries of its own native land."[33]

Having presented the arguments in support of the emperor's claim to universal jurisdiction, Solórzano then went on to deal with what he termed "the more true and more general" opinions about the extent of imperial jurisdiction. According to the authors of these opinions, "neither when Rome flourished long ago nor afterwards, when the Roman Empire was transferred to the Greeks, the French and the Germans" did the emperors have jurisdiction over any peoples other than those directly subject to them.[34] Imperial jurisdiction was thus limited to the defined borders of the Empire, that is, to the territory and the people over whom the emperor clearly exercised governing power. The history of the Roman Empire itself at the time of its greatest extent demonstrated that there were nations that Rome never controlled. Some lawyers argued that the Persian Empire and other peoples may have possessed "exemption from the Roman Empire on a *de facto* basis but not *de jure* . . . ," an argument that Solórzano found unacceptable, even "silly and shallow." Furthermore, not only were such arguments baseless with regard to the jurisdiction of the ancient Roman Empire, they were also irrelevant to the status of the Empire in the contemporary era. In fact, the freedom of the ancient Persians and the seventeenth-century Indians from imperial jurisdiction was not *de facto* but *de jure*. Indeed, "it was not just nor was it appropriate or was it even possible for the whole of mankind to dwell under a single ruler and overseer."[35]

In the long run, the history of the Roman Empire demonstrated that there were numerous peoples who successfully resisted Roman efforts to conquer them. Pointing to the great historian of the Roman state, Solórzano wrote that "if Polybius was as great a cosmographer as he was an historian, he would not have asserted that the Romans had conquered the entire world."[36] Indeed, the historical evidence demonstrated that only the Christian Church extended its jurisdiction to all people.[37] Where the lawyers, the authors of the various books of the Bible, and other writers had described the imperial power as universal in extent, they were only exercising literary license.[38] The Romans had conquered so much of the known world that it appeared as if they had conquered all of it, or Rome was such a dominant power that it seemed as if no one could stand in its way. Nevertheless, this was only a piece of exaggerated rhetoric, a synecdoche (*aut per figuram Synecdochem*), not a description of political or legal reality. After all, as one writer had noted, in addition to calling themselves the Lords of the World, Roman emperors also referred to themselves as "gods" as well. No one would accept the latter term as an accurate description of the emperor's role in the world, so why should anyone take seriously the other obviously exaggerated claim as a description of imperial power?[39]

The final step in this stage of the argument about the extent of imperial jurisdiction was to refute the argument of St. Jerome and others about the need for a single world ruler analogous to the single head of a beehive. Solórzano argued that Jerome only meant that within any beehive there is a single leader whom the others follow. Thus, "in any well-established republic, kingdom or province a specific emperor, king or rector exists" to render justice to all who are subject to him.[40] It does not follow logically, at least on the analogy of the beehive, that all human beings formed a single entity requiring a single head.

Having proved that the imperial claim to universal jurisdiction was, at best, a rhetorical statement, Solórzano then proceeded to demonstrate that the emperor could not award the New World to the kings of Spain or to anyone else. The emperor's jurisdiction extended only to his subjects. He has no right "to take from them [the inhabitants of the New World] their *dominium* of goods and lands."[41] Furthermore, Solórzano pointed out, even with regard to his own subjects, the emperor, or for that matter any other ruler, does not have the right to take any of his subjects' possessions arbitrarily.[42] Such behavior characterized the tyrant, not the king. The function of a ruler is to protect and govern his people, not to rob them.[43]

With this demonstration of the falsity of the claim that the emperor possessed a universal jurisdiction that could legitimize the conquest of the New World, Solórzano might have ended the discussion of imperial power. Nevertheless, he went on to assert one more point about imperial jurisdiction, namely that not only did the emperor not possess jurisdiction over the New World, he did not possess any over Spain either. Under the Gothic kings, the Spanish had become independent of the Empire. If this was not enough to demonstrate the independence of Spain from imperial jurisdiction, after the Muslims had invaded and occupied Visigothic Spain, the Spanish subsequently regained control of their land "by their own virtue and effort." Since the Roman emperors had not protected Spain from invasion and had not led the *reconquista*, they had lost any claim to jurisdiction over Spain and its inhabitants.[44]

Finally, Solórzano described the Spanish monarchs as possessing in their own kingdoms the power that the emperor possessed in his Empire; in other words, these rulers were the emperor's equals, not his subordinates.[45] In such circumstances, the emperor could not legitimize any action of the Spanish rulers, because he possessed no basis for exercising jurisdiction over them. Furthermore, lest anyone think that Charles V's possession of the imperial throne along with the Spanish thrones meant that the Empire had regained some kind of jurisdiction over Spain, Solórzano pointed out that Charles V had publicly promised to recognize the independence of Spain from the Empire's jurisdiction.[46] In support of this, Solórzano added that Charles V also promised that any titles of nobility and other privileges that he granted to his Spanish subjects in his capacity as emperor would be valid only in the Empire and not in Spain.[47] In fact, the Spanish were so sensitive to potential imperial infringements of their sovereignty that one legal writer even asserted the existence of a law in Spain making it a capital offense to attempt to use imperial laws in the Spanish courts.[48]

With this rejection of the imperial claim to universal jurisdiction, one might ask if there was any remaining figure who could claim such jurisdiction and so provide a legitimate basis for the Spanish conquest of the Americas. Solórzano was, of course, leading the reader to the only possible basis for acquiring any of the lands of the infidels in the New World, the pope's role as spiritual *dominus mundi*.

Part II — The Pope as *Dominus Mundi*

In concluding the second book of the *De Indiarum Jure* with a discussion of the pope's role as the Lord of the World, Solórzano came to terms with the political realities that determined the limits of the debate about the legitimacy of the Spanish conquest of the Americas. Obviously a high-ranking Spanish official in the seventeenth century was not about to conclude a discussion of the conquest with a condemnation of the legal basis upon which the Spanish had constructed the first modern overseas empire. He could, of course, criticize the ways in which the conquistadores failed to adhere to the high moral principles that should have guided them in their work of converting and civilizing the Indians, but he could not deny the legitimacy of Spanish government of the New World.

At the same time, Solórzano recognized that the papal grant to the Spanish monarchs involved more than simply authorizing them to support the efforts of missionaries in the New World. The Spanish monarchs could acquire possession of the Americas as well. Furthermore, the papal grant included a prohibition against "other Christian kings, princes, or private individuals to come near that [New] World or to navigate its sea."[49] In fact, these three elements of Alexander VI's grant of the New World to the Spanish were, of course, inextricably linked. The costs involved in the work of converting the Indians were to be defrayed by the profits that the Spanish made in trade with the New World. To insure the flow of profits of such trade, it was reasonable to authorize the Spanish a monopoly of it and thus to ban ships of other nations from entering the seas around the Americas. The pope himself could not afford the great costs involved in this enormous task. The number of men and ships required, and the quantity of equipment that the conquest of the Americas would require, far exceeded the papacy's resources.[50]

Even if the papacy did possess the human and financial resources that the conquest of the New World required, it was not proper for the popes to participate directly in the work of conquest that would accompany the initial stages of missionary work.[51] Here, Solórzano was stressing the distinction between the *auctoritas*, the moral authority of the papacy, and the *potestas*, the power exercised by secular rulers, a distinction that the canon lawyers had traditionally made. Christian rulers "are the ministers of God and of the Church," that is, subordinates who act at the instructions of another.[52] The Christian view of the world assumed a hierarchy of powers and a division of labor. At the same time, there was also the tradition that neither power should intervene in the realm of the other. Secular rulers, therefore, could not exercise spiritual jurisdiction over infidels without papal licence, and ecclesiastical leaders could not raise armies and wage wars in their spiritual capacity.[53] The goal was cooperation between the representatives of the two powers by which this world was ruled, each functioning within its proper sphere of activity and with respect for the role of the other power.

Having set out the framework within which the spiritual and the secular powers should operate, Solórzano then went on to consider the role of the Spanish in the New World. "If this work [of converting the New World] is to be enjoined upon and demanded of any Christian ruler, no one can deny that it ought to be committed as by right to the Catholic kings of Spain" who were the first "to explore and occupy those lands of the New World that had been unknown to the ancients.[54] Furthermore, the Spanish had the men and ships necessary for such a great task as well as the power to achieve great deeds. Even Las Casas, otherwise so critical of the effects of the Spanish role in the Americas, agreed that the Spanish discovery of the New World justified Spanish control of the newly discovered regions.[55]

Above all, however, more important than priority of discovery or possession of the necessary resources, the Spanish deserved to possess the Americas under papal licence "because of the purity of their faith and their ardent zeal for the true faith."[56] The devotion of the Spanish to the true faith was in marked contrast to the English and the French, who also sought to possess the newly discovered lands. These kingdoms were "disfigured by the various wicked errors of heretics" instead of being graced by the true faith of the Christian Church. If the rulers of these kingdoms had been authorized to send their subjects to the New World, they might have "disseminated the wicked and evil doctrine of Luther or Calvin," thus casting sterile spiritual seed "among the simple and unprotected Indians" who lived in the Americas.[57] God, foreseeing that England and France would one day harbor heretics who denied the truths of the faith, had even prevented the kings of England and France from appreciating the theories of Christopher Columbus when he approached them for assistance.[58] As a result, God, being anxious to protect the Indians from heretics and their teachings, entrusted the conversion of the New World to the Spanish, who had avoided the lure of heresy and had remained faithful.[59]

Indeed, Solórzano pointed out, the kings of Spain would seem to be the Church's designated agent "for the defence of the faith and for the conversion and protection of the newly discovered islands and infidel peoples and the holy Gospel of Christ" throughout the entire world.[60] This sacred duty to act as the Church's instrument in the divine work of spreading the faith was a task that the Spanish kings did not shirk.

At this point, Solórzano moved to a discussion of the titles that the kings of Spain and of France bore in order to make a point about the role of Spain in both the Church and in the world at large. Ever since the ninth century, the kings of Spain rejoiced in the title of the "Most Christian kings," a title by which Pope John VIII addressed one of the kings in Spain.[61] As for the kings of France, who now used the title "Most Christian," they did so improperly. They were known by that title at one time "because of the power (*imperium*) that they once possessed and not because of their kingdom," by which Solórzano apparently meant the spiritual quality of their rule and of their subjects. Now that the French no longer possessed such *imperium*, they should surrender that title. Unfortunately, Pope Pius II (1458–1464) confirmed that title in a letter to King Louis XI (1461–1483).[62]

In order to demonstrate that the Spanish kings bore a title even older than that of the French kings, Solórzano then discussed the title borne by the Spanish monarchs, that of The Catholic Kings. While he recognized that this title was generally identified with Ferdinand and Isabella because Pope Alexander VI addressed them by that name, he argued that Spanish rulers had used this title well before the end of the fifteenth century. Indeed, the title was to be found in the time of the Visigoths. One of these kings, Reccared (586–601) was called The Catholic by the bishops at the Council of Toledo "because he was the first to protect inviolate the Catholic faith and because he freed the whole of Spain from the Arian heresy." Later, Alfonso VIII (1158–1214) was known by the same name for similar reasons.[63] In the final analysis, the title of Catholic Kings identified Spanish rulers who from the days of the Visigoths, whose rulers first converted Spain to orthodox Christianity, to Ferdinand and Isabella, who ousted the Muslims from their last foothold in the peninsula.

In the debate about the relative tradition and importance of the titles that the Spanish and French kings bore, Solórzano pointed to the power of healing the sick that some kings claimed to possess. The "king's touch," the power of curing disease, usually scrofula, that some kings claimed was obviously a sign of divine favor. The kings of France and England claimed this power, according to their supporters.[64] To counter any argument that the possession of such powers by these other monarchs demonstrated that they possessed a higher status within the Christian world than did the Spanish rulers, Solórzano cited other sources that proved that the Spanish rulers also had them. For example, the Spanish rulers had the power to expel demons because of their zeal for the faith.[65] In addition, another writer claimed that the kings of Aragon also had the power of curing scrofula.[66] According to some other scholars, all Christian kings possessed this power by virtue of the anointing with holy oil that took place in the course of royal coronation ceremonies.[67] In other words, where the supporters of the English and French monarchs saw the power of curing the sick claimed by these kings as a demonstration of their exalted spiritual status, defenders of the Spanish monarchs saw only the exercise of a power that every Christian ruler possessed by virtue of his coronation and anointing.

The discussion of the powers of kings to cure the sick, like that which dealt with the relative antiquity of the titles of kings, was of more than theoretical interest. It was not only a discussion about the relative status of European Christian kings, it was also about the right of these non-Spanish kings to enter the Americas. If these kings were as spiritually exalted as the Spanish monarchs and if they had assisted the Church in its work over the centuries as attested by titles such as "Most Christian," then why could they not continue to support the work of the Church in the New World? Why did the papacy grant a monopoly of the New World to the Spanish rulers?

Solórzano suggested at this point that criticism of the papal grant of the New World to the Spanish was the work of heretics. They ridiculed the papal claim to determine who could go to the Americas.[68] Thus, the debate about the right of Alexander VI to award responsibility for the conquest of the New World and the conversion of its inhabitants to Christianity to the Spanish was, for Solórzano, a debate about the very nature of the Church and the role of the pope in it. In order to deal with these issues, Solórzano presented three arguments in support of the opinion that the pope did not possess the right to restrict entry to the New World only to Christians of his selection.

In the first place, there was the argument that responsibility for the conversion of the infidels belonged to all Christian rulers as a consequence of Christ's own injunction.[69] This being the case, no one, even the pope, could legitimately forbid any Christian ruler from engaging in the task of converting the Indians of the Americas or any other infidels anywhere.

The second argument stemmed from Vitoria's opinion about the right of all people to engage in trade throughout the world without interference, a right derived from the *ius gentium*.[70] If this right existed, then it would seem that the Spanish could no more prohibit other people from entering the New World than "the French could prohibit the Italians from trading with the Spanish or from sailing in Spanish waters."[71]

The final argument in this section was that if the papal award of the New World to the Spanish was designed for the good of the Indians, then this goal would be achieved more readily if as many people as possible came to the New World. The more Christians in the Americas, the sooner the Gospel message would be preached to the infidels and the sooner they would be converted. In addition, the more contact the Indians had with Europeans, the more trade would ensue, to the advantage of Indians and Europeans alike.[72]

Attractive though these arguments might be, however, Solórzano countered that the opposite opinion, the one defending the pope's right to limit access to the New World, "was the more true and the more received" among scholars. Limiting access to the New World to people whom the papacy had authorized to go there "was not only just and useful but, for the activity of which we treat [the conversion of the Indians], put forth as being necessary."[73] The leading Catholic thinkers who had dealt with this matter agreed that since the pope was responsible for the salvation of all people, "using his own judgment he can order and dispose of all things that he determined pertained to the achievement of that goal." This meant that he could assign to Christian rulers specific regions of the New World within which these rulers would have a monopoly of preaching the Gospel and trade. At the same time, such rulers were also forbidden to interfere in the zones of responsibility assigned to other rulers.[74] Solórzano summed up this stage of the argument in a way reminiscent of Aristotle's discussion of causality:

> All this [power] belongs to the pope, so these writers say, as if to the prime mover (*principalem motorem*) (so to speak). For kings are like his tools and instruments, and no one can transgress the boundaries he has established because only the [prime] mover can move them.[75]

For Solórzano, the pope, then, was not unlike God in that he was the first cause of political order, possessing the power to assign newly discovered lands to Christian rulers of his own choosing. His decisions in this matter would thus not be subject to appeal.

In addition to the pope's power in matters involving the infidels resulting from his spiritual responsibility for all people, there was also a pragmatic argument to support the papal role in the European encounter with the newly discovered lands and peoples. How could there be peaceful relations among the several European powers involved in the work of preaching the Gospel to the infidels if "they enter upon that work helter-skelter (*promiscue*)," without any guidance or direction? Even those who sought to carry out this work with the best of intentions, "free from all selfish motives," could find themselves at odds over spheres of jurisdiction and other practical problems.[76] The experience of the Castilians and the Portuguese in the aftermath of Columbus's first voyage, their quarrel over whether or not the Genoese had in fact sought to claim for Castile lands that the papacy had earlier assigned to the Portuguese, nearly led to war. Even though these rulers "were Christians and bound by the greatest bonds of friendship and interest," Columbus's report of his discoveries so embittered relations between the two kingdoms that Pope Alexander VI had to intervene. His three famous bulls contained the basis for drawing the line of demarcation delineating the respective Castilian and Portuguese spheres of responsibility in the New World, with the result that war was avoided.[77] Without papal determination of spheres of jurisdiction, these two Christian kingdoms might have gone to war, thus frustrating the ultimate goal of converting the peoples whom the explorers had encountered.

The power of the pope to determine spheres of missionary responsibility was not only a practical necessity, however, it was also based on the experience of the Apostles. The Gospels described how the Apostles implemented Christ's injunction to preach His message to all people throughout the world. The Apostles "divided up among themselves all the regions of the world among themselves" and each took responsibility for preaching to the people of one of these regions. In this way, the Apostles avoided the kinds of jurisdictional conflicts that might otherwise have hindered the fulfillment of their assigned task.[78] Subsequently, the Church was subdivided into dioceses and parishes, each with a single official responsible for ecclesiastical matters within the clearly defined boundaries of his sphere of jurisdiction.[79] The result was an ecclesiastical structure with a single head, the pope, ruling over a series of individual administrative units, dioceses, each of which had its own head and within which there were parishes, each with its head. By analogy, the Church was thus a single hive subdivided into separate units, but all were governed by a single head.

Here again, in support of these arguments based on the experience of the early Church, Solórzano pointed to the pragmatic reasons for drawing clear-cut lines of responsibility. Citing a traditional legal maxim, "where there are many people there is much confusion," he pointed out that "there is a natural inclination for dissention among men."[80] In matters affecting religion, this natural human tendency to wish to do things in different ways would have disastrous consequences in the work of converting infidels. The Indians, for example, "might become imbued with differing and even conflicting opinions . . . if men from opposing nations and lands and operating under different kings and laws" undertook missionary work in the same place. The fact that such men would all be Christians would not prevent differences and conflicts.[81] Indeed, the historical experience of the human race suggests that competition and conflict are the natural human condition.[82] This being the case, some authority should exist to insure order and uniformity in the great work of converting people to the true faith. The pope, then, is the logical figure to do this, because it is he who is responsible to God for the performance of this work.

In the second stage of this argument, Solórzano pointed out that not only would the presence of numerous European Christians in the New World lead to confusion in the missionary effort, it would also be inefficient. After all, popular wisdom had it that a task "entrusted to many individuals is generally carried out in a slothful manner," because in such circumstances "each person places the responsibility for completing the task on someone else."[83] Curiously, Solórzano did not see this situation in terms of spiritual competition in which representatives of different Christian societies competed in a pious contest to develop the best means for converting the infidels. Instead, he perceived it as demonstrating that diffused responsibility for a task meant that it would not be efficiently carried out. In support of this position, he cited, among others, Aristotle, who demonstrated the fatal flaws in any theory of society that insisted upon communal ownership of goods.[84] Communal ownership would mean a lack of individual responsibility and thus the collapse of the community. Not only did the greatest political thinker of the ancient world oppose communal ownership, the Church opposed it. The possession of goods in common was also characteristic of heretics such as the Waldensians, and the Anabaptists as well. Thus, the best thinking among both the pagans and the Christians was that private and personal possession of property was the most efficient basis upon which a society could function. Private possession of goods being the best means of insuring a sense of responsibility for the public good, the papal grant of the New World to the Spanish as a private possession was the most suitable way to insure the conversion of the Indians to Christianity.

It could be objected that by granting responsibility for the conversion of the New World to one Christian ruler, the pope was infringing on the general responsibility of all Christian rulers to engage in this work. Solórzano responded that the pope possessed an overriding responsibility for the efficient achievement of that goal that gave him the power to assign responsibility for missionary efforts in specific places to specific Christian rulers. In particular, he noted, the pope had to insure that no heretics entered the New World to preach their evil doctrines, an obvious allusion to the existence of the Huguenots in France.[85] Presumably the rulers of Spain, who had ruthlessly eliminated heresy from their dominions, were the only Christian rulers who could guarantee the exclusion of heretics from the Americas.[86]

If the ban on other Christian rulers supporting missionary efforts in the New World was a reasonable exercise of papal administrative authority over Christians, the ban on other Christian rulers trading with the infidels posed another problem. The prohibition of trade with the peoples of the

New World went hand in hand with the ban on missionary activity. Heretics could enter along with merchants if they had free access to the newly discovered lands. Furthermore, the costs of missionary work were underwritten by the trading monopoly granted to the power assigned responsibility for the task of conversion. This limitation, however, violated the right to travel freely and to engage in peaceful trade, a right derived "from the natural law and from the common law of all nations."[87] The mission of the Church, however, to insure the conversion of the infidels could override these rights to travel and to trade because they were derived from laws that themselves were subordinate to Church law in certain matters. This should not surprise anyone, added Solórzano, because it was well known that on occasion "principal or primordial precepts of natural law either yield, give way or are turned aside when by chance they collide with other rights, in which is to be found the greater and more pressing reason, need or requirement of the common good."[88]

Furthermore, merchants did not possess an absolute right to travel anywhere they wished. It was true, Solórzano pointed out, that once foreign merchants had entered into another country they could not be ordered to leave "because it appears that the world is the common fatherland of all men." On the other hand, the ruler of a particular area could forbid foreigners to enter his lands if he judged such a ban to be advantageous.[89] To illustrate this point, Solórzano observed that if merchants of all nations could enter the New World, "the Indians might be cheated in the purchase of foreign goods and the sale of their own goods." On the other hand, by restricting entry to the New World to the Spanish alone, the Indians might have received less for their goods than otherwise would have been the case. Nevertheless, "they should be content because of the other great advantages" that contact with the Spanish provided. Solórzano pointed out that "no heresies or other wicked sects flourished among them" and no foreigners "brought arms and other damnable and forbidden merchandise to them."[90] The Indians should accept the Spanish monopoly of trade with the New World as a positive benefit, a barrier against the evils that the entry of non-Spaniards would bring to them. Solórzano added that Roman and canon law contained numerous references to the need to protect infidels and barbarians from the destructive consequences of contact with other peoples.[91]

Thus, when Alexander VI authorized only the Castilians to enter the Americas, he was acting in a just and proper manner. The legitimacy of the bulls arose not only "from the papal will but also from the pressing, legitimate motive of the conversion of the Indians" and to protect them from those "obstinate and disobedient" individuals who would only do them harm.[92] Furthermore, the publicity given to Alexander VI's bull meant that no Christian could plead ignorance of its terms.[93]

The theme of this chapter, the last chapter of the second book of the *De Indiarum Jure*, was that there existed a world order that should determine the nature of relations among states and peoples. In asserting the papal responsibility for allocating spheres of responsibility in the New World, Solórzano was implying the responsibility of the pope for the good order of Europe as well. Solórzano's view of the world was very like that of the thirteenth-century popes who saw themselves at the apex of a hierarchy of powers. The pope stood at the peak and below him, acting on his instructions, stood the Christian rulers of Europe. In a general sense, this conception of an ordered hierarchy of powers, spiritual and temporal, existing to insure the fulfillment of Christ's injunction to preach His gospel to all people, was typical of medieval thinking on the nature of society.

Furthermore, the philosophers and the lawyers, working on premises drawn from the writings of the ancient Greeks and Romans, supported this conception of society. Aristotle, for example, saw the right order of society as one in which the wiser ruled the less wise. While he was describing the individual city states of Greece, the same concept, on a grander scale, underlay the Hellenistic conception of a *cosmos polis*, the world city in which people would be as close to one another as were the citizens of a single *polis*.[94] As for the lawyers, they agreed in principle that the existence of wars and conflicts among human societies was the result of a lower order of existence than should exist. War and its associated evils were part of the world as it actually is, the world that the *ius gentium* described. On the other hand, the world of the *ius naturale* was a better, peaceful world where people operated in harmony with one another. Thus, the major medieval intellectual traditions all agreed at a theoretical level about the possibility, even the necessity, of a harmonious world order.

What was lacking in these traditions was any serious discussion of the machinery that could bring about the creation of a harmonious world order. Roman law did describe the emperor as the *Dominus mundi*, the Lord of the World, but this received little attention in classical Roman legal thought. During the Middle Ages, however, this concept took on new life. In the *De Monarchia*, for example, Dante argued for an orderly, harmonious world order directed by the Holy Roman emperor.[95] While this was clearly part of the fourteenth-century polemical battle between Guelfs and Ghibellines in Italy, nevertheless the argument had its attractions as a solution to the church-state conflict. When this solution to the problems of conflict was being proposed in the Middle Ages, the Holy Roman Empire had reached the nadir of its power and could not be seen as a serious solution to the problem of order.

From the papal perspective, the one feasible instrument of political order was the papacy itself. In the golden age of the strong papacy, from the pontificate of Innocent III (1199–1216) to that of Boniface VIII (1294–1303), popes actively intervened in the temporal order to end wars between Catholic rulers. While these efforts were not always successful, they represented the most tangible attempt to resolve disputes among Christian nations without recourse to warfare.

Solórzano's *De Indiarum Jure* represented a seventeenth-century variation of the thirteenth-century papacy's conception of world order. It linked the papal theory of responsibility for the souls of all people to the power and achievements of the Spanish monarchs in the New World. It reasserted the medieval notion of a Christian order in which the Church and secular rulers cooperated harmoniously for the common good of people, a common good that possessed both spiritual and temporal elements. The pope was the general overseer of the spiritual good of all people and secular rulers, acting under his direction, would insure that the laws of the Church were enforced and that society was organized in such a way as to encourage people to the spiritual end, which was the goal of human existence.

At the same time, it is important to realize that Solórzano's conception of the relation between the spiritual and the temporal powers, rooted though it was in the medieval legal tradition, differed with that tradition in one important respect. While Solórzano recognized the pope in theory as the ultimate source of Spanish jurisdiction in the New World, he saw the actual papal role in quite limited terms. That is, once Alexander VI had authorized the Spanish to take charge of the conversion of the Indians, the pope no longer had any role to play in that work. Solórzano did not suggest, for example, that the pope had the right to judge the way in which the Spanish carried out their papally assigned task in the New World and to reassign jurisdiction over the Americas to another Christian ruler if the Spanish failed to implement the terms of *Inter caetera*. The pope could transfer the Roman Empire from one people to another but not, apparently, Spain's responsibility for the spiritual well-being of the Indians.

The papacy appears to have recognized that the *De Indiarum Jure* was subversive of papal interests, and placed it on the Roman Index in 1647.

Specifically, the Latin text, not the Spanish version, was condemned. The reason for the condemnation was that Solórzano concluded elsewhere in the *De Indiarum Jure* that, although Spanish control of the Americas was derived from a papal grant, the length of Spanish control of the Americas effectively meant that according to "custom and prescription," such jurisdiction was "inalienable and non-transferable." Having provided the initial legal basis upon which the conquest could begin, the papacy, in Solórzano's opinion, then receded into the background. The fact of Spanish control of the Americas was becoming, in his opinion, the effective basis for continued Spanish control. As the clerics who prepared the condemnation of the *De Indiarum Jure* realized, in the final analysis, Solórzano did not want a world in which church and state, pope and kings, cooperated in the governance of the entire human race, the kind of world that papal theorists had described. He wanted to defend the existence of a Spanish world monarchy in the modern world within the framework of the medieval legal tradition. In the long run, such an endeavor was doomed to failure, if only because Solórzano's formulation of the papal relationship to secular rulers would have built into the system of world order that he outlined the conditions for a renewal of the medieval church-state conflict. That struggle was over the boundaries between the spiritual and the temporal powers and had grown more heated as the secular powers sought to limit the Church's role in society.[96]

It is not surprising, then, that when Hugo Grotius came to create the basis for modern international law, he began by rejecting this entire medieval approach to international law and relations. Like the papacy, though for different reasons, he too wished to avoid the divisive struggle between the two powers that had characterized the medieval experience. Where the papacy insisted upon a fuller role in public life, Grotius and his successors took Solórzano's position one step further: There was to be no role for the papacy in the new international law, not even a nominal role as the legitimator of conquest, because human beings did not form the flock that Innocent IV had described it as being long ago. Humanity was not some kind of metaphysical unity, there were only states that had to cooperate for clearly defined ends. The salvation of souls was not one of these ends.

Conclusion

Juan de Solórzano Pereira's *De Indiarum Jure* stands as a monument to a particular response to the problem of world order that Columbus's voyages created. If it had been the work of a cloistered academic, it might have been of some limited interest, because of the conception of a rightly ordered international society that it contained. What makes Solórzano's treatise significant, however, was his experience at the highest levels of government in the Americas and in Spain. Like his contemporary, Hugo Grotius, Solórzano was actively involved in dealing with the problems that the discovery of the New World created and was anxious to use his knowledge and experience to advance his career. Rather than raising doubts about his credibility, Solórzano's personal ambition is an assurance that his work accurately reflects the way in which a learned, ambitious Spanish bureaucrat of the seventeenth century perceived Spain's role in the New World. He was not an alienated intellectual criticizing the power structure of his own day; he was a man anxious to play a part in that structure, yet fully aware of the evils associated with the conquest of the New World and anxious that the Spanish reform their colonial administration. When Solórzano criticized the Spanish government, he did so from the inside and as a man who believed in the Spanish mission in the New World. It was not the theory of Spanish world monarchy that he criticized, it was the practice, a position that echoed the views of Bartolomé de Las Casas. To some extent, Solórzano's analysis and defense of the conquest of the Americas clearly places the *De Indiarum Jure* within what Professor John Elliott has described as the "orgy of national introspection" that characterized intellectual life at the beginning of the seventeenth century in Castile. This work was but one of the "innumerable projects, both sensible and fantastic," that proposed ways to restore the greatness of Castile.[1]

To the extent that it focused on the personal responsibility of the Spanish monarchs to deal in a just and Christian manner with the people of the Americas, the *De Indiarum Jure* also has some of the character of a "mirror of the prince," a guide for the good Christian ruler, a genre dating back to the twelfth century. In keeping with the traditional "mirror of the prince" literature, Solórzano saw the fundamental responsibilities of rulers in moral terms. By asserting the importance of moral means and goals in politics, Solórzano thereby became a participant in the contemporary debate about the relationship between politics and morality identified with Machiavelli's (1469–1527) *Prince*. The *Prince* was a "mirror of the prince" that told the ruler (or was understood to have told the ruler) that political success depended on practices that violated Christian principles.[2] As Robert Bireley recently phrased Machiavelli's position, the core of "this new gospel was the message that one could not be a serious Christian and prosper in politics."[3] Like the anti-Machiavellians whom Bireley discusses, Solórzano "sought to elaborate a Christian statecraft or reason of state, that is, a Christian method for the preservation and development of a powerful state."[4] The *De Indiarum Jure* was a defense of the spiritual mission that God had assigned to the Spanish monarchs and that Alexander VI had authorized on behalf of the Church, a mission that demanded the highest standards of virtue on the part of the rulers. The success of the mission depended on the moral qualities of those who led the Spanish effort. Unlike Machiavelli, Solórzano would argue that the good Christian ruler would be more successful in dealing with the peoples of the New World, because he would be seeking their civil and moral good, unlike the self-seeking, Machiavellian ruler, who would exploit them for this own purposes.[5]

The anti-Machiavellian theme found in Solórzano's writings was rooted in the revival and development of medieval scholastic thought associated with Vitoria and the other Spanish scholastics who followed him. Vitoria sought to reconnect law and moral theology, reasserting a connection, that if not entirely lost, had been little stressed since the twelfth century.[6] The work of Vitoria and his colleagues belies the still-popular notion that scholasticism was dead by 1500 either because it was sterile to begin with or because, although it was adequate for medieval intellectual needs, the modern world and its problems required a more sophisticated philosophical structure than medieval scholasticism could provide. The line of Spanish scholastics from Vitoria to Solórzano did not simply regurgitate thirteenth-century philosophical concepts. These thinkers employed the medieval scholastic method and its fundamental premises in order to deal with what they perceived to be the great moral problem of their age, the relationship between Europeans and the newly discovered peoples of the Americas.[7]

In fact, what Vitoria, Solórzano, and other Spanish thinkers were doing was what other Europeans had been doing and continued to do, seeing the New World in terms of the experience of the Old, placing the new experience within the intellectual framework provided by ancient texts. The term ancient here is, of course, being employed in a double sense. As Anthony Grafton has pointed out, ancient texts, that is, the writings of the ancient Greeks and Romans, provided much of the intellectual framework within which sixteenth- and seventeenth-century Europeans sought to understand the new worlds that were opening up to them. These ancient texts were stretched, as it were, to cover new circumstances that the ancient writers could not possibly have envisioned, and were so authoritative that centuries after Columbus's first voyage they continued to shape and inform the European outlook.[8] What Grafton and many other writers have missed is the fact that in the sixteenth and seventeenth centuries, ancient texts, in the sense of old but not classical authors, also played a significant role in shaping the European outlook. Medieval authors, such as the scholastic philosophers and canon lawyers, not to mention travelers such as Marco Polo and the mythical John Mandeville, and the various missionaries who went to Asia, also shaped the European outlook.[9] Their ideas and perceptions went into the creating of the European minds that worked to assimilate the new worlds, along with the ancient classical texts. As the writings of a long line of Spanish thinkers from Vitoria to Solórzano demonstrated, medieval texts could be stretched to accommodate the New World just as classical texts were.

The *De Indiarum Jure* was more than a compendium, however, even a sophisticated compendium, of ancient and medieval thought. It also reflected the major currents that characterized sixteenth- and seventeenth-century intellectual life in Spain and throughout Europe, underscoring the fact that Spanish intellectual life, though deeply rooted in the medieval scholastic tradition, shared many of the preoccupations and interests of contemporary humanism as well. Solórzano was able to call upon a wide range of classical authors as well as medieval writers in the course of his work, and, like the humanists (and like Aquinas), he paid close attention to the natural or secular order. While ancient pagan authors could not provide guidance with regard to the Christian life, they could provide guidance for those involved in the political and governmental realm. As *dominium* belongs to all people regardless of spiritual condition, so pagans such as Aristotle and Cicero could provide valuable guidance to Christian rulers in the execution of their temporal functions. Here again, Solórzano was building upon a medieval tradition associated with Aquinas but popularized and expanded by the humanists of the Renaissance.

We can also see in Solórzano's work a strong interest in the natural order by way of the early ethnological work of writers such as Acosta and the historical writings of Baronius and others. These materials provided him with a wide range of human experience that he used to understand the newly encountered peoples of the Americas. His ideas about world order were always tempered by a kind of realism about the human experience that stemmed from historical accounts of the European experience and contemporary descriptions of the ways of life found among the inhabitants of the Americas.

In many ways, Solórzano's *De Indiarum Jure* provides a guide to the intellectual milieu within which two centuries of Spanish thinkers wrestled with the problem of how to deal with the peoples of the new worlds that were almost daily being revealed to Europeans. A careful analysis of the citations he provides would enable the reader to re-create the holdings of a seventeenth-century Spanish intellectual's library. In that sense, it is Solórzano's very traditional intellectual outlook that is useful to the twentieth-century scholar who wishes to understand how the Spanish perceived their role in the emerging modern world.

Solórzano's *De Indiarum Jure* was, however, more than a guide to seventeenth-century intellectual history. Out of the milieu that produced Solórzano came the modern theories of international law and relations that we now associate with the names of Hugo Grotius and his successors. To a great extent, contemporary scholars have seen the development of international law from Grotius onward as owing little or nothing to the work of the Spanish writers of the sixteenth and seventeenth centuries and to their medieval predecessors. The names of Vitoria and Suárez are remembered largely because of the work of a number of Spanish writers and, above all, because James Brown Scott took up their cause so enthusiastically in this century. The attention paid to these writers, moreover, has in some ways contributed to the neglect of Solórzano, because those scholars who have sought to place the roots of modern international law in the Spanish predecessors of Hugo Grotius have identified a straight line of intellectual influence running from Vitoria and Suárez to Grotius. The Spanish international law thinkers have thus derived their significance from the way in which they contributed to Grotius's work. Seen in this light, Solórzano would be of little importance because, although a contemporary of Grotius, he was moving along traditional lines rather than contributing to the development of Grotian international law.

If the development of international law is approached from a different perspective, however, Solórzano's significance becomes obvious. Rather than being just another example of the work of an official whose thought was influenced by Vitoria, perhaps the last of the line from Salamanca, which is an approach to international relations that Hugo Grotius's work eventually overshadowed and displaced, the *De Indiarum Jure* may be seen as the fullest expression of a conception of world order that first emerged in the early thirteenth century. His significance, and that of the Spanish school in general, does not depend therefore on his relationship to the creation of Grotius's thought. The Spanish thinkers, building on the foundation established by the medieval canon lawyers, created a theory of international law and relations that would create a different kind of world order than that which Grotius envisioned.

The line of medieval thought that reached back to the thirteenth-century writers who sought to understand the nature of relations between Christian and non-Christian societies has seemed to many modern scholars irrelevant to the conditions created by the discovery of the New World. In a sense, so this line of argument goes, the failure of Spanish thinkers to develop a modern, that is, a Grotian, theory of international law and relations paralleled the failure of the Spanish to create a lasting empire. In each case, the Spanish are condemned for failing to grasp the essence of modernity, seeking instead to create an essentially medieval-style empire on the basis of a thirteenth-century conception of political order.

That the Spanish failed to understand the modern world, indeed, the opinion that the Spanish refused to enter the modern world, retaining an outmoded medieval view of the world, happened to fit a particular moralistic view of early modern history nicely. Spain was the wicked, backward, evil empire that flourished only to be destroyed by its own corruption. To English Protestants, Spain deserved to lose her empire because she had sought to impose a reactionary Catholic order on Europe. The treatment of the peoples of the New World illustrated what would happen if the Spanish had remained the dominant power in Europe. The result of this outlook was the Black Legend, which demonized Spanish activities in the New World.

The great irony in the development of the Black Legend was that the sources for criticizing the Spanish role in the Americas were largely Spanish and Catholic. When English Protestant writers constructed the Black Legend, they did so using the materials that Spanish critics of the conquest of the New World had provided, critics who often had firsthand knowledge of the conquest and the evils associated with it. The most famous critic of the conquest, Bartolomé de Las Casas, was the son of a man who had sailed with Columbus, was himself one of the first Spanish settlers in the New World, and, subsequently, an associate of the Columbus family. Long before foreign writers criticized the conquest, the conquerors themselves had done so.

The reason the Spanish could analyze and criticize the manner of the conquest of the New World so thoroughly was that they continued to perceive relations between Europeans and the non-European world within the framework that medieval lawyers, philosophers, and theologians had created. They possessed a set of moral standards against which they could measure the activities of the conquistadores before passing judgment on them, as well as a language that could articulate their views. This moral language the Spanish shared with the larger European intellectual community, so it has always been puzzling to observers that only Spanish clerics, intellectuals, and officials chose to apply these standards to the situations that Columbus's voyages created, and then present their conclusions to the public in both oral and written fashion. The obvious explanation, which might not explain very much, is simply that at the time Spanish explorers found the New World, Spanish intellectual life was flourishing. The nature of this intellectual life, its emphasis on the medieval scholastic tradition as well the encouragement of Christian morality, found in the problems that the discoveries created a fertile field for examination and analysis. The schools that trained academics and the lawyers who staffed the royal bureaucracy continued to rely heavily upon the important thinkers of the Middle Ages. To a student of Solórzano's generation, Thomas Aquinas and Innocent IV were living figures whose work bore directly upon the contemporary world. While a late sixteenth- or early seventeenth-century Spanish student may have read these and other medieval writers only in excerpts found in more recent works, nevertheless they remained important, relevant figures in a society where religious and intellectual orthodoxy were extremely important.

Thus, when Solórzano came to consider the legitimacy of the conquest of the New World, he could do so within an agreed-upon intellectual framework. He could rest his entire justification on two traditional bases, both of which originated in the thirteenth century: one, infidels were true human beings; and two, the pope was responsible for the spiritual well-being of all people, Christians and non-Christians alike.

The consequence of Solórzano's starting point was that in order to defend the legitimacy of the Spanish conquest of the New World, he had to place it within the context of a world order. The only legitimate, morally correct justification for the Spanish occupation of the Americas was that it aided in the fulfillment of the Church's mission to all people. He could have, in fact, simply reproduced the arguments based on Innocent IV's discussion of infidel *dominium* that writers from Vitoria onward had developed, and thus provided a traditional defense of the conquest.

Instead, Solórzano chose to develop the defense of the conquest in a more complex way, relying not simply on legal and theological theory but on ethnological and historical material as well. One reason for this broader approach was that he, unlike Vitoria, was forced to defend the conquest on a series of fronts. When Vitoria, his contemporaries, and his students began to discuss the legitimacy of the conquest, they had only to deal with the theory of universal papal responsibility. Either the pope had such responsibility or he did not. Vitoria and his immediate followers could take for granted the existence of the papacy and could accept the existing theories about the nature and extent of that power.

When Solórzano came to discuss the conquest, he was dealing with a new situation, one in which the existence and role of the papacy was under attack. In order to defend Alexander VI's award of the West Indies to the Castilians and the award of the East Indies to the Portuguese, Solórzano had first to defend the existence of the papacy itself. Protestants pointed to the papacy as the symbol of the corruption of the Christian faith; some Catholics, critical of the state of the Church, though not inclined to leave it, were questioning the nature and extent of papal power. Solórzano's lengthy defense of the papacy was therefore essential to his overall goal. If the papacy did not possess the powers that the theologians, the canon lawyers, and the popes themselves had claimed, the monopolies that Alexander VI had granted to the Castilians and the Portuguese were invalid.

If Alexander VI did not have the right to determine who could enter the New World, then the Castilians and the Portuguese would have to make some difficult and expensive choices if they wished to retain their overseas possessions. If the threat of papal condemnation did not scare off Protestant and Catholic interlopers seeking to establish footholds in the New World, then those governments would have to strengthen their military positions, a costly process. In Solórzano's own lifetime, the Portuguese were already losing control of the East Indies to the Dutch, while the Spanish were facing increasing competition in the Americas from the English and the French. There was a strong element of naive hope in Solórzano's description of a world order with the pope at its head, serving as the arbiter of international disputes. Like Innocent III, Innocent IV, and

Boniface VIII four centuries earlier, he seemed sure that the logic of a universal legal basis for world order would be convincing to his audience.[10] Under such circumstances, as long as the Spanish were seeking the spiritual welfare of the Indians, the English, French, and other European peoples would, or at least should, refrain from interfering in the Americas without Spanish permission.

Solórzano presented the description of the Indians' way of life in order to demonstrate that indeed these people were in need of guidance toward a civil, Christian life, the twin goals, presumably, of all reasonable people. In defending the right of these Indians to *dominium*, Solórzano was providing a basis for condemning all forms of intervention in the New World except that which was designed to assist the Indians to rise toward a civilized, Christian way of life. This being the case, Solórzano logically defended the humanity of the Indians. If they were not human, after all, then they could not possess *dominium* and so would have no rights to be infringed if Europeans decided to occupy their lands. Their behavior, savage though it might be, was susceptible to change under the direction of Spanish missionaries and officials. The danger was that if heretics or other Catholics attempted to operate in the New World, the Spanish efforts at improving the Indians would be undercut. The papally created Spanish monopoly of the New World was, therefore, the only logical way to insure the fulfillment of the papacy's spiritual mission.

The history of the barbarians who invaded Europe provided Solórzano with another defense of the Spanish monopoly. The Europeans who looked down upon the Indians had once been looked down upon by others. The inhabitants of the Americas were like the Goths, the Britons, or the Iberians from the fourth to the tenth century. Spain was playing the role of the Christian empire, bringing civilization and Christianity to the barbarians. There was a strong element of providentialism in all of this. Solórzano had to be careful not to use the term *imperium*, that is, empire, to describe what the Spanish were doing, but there was an echo of the medieval notion of the *translatio imperii*, the transfer of the seat of the world empire from one society to another, in this discussion. The imperial power and status once associated with Rome had moved to Constantinople with Constantine in the fourth century. In 800 the pope brought that power and status back to the West when he crowned Charlemagne as emperor in Rome. There is a hint of another transfer of empire, this time to Castile, in Solórzano's discussion of Alexander VI's *Inter caetera*.[11] God was now using Castile as He once used the Roman Empire. The mission that Virgil assigned to the Romans, now Christianized, in Book 6 of the *Aeneid*, was assigned to the Castilian monarchs.

Solórzano's history of papal-royal cooperation in the work of civilizing and converting the infidels, a history that began with the discussion of the English bringing the Irish into conformity with the reforms of the eleventh and twelfth centuries, illustrated how the good Christian ruler should cooperate with the papacy. In his history, there is no conflict between the interests of the Church and those of the good Christian ruler. The good of the Church is to the advantage of the Christian king. As even *Inter caetera* pointed out, there were economic benefits that would accrue to the Castilians and Portuguese as a result of assisting the papacy in its mission to the infidels.[12] This discussion also demonstrated that cooperation between papal and royal power in the fulfillment of the Church's mission had existed for a long time and had been to the advantage of both parties. Solórzano's history of papal-royal relations also quietly stated the message that while the rulers of the other European kingdoms at least occasionally did battle with the papacy, the Castilian monarchs did not.

One of the curious aspects of the *De Indiarum Jure* is that, in spite of Solórzano's discussion of religious conversion as the overriding motive for European involvement in the New World, there is little discussion of what conversion meant and how it occurred. It would seem to have been his belief that once the Indians became civilized they would automatically proceed to the baptismal font. Christianization would thus seem to be the product of the civilizing process. Given what we would now label his anthropology, namely that all people, Europeans and Americans, Christians and infidels, shared a common humanity, and his history, namely that the Goths and other barbarians easily moved from savagery and idolatry to civilized and Christian ways of life, it is probably understandable that he saw the process in these terms. The Indians would progress as had the Goths and others, or, more precisely, as Solórzano's history said they had progressed.

What this theory of the relationship between the process of becoming civilized and the process of becoming Christianized suggests is that Solórzano had not read his sources for the history of early medieval Europe very closely. He did not point to the number of martyred missionaries whose deaths preceded the conversion of the barbarians, nor did he point to Charlemagne's continuing problems with the Saxons. He took a very optimistic position on the speed and effectiveness of the missionary endeavor. The *De Indiarum Jure* would encourage its readers to believe that the conversion of the infidels was a comparatively easy task, one that was much simpler than the task of civilizing them.

Furthermore, Solórzano's conception of religious conversion seems untouched by the Reformation debate about the nature of conversion and the significance of baptism. Protestant theologians and polemicists criticized the Catholic Church for reducing what they saw as an intense personal experience to a simple ritual. Supporters of the Black Legend often pointed to the manner in which numbers of infidels were baptized in a public ceremony as a sign of the corrupted version of Christianity that the Church of Rome represented. Solórzano's conception of conversion and baptism seems based on the assumption that baptism begins a process of growth in the Christian life that will continue over a lifetime. The Protestant view of conversion and baptism, roughly speaking, assumed that baptism marked the end of a process or experience of conversion, not the beginning. It might be that, indeed, he knew of the debate about conversion and baptism, but simply chose the conservative, orthodox position to avoid problems with ecclesiastical officials.

The overall significance of the *De Indiarum Jure* is that it provided a conception of world order based on a set of premises derived from thirteenth-century scholastic, especially canonistic, thought. It differed from the modern notions of international order not so much in its sources as in its goals. That is, Grotius had read and commented upon many of the materials that Solórzano employed, but he understood and deployed them in a different way. To employ current terminology, Solórzano wrote to defend the existence of a territorial empire, not a trading one.[13] His conception of empire (used in the general sense, not the legal) meant the acquisition of large amounts of populated land that had to be governed. In the Americas, for example, Castile was not simply engaging in trade with the local population — a process that would necessitate acquiring only the small amounts of land that trading posts would require — it was ruling millions of people. To some extent, of course, this policy reflected the attitude of a society that identified land with power and status as well as income. Grotius, on the other hand, wrote in the defense of a commercial society, one that sought free access to the sources of the goods that Europeans wished to obtain from Asia and elsewhere.

Solórzano and Grotius were dealing with the same fundamental problems, but Grotius had the simpler task. He had only to justify the existence of a right to travel freely in peace and to engage in trade. Solórzano had to justify the conquest of a large number of people living over an area much larger than the whole of Europe, let alone Castile or even Spain itself. Furthermore, the *De Indiarum Jure* dealt with the problems arising from contact with people whom Europeans generally defined as savage barbarians. Grotius's conception of world order fitted the trading world of the East Indies, but would have been virtually useless as a basis for dealing with the inhabitants of the Americas, who did not engage in the sort of large-scale trade found in Asia and the Indian Ocean.

To bring the Americas into regular relations with the wider world would necessitate major changes in the societies that existed there. The Grotian system could provide no guidance. The morally based view of the world that the medieval canonists and theologians outlined did, however, provide a theoretical basis for constructing a government to rule over the kinds of societies that the Spanish found in the Americas. This is not to say, of course, that the Spanish acted in the Americas in full accord with these high moral principles. They clearly did not; but the Spanish tried harder than any other people in the sixteenth and seventeenth centuries to reconcile economic and moral interests in the conquest of the New World.

In the final decade of the twentieth century, 500 years after the debate about the relationship between Europe and the non-European world began, the West finds itself once again debating the issues that concerned Solórzano. While contemporary governments do not concern themselves with idolatry or polygamy in other states, they might intervene in the internal affairs of states whose governments are accused of oppressing and abusing their own citizens or attempt to provide basic social services in the absence of indigenous government. The notion that sovereign states can do, or not do, as they wish within their own borders has become an increasingly questionable assumption. Furthermore, the decline of some former colonial nations into a Hobbesian state of nature and the re-emergence of longstanding ethnic animosities amid the ruins of the USSR and its satellites have caused a reconsideration of what it means to be a sovereign state. In addition, the question of the relation of power to morality and the related issue of whether or not strong states have a moral responsibility to intervene in situations where local governments have failed to live up to international standards of behavior is of increasing importance in the development of foreign policy. International conferences are held to determine what, if any, universal standards of human rights exist and what, if any, responsibility powerful states have to insure that all governments adhere to such standards. Spanish thinkers from Vitoria to Solórzano might be forgiven for believing that after three hundred years, twentieth-century governments would be closer to solving these problems than they actually are. In fact, the Grotian notion of world order, based as it was on the existence of sovereign states, is passing into history, as the Spanish conception of order had done by the eighteenth century.

Recently, discussing what should be the American response to the degenerating situation in several African countries, most notably Somalia, a well-known political analyst observed that in these regions

> the level of political development is simply insufficient for a modern state. . . . In each case, therefore, nothing of value can be gained by brief interventions, which end up leaving the populations at the mercy of the same authorities. Unless the enormity of recolonization is accepted, turning the U.N. into the long-term administrator of a growing number of African colonies, each country and its peoples can only be left to its own fate.[14]

The call for the return to European colonial control of Africa, the demand for American and western European intervention in the crises afflicting eastern Europe at the moment strongly echo the arguments made by sixteenth- and seventeenth-century Europeans as they came to know the new worlds that were opening up to them. The optimistic expectation that decolonization would automatically lead to the creation of western-style states has been frustrated. The hard questions that the Spanish were asking four hundred years ago are being asked again. Are there universal standards of humane existence? What, if any, universal human rights do all people possess? Do developed states have any moral obligation or any right to impose universal standards of behavior on other peoples? Perhaps Grotius was not so modern after all and Vitoria, Solórzano, and their contemporaries had a clearer understanding of what the expansion of Europe overseas would ultimately mean in terms of international and intercultural relations.

Notes

Preface

1. Brian Tierney, *Religion, Law, and the Growth of Constitutional Thought, 1150–1650* (Cambridge: Cambridge University Press, 1982).

Introduction

1. It is conventional to refer to the Spanish conquest of the Americas, although strictly speaking it was the Crown of Castile that supported Columbus. There was no Spanish Crown as such in this entire period. Furthermore, although it is also conventional to refer to the Spanish Empire, there was, legally, no such institution. Charles V, Philip II, and their successors were kings of the individual kingdoms and lesser units that formed the patchwork quilt of political units they ruled. See John H. Elliott, *Imperial Spain, 1469–1716* (New York: St. Martin's Press, 1963; reprint ed. New York: New American Library, 1966), 164.

2. Kirkpatrick Sale, *The Conquest of Paradise: Christopher Columbus and the Columbian Legacy* (New York: Knopf, 1990). Concerning the criticism of the Columbian quincentenary by the National Council of Churches, see James Muldoon, "The Columbus Quincentennial: Should Christians Celebrate It?" *America* (October 27, 1990): 300–303; see also "Good Guy or Dirty Word?" *Time* (November 26, 1990): 79.

3. There has been an extensive discussion of the demographics of the New World in the sixteenth and seventeenth centuries. For a brief introduction to the numbers involved and to the basic literature, see John Lynch, *Spain Under the Habsburgs*, 2 vols., 2nd ed. (New York: New York University Press, 1984), 2: 220–21. By comparison, the worst recorded plague in Europe, the Black Death, killed one-third or so of the population during the mid-fourteenth century and then continued to re-appear periodically until the eighteenth century: see Philip Ziegler, *The Black Death* (New York: John Day Co., 1969), 230–31. A more recent study argues that the European population had already begun to fall before the plague reached Europe and, as a result, the older opinion that from one-third to two-thirds of the population died overestimated the death rate. This author suggests that the death rate in the period 1348–50 was "perhaps nearer 20 per cent of the population." Graham Twigg, *The Black Death: A Biological Reappraisal* (New York: Schocken Books, 1985), 70–71.

4. On the background to American slavery, see William D. Phillips, Jr., *Slavery from Roman Times to the Early Transatlantic Trade* (Minneapolis: University

of Minnesota Press, 1985); David Brion Davis, *The Problem of Slavery in Western Culture* (Ithaca, NY: Cornell University Press, 1966).

5. The term "ecocide" is used by the National Council of Churches in its list of charges against Columbus: see Muldoon, *America*, 300.

6. Alfred W. Crosby, *The Columbian Exchange: Biological and Cultural Consequences of 1492* (Westport, CT: Greenwood Press, 1972), 86–94; see also his *Ecological Imperialism: The Biological Expansion of Europe, 900–1900* (Cambridge: Cambridge University Press, 1986). Crosby's work on the ecological and biological consequences of the discovery of the New World has had a significant impact, although not without criticism. See, for example, the review by G. V. Scammell, *English Historical Review* 103(1988): 108–10.

7. In the struggle among the religious orders that did the bulk of the missionary work with the native peoples and the bishops and the secular clergy who administered the parishes that were established, each side leveled a good deal of criticism at the others' dealings with the Indians; see Robert Ricard, *The Spiritual Conquest of Mexico*, trans. Lesley Byrd Simpson, reprint ed. (Berkeley: University of California Press, 1982), 243–55.

8. William S. Maltby, *The Black Legend in England: The Development of Anti-Spanish Sentiment, 1558–1660* (Durham, NC: Duke University Press, 1971), 30–31. For an introduction to the literature concerning the Black Legend in American historiography see Benjamin Keen, "Main Currents in United States Writings on Colonial Spanish America, 1884–1984," *Hispanic American Historical Review* 65(1985): 657–82, esp. 663–69.

9. These techniques had first been employed in late medieval Ireland as the English sought to pacify the native population; see James Muldoon, "The Indian as Irishman," *Essex Institute Historical Collections* 111(1975): 267–89; see also Neal Salisbury, "Red Puritans: The 'Praying Indians' of Massachusetts and John Eliot," *William and Mary Quarterly* 31(1974): 27–54; and James Axtell, *The Invasion Within: The Contest of Cultures in Colonial North America* (New York: Oxford University Press, 1985), 131–78.

10. J. H. Parry, *The Spanish Seaborne Empire* (New York: Knopf, 1970), 161–65. The most important study on missionary techniques remains Ricard, *The Spiritual Conquest of Mexico*.

11. The National Council of Churches, for example, has taken this position: see Muldoon, *America*, 302. In the late twentieth century, some critics of the growing evangelical Protestant movements in Latin America, movements often directed by missionaries from the United States, have seen them as leading inevitably to the North Americanization of Latin America, in effect, another wave of cultural genocide; see David Martin, *Tongues of Fire: The Explosion of Protestantism in Latin America* (Oxford: Basil Blackwell, 1990), 282–88.

12. W. H. Prescott, *The History of the Conquest of Mexico*, 2 vols. (London: George Routledge and Sons, n.d. [1878]), 1: 44.

13. Ibid.: 44–45. Concerning the attitude of Prescott, Parkman and their contemporaries toward the indigenous peoples of the Americas, see David Levin, *History as Romantic Art: Bancroft, Motley, Prescott, and Parkman* (Stanford, CA: Stanford University Press, 1959), 126–59.

14. John Emmerich Acton, "Inaugural Lecture on the Study of History," *Lectures on Modern History*, reprint ed. (London: Collins, 1960): 38. Concerning Acton's view of history and of the historian's role, see Gertrude Himmelfarb, *Lord Acton: A Study in Conscience and Politics* (Chicago: University of Chicago Press, 1952), 190–204 and *Victorian Minds* (New York: A. A. Knopf, 1968), 195–96.

15. "It might be true to say that in Lord Acton, the whig historian reached his highest consciousness; . . . in his writings moral judgments appeared in their most trenchant and uncompromising form." Herbert Butterfield, *The Whig Interpretation of History* (London: G. Bell, 1931; reprint ed., New York: W. W. Norton, 1963), 109.

16. Elliott, *Imperial Spain*, 68.

17. There is an extensive literature on these bulls: see James Muldoon, "Papal Responsibility for the Infidel: Another Look at Alexander VI's Inter Caetera," *Catholic Historical Review* 64(1978): 168–84; Brigitte F. P. Lhoest, "Spanish American Law: A Product of Conflicting Interests," *Itinerario* 16(1992): 21–34; Patricia Seed, "Taking Possession and Reading Texts: Establishing the Authority of Overseas Empires," *William and Mary Quarterly* 49(1992): 183–209 at 200–202; Delno West, "Christopher Columbus and His Enterprise to the Indies: Scholarship of the Last Quarter Century," *William and Mary Quarterly* 49(1992): 224–27, note 73.

18. Antonio Domínguez Ortiz, *The Golden Age of Spain, 1516–1659*, trans. James Casey (New York: Basic Books, 1971), 229–45, esp. 238–42.

19. For general background to the Spanish conquest of the Americas, see Elliott, *Imperial Spain*, and *The Old World and the New, 1492–1650* (Cambridge: Cambridge University Press, 1970); Parry, *The Spanish Seaborne Empire*; and also his *The Spanish Theory of Empire in the Sixteenth Century* (Cambridge: Cambridge University Press, 1940; reprint ed. New York: Octagon Books, 1974); Mario Góngora, *Studies in the Colonial History of Spanish America*, trans. Richard Southern (Cambridge: Cambridge University Press, 1975); and most recently Colin M. MacLachlan, *Spain's Empire in the New World: The Role of Ideas in Institutional and Social Change* (Berkeley: University of California Press, 1988). All of these books have extensive bibliographies. An older work still of great value is Roger Bigelow Merriman, *The Rise of the Spanish Empire in the Old World and in the New*, 4 vols. (New York: Macmillan, 1918–34; reprint ed. New York: Cooper Square, 1962).

20. For an introduction to the legal literature, see; James Muldoon, "The Contribution of the Medieval Canon Lawyers to the Formation of International Law," *Traditio* 28(1972): 483–97; see also Robert A. Williams, Jr., *The American Indian in Western Legal Thought: The Discourses of Conquest* (New York: Oxford University Press, 1990).

21. Among the more important works in English alone that have examined Spanish political thought of this period in some detail are Guenter Lewy, *Constitutionalism and Statecraft During the Golden Age of Spain: A Study in the Political Philosophy of Juan de Mariana, S.J.* (Geneva: Librairie E. Droz, 1960); Bernice Hamilton, *Political Thought in Sixteenth-Century Spain: A Study of the Political Ideas of Vitoria, De Soto, Suárez, and Molina* (Oxford: Oxford University Press, 1963); J. A. Fernández-Santamaria, *The State, War and Peace: Spanish Political Thought in the Renaissance, 1516–1559* (Cambridge: Cambridge University Press, 1977); and *Reason*

of State and Statecraft in Spanish Political Thought, 1595–1640 (Lanham, MD: University Press of America, 1983). All of these books have extensive bibliographies.

22. Lewis Hanke, *The Spanish Struggle for Justice in the Conquest of America* (Philadelphia: University of Pennsylvania Press, 1949), 109–32. For a more recent and more extensive discussion of the debate, see Hanke, *All Mankind Is One* (DeKalb: Northern Illinois University Press, 1974). The text of Las Casas's position is also available: Bartolomé de Las Casas, *In Defense of the Indians*, trans. and ed. Stafford Poole, C.M. (DeKalb: Northern Illinois University Press, 1974).

23. Hanke's views on this debate can be found in "More Heat and Some Light on the Spanish Struggle for Justice in the Conquest of America," *Hispanic American Historical Review* 44(1964): 293–340; "A Modest Proposal for a Moratorium on Grand Generalizations: Some Thoughts on the Black Legend." *Hispanic American Historical Review* 51(1971): 112–27. For criticism of Hanke's views, see Benjamin Keen, "The Black Legend Revisited: Assumptions and Realities," *Hispanic American Historical Review* 49(1969): 703–19; and "The White Legend Revisited: A Reply to Professor Hanke's 'Modest Proposal,'" *Hispanic American Historical Review* 51(1971): 336–55.

24. James Brown Scott, *The Spanish Origin of International Law: Francisco de Vitoria and His Law of Nations* (Oxford: Clarendon Press, 1934). For a discussion of Scott's work and the criticisms that it received, see Muldoon, "The Contribution," *Traditio*: 486–90. The importance of the Spanish scholastics and Grotius for the subsequent history of another branch of legal development, the law of contract, has recently been examined by James Gordley, *The Philosophical Origins of Modern Contract Doctrine* (Oxford: Clarendon Press, 1991).

25. John H. Elliott, *The Count-Duke of Olivares: The Statesman in an Age of Decline* (New Haven: Yale University Press, 1986), 677–80. This volume climaxed a series of major publications on the history of seventeenth-century Spain, beginning with an article on the problem of Spanish decline; "The Decline of Spain," *Past & Present* 20(Nov. 1961): 52–75; reprinted *Crisis in Europe, 1560–1660*, ed. T. H. Aston (New York: Basic Books, 1965); 167–93. There is also now a biography of Olivares's master, Philip IV: see R. A. Strading, *Philip IV and the Government of Spain 1621–1665* (New York: Cambridge University Press, 1988). See also his *Europe and the Decline of Spain: A Study of the Spanish System, 1580–1720* (Boston: Allen & Unwin, 1981).

26. Elliott, *Olivares*, 684. Professor Elliott has pointed out that later proposals and programs for reform that historians usually assign to Enlightenment thinkers in Spain in fact are quite similar to the proposals of Olivares. Ibid., 684–85.

27. The key issues and positions in the debate have been discussed in a series of articles in *Past & Present*: Henry Kamen, "The Decline of Spain: A Historical Myth?" 81(Nov. 1978): 24–50; John J. TePaske and Herbert S. Klein, "The Seventeenth-Century Crisis in New Spain: Myth or Reality?" 90(Feb. 1981): 116–35; J. I. Israel and Henry Kamen, "Debate: The Decline of Spain: A Historical Myth?" 91(May 1981): 170–85; Henry Kamen, J. I. Israel, John J. TePaske, and Herbert S. Klein, "Debate: The Seventeenth-Century Crisis in New Spain: Myth or Reality?" 97(Nov. 1982): 144–61.

28. Paul Kennedy, *The Rise and Fall of the Great Powers: Economic Change and Military Conflict from 1500 to 2000* (New York: Random House, 1987), 41.

29. Elliott, *Imperial Spain*, 296; see also his *Olivares*, 84–89.

30. One of the most important practical issues facing those who would reform the Spanish government was the corruption that marked official life at all levels. To understand this aspect of the world within which Solórzano functioned, see Stafford Poole, C. M., "Institutionalized Corruption in the Letrado Bureaucracy," *The Americas* 38(1981–82): 149–71; and Kenneth J. Andrien, "Corruption, Inefficiency, and Imperial Decline in the Seventeenth-Century Viceroyalty of Peru," *The Americas* 41(1984): 1–20.

31. The universities of Salamanca, Alcalá, and Valladolid were the major Castilian universities in the sixteenth and seventeenth centuries. Contrary to common opinion, law, not theology, was by far the most popular field of study. "At Salamanca and Valladolid . . . law students outnumbered theologians by twenty to one"; Richard L. Kagan, "Universities in Castile 1500–1810," *The University in Society*, ed. Lawrence Stone, 2 vols. (Princeton, NJ: Princeton University Press, 1974), 2: 355–405 at 373. See also his *Students and Society in Early Modern Spain* (Baltimore: Johns Hopkins University Press, 1974).

32. Little has been written on Solórzano Pereira. The most extensive discussion of the man and his work is Javier Malagón and José M. Ots Capdequí, *Solórzano y la Política indiana*, 2nd ed. (México: Fondo de Cultura Económica, 1983). There is a brief biographical note in the *Encyclopedia universal ilustrada Europeo-Americana*, vol. 57 (Bilbao, Madrid, Barcelona: Espasa-Calpe, 1930–1933): 198–99.

33. Malagón and Capdequí, *Solórzano*, 41–42; see also C. H. Haring, *The Spanish Empire in America* (New York: Oxford University Press, 1947): 113.

34. Humanism in Spain has been little studied, but it is clear that the movement had a significant influence there; see Carlos G. Noreña, *Studies in Spanish Renaissance Thought* (The Hague: Martinus Nijhof, 1975); also O. Carlos Stoetzer, *The Scholastic Roots of the Spanish American Revolution* (New York: Fordham University Press, 1979), esp. 16–59; Luis Gil Fernández, *Panorma social del humanismo espanol (1500–1800)* (Madrid: Editorial Alhambra, 1981). On the spread of humanist thought see Paul Oskar Kristeller, "The Moral Thought of Renaissance Humanism" and "The European Diffusion of Italian Humanism" in *Renaissance Thought and the Arts* (Princeton, NJ: Princeton University Press, 1990), 20–88. Humanism also had a long history of association with the legal profession; see Guido Kisch, *Studien zur humanistischen Jurisprudenz* (Berlin and New York: Walter de Gruyter, 1972). In addition, Solórzano appears to have been influenced by the once-famous and widely read neostoic philosopher Justus Lipsius (1547–1606). On Lipsius, see Jason Lewis Saunders, *Justus Lipsius: The Philosophy of Renaissance Stoicism* (New York: The Liberal Arts Press, 1955); Mark Morford, *Stoics and Neostoics: Reubens and the Circle of Lipsius* (Princeton, NJ: Princeton University Press, 1991); Robert Bireley, *The Counter-Reformation Prince: Anti-Machiavellianism or Catholic Statecraft in Early Modern Europe* (Chapel Hill: University of North Carolina Press, 1990), ix–x, 72–100. For an introduction to the state of political and legal thought in Solórzano's day, see Anthony Grafton, "Humanism and Political Theory," Donald R. Kelley,

"Law," and Peter Burke, "Tacitism, Sceptisism [sic], and Reason," *The Cambridge History of Political Thought 1450–1700*, J. H. Burns and Mark Goldie, eds. (Cambridge: Cambridge University Press, 1991), 9–29, 66–94, esp. 75–78 and 479–98. Concerning the role of humanism in the age of Spanish expansion overseas, see Berta Ares, Jesus Bustamante, Francisco Castilla, and Fermin del Pino, *Humanismo y vision del otro en la España moderna: cuatro estudios* (Madrid: Consejo Superior de Investigaciones Científicas, 1992).

35. Parry, *The Spanish Seaborne Empire*, 276.

36. See, for example, the judgments of Sir Arthur Helps, *The Spanish Conquest in America and Its Relation to the History of Slavery and to the Government of Colonies*, 4 vols., reprint ed. (New York: AMS Press, 1966), 4: 243; also Haring, *The Spanish Empire in America*, 113; Lynch, *Spain Under the Habsburgs*, 2: 175.

37. Góngora, *Studies*: 62.

38. See Salvador de Madariaga, *The Rise of the Spanish American Empire* (New York: Macmillan, 1947); *El Auge del Imperio Español en America*, 2nd ed. (Buenos Aires: Editorial Sudamericana, 1959); and *El Ocaso del Imperio Español en America*, 2nd ed. (Buenos Aires: Editorial Sudamericana, 1959).

39. Lewis Hanke, *Aristotle and the American Indians: A Study in Race Prejudice in the Modern World* (Bloomington: Indiana University Press, 1959), 92.

40. For example, Adam Smith, *An Inquiry into the Nature and Causes of the Wealth of Nations* (New York: Modern Library, 1937), 201.

41. Richard Bland, *An Enquiry into the Rights of the British Colonies . . .* (Williamsburg: Alexander Purdie, 1766; reprinted London: J. Almon, 1769), 13; and James Otis, "The Rights of the British Colonies Asserted and Proved," *Pamphlets of the American Revolution*, ed. Bernard Bailyn, vol. 1 (Cambridge, MA: Belknap Press, 1965), 419–82 at 438. These references to Solórzano came from the translator's introduction to Jean Domat, *The Civil Law in Its Natural Order*, trans. William Strahan, 2 vols. (London: J. Bettenham, 1722): xviii–xix. Solórzano was cited much more extensively by a defender of the English Parliament's jurisdiction over the American colonies; see William Abercrombie, *Magna Carta for America* (Philadelphia: American Philosophical Society, 1986), 70, 199, 312. Abercrombie, like Solórzano, had served in the Americas as a royal official, and then wrote two long essays on the imperial situation upon his return to Europe. His essays were not, however, published until recently. According to one survey of eighteenth-century law libraries, there were six copies of Strahan's translation of Domat's work in eighteenth-century North America and one copy of the French edition; see Herbert A. Johnson, *Imported Eighteenth-Century Law Treatises in American Libraries, 1700–1799* (Knoxville: University of Tennessee Press, 1978), 18–19, 62. By contrast, there were ten copies of Blackstone's *Commentaries*, ibid., 59.

42. *A New Collection of Laws, Charters and Local Ordinances of the Government of Great Britain, France and Spain relating to the concessions of land in their respective colonies; together with the laws of Mexico and Texas on the same subject*, ed. Joseph M. White, 2 vols. (Philadelphia: T. & J. W. Johnson, 1839), 1: 367–72.

43. Juan de Solórzano Pereira, *De Indiarum Jure sive de justa Indiarum Occidentalium Inquisitione, Acquisitione, & Retentione*, 2 vols. (Madrid: Ex Typographia Francisci Martinez, 1629–1639). There were several other later editions. In the

course of writing this book, the Madrid edition of 1629–1639 was used as well as that of 1777 (Madrid: In Typographia Regia, 1777); see also the *Política indiana*, Biblioteca de autores españoles desde la formacion del lenguaje hasta nuestros dias, ed. Miguel Angel Ochoa Brun, 5 vols. (Madrid: Ediciones Atlas, 1972). A comparison of the two versions of the book would an interesting exercise.

44. For a list of Solórzano's publications, see Malagón and Capdequí, *Solórzano*, 96–110.

45. Ibid., 46.

46. Guenter Lewy, *Constitutionalism and Statecraft*: 23.

47. Ibid., 24.

48. In seeking to protect Cervantes from the charge of hypocrisy leveled at him by Américo Castro, Aubrey F. G. Bell argued that Cervantes "was a devout son of the Church and a fervently patriotic Spaniard who was willing to curb or modify, suppress or alter his happiest inventions and most telling criticisms if it occurred to him that they might prove a stumbling-block to the illiterate or a handle to the enemies of Spain." Aubrey F. G. Bell, "Liberty in Sixteenth-Century Spain," *Bulletin of Spanish Studies* 10(1933): 164–79 at 168. In the debate about the legitimacy of the conquest of the New World, something similar took place. Both Las Casas and Sepúlveda produced works in Spanish designed to win popular support for their respective positions; see Lewis Hanke, *Spanish Struggle for Justice*, 114–15. Concerning the rising literacy rate among the Castilians, see Sara T. Nalle," Literacy and Culture in Early Modern Castile," *Past & Present* 125(Nov. 1989): 65–96.

49. Hanke, *Spanish Struggle for Justice*, 90.

50. The importance of the medieval background, especially the medieval legal tradition, in the intellectual outlook of the sixteenth-century Spanish, has been stressed in the work of Luis Weckmann, *The Medieval Heritage of Mexico*, trans. Frances M. Lopez-Morillas (New York: Fordham University Press, 1992).

51. Fernández-Santamaria, *Reason of State*, xi. Although he does not discuss Solórzano, the observation describes Solórzano's situation among scholars quite well.

52. On the development of this legal tradition, see; James Muldoon, *Popes, Lawyers, and Infidels: The Church and the Non-Christian World, 1250–1550* (Philadelphia: University of Pennsylvania Press, 1979).

53. "Protestant history became the handmaiden of Protestant theology and Protestant politics." James Westfall Thompson, *A History of Historical Writing*, 2 vols. (New York: Macmillan, 1942), 1: 527. In addition, see Harry Elmer Barnes, *A History of Historical Writing*, 2nd rev. ed. (Norman: University of Oklahoma Press, 1937; reprint ed. New York: Dover Publications, 1962), 121–35. The goal of Protestant reformers was to "return to the 'pure' holy Christian Church" that had existed before the rise of Roman popes who had corrupted the Church. Ernst Breisach, *Historiography: Ancient, Medieval, & Modern* (Chicago: University of Chicago Press, 1983), 166. For Martin Luther, Pope Gregory I (590–604) was "the last acceptable figure of the early Church." John M. Headly, *Luther's View of Church History* (New Haven, CT: Yale University Press, 1963), 192.

54. For Grotius's opinion of his Spanish and Catholic predecessors, see Hugo Grotius, *De Jure Belli ac Pacis Libri Tres [The Law of War and Peace]*, trans. Francis W.

Kelsey, *The Classics of International Law* (Washington, DC: Carnegie Endowment for International Peace, 1925; reprint ed. Indianapolis: Bobbs-Merrill, 1962), 22.

Chapter One

1. The fundamental work on the development of the theory of the just war is Frederick H. Russell, *The Just War in the Middle Ages* (Cambridge: Cambridge University Press, 1975). Concerning the subsequent application of the theory of the just war in the early modern world, see James Turner Johnson, *Ideology, Reason, and the Limitation of War* (Princeton, NJ: Princeton University Press, 1975); see also his *The Just War Tradition and the Restraint of War* (Princeton, NJ: Princeton University Press, 1981).

2. Walter Ullmann, *Medieval Papalism* (London: Methuen & Co., 1949), 28. According to another scholar, "Gratian himself seems to have been the last great figure to write on canon law from the point of view of the moral theologian." Michael B. Crowe, *The Changing Profile of the Natural Law* (The Hague: Martinus Nijhoff, 1977), 74.

3. It is worth noting that a number of important popes from the late twelfth century onward had been trained as lawyers as well and made significant contributions to the law's development. These included Alexander III (1159–1181) and Innocent III (1198–1216), although their legal background and training has been questioned: see J. T. Noonan, Jr., "Who was Rolandus?" in *Law, Church and Society: Essays in Honor of Stephan Kuttner*, ed. Kenneth Pennington and Robert Somerville (Philadelphia: University of Pennsylvania Press, 1977), 21–48; Kenneth Pennington, "The Legal Education of Pope Innocent III," *Bulletin of Medieval Canon Law*, n.s. 4(1974): 70–77. F. W. Maitland described Innocent IV (1243–1254) as "the greatest lawyer that ever sat upon the chair of St. Peter," Muldoon, *Popes, Lawyers*, x. Boniface VIII (1294–1303) boasted of his legal training and career as a teacher of law; see Muldoon, "Boniface VIII's Forty Years of Experience in the Law," *The Jurist* 31 (1971): 449–77.

4. James Brundage, *Medieval Canon Law and the Crusader* (Madison: University of Wisconsin Press, 1969), 190.

5. Ibid., 31.

6. The most extensive discussion of this commentary is in Muldoon, *Popes, Lawyers*, 6–15.

7. On the theory of the just war of recuperation, see Russell, *The Just War*, esp. 199–201, 253; Johnson, *Ideology*, 154–58.

8. Muldoon, *Popes, Lawyers*, 9, n.27.

9. On Innocent IV as the first theorist of world society, see William R. Garrett, "Religion, Law and the Human Condition," *Sociological Analysis* 47(1987): 1–34 at 7.

10. Innocent IV, *Commentaria*, 3.34.8.

11. The organic analogy, the comparison of the body politic with a human body, was a common medieval image. There is a brief, classic statement of it in Otto Gierke, *Political Theories of the Middle Age*, trans. F. W. Maitland (Cambridge:

Cambridge University Press, 1900), 22–30; see also Ernst Kantorowicz, *The King's Two Bodies: A Study in Mediaeval Political Theology* (Princeton, NJ: Princeton University Press, 1957), 193–232.

12. The nature and extent of the papal vicarate had changed over time. Originally the pope was the Vicar of St. Peter, and only around 1200 did the title become Vicar of Christ; see Michele Maccarrone, *Chiesa e stato nella dottrina di papa Innocenzo III* (Rome: Facultas Theologica Pontificii Athenaei Lateranensis, 1940).

13. Muldoon, *Popes, Lawyers*, 10–11; Edward A. Synan, *The Popes and the Jews in the Middle Ages* (New York: Macmillan, 1965), esp. 111–15; B. Z. Kedar, "Canon Law and the Burning of the Talmud," *Bulletin of Medieval Canon Law*, n.s. 9(1979): 79–82; Jeremy Cohen, *The Friars and the Jews: The Evolution of Medieval Anti-Semitism* (Ithaca, NY: Cornell University Press, 1982), 60–76, 96–99.

14. "si non obediant, compellendi sunt brachio seculari, & indicendum est bellum contra eos per Papam . . . ." Innocent IV, *Commentaria, ad* 3.34.8.

15. Muldoon, *Popes, Lawyers*, 16.

16. Ibid., 18.

17. On Donatism, Herbert A. Deane, *The Political and Social Ideas of St. Augustine* (New York: Columbia University Press, 1963), 4, 34–36, 179–97.

18. Hostiensis's opinion on this issue appears to have undergone a significant change in the course of writing his commentary; see the recent article by Kenneth Pennington, "An Earlier Recension of Hostiensis's Lectura on the Decretals," *Bulletin of Medieval Canon Law*, n.s. 17(1987): 77–90 at 84–85.

19. Muldoon, *Popes, Lawyers*, 107–14.

20. Johannes Andreae, *In quinque decretalium libros novella commentaria* (Venice: 1581; reprint ed., Turin: Bottega d'Erasmo, 1963), *ad* 3.34.8. Concerning Johannes Andreae and his significance, Stephan Kuttner's introduction to this edition, especially XIII–XIV; see also *The New Catholic Encyclopedia* (New York: McGraw-Hill, 1967) 7: 994–95 and the *Dictionnaire de droit canonique*, ed. R. Naz, 7 vols. (Paris: Letouzey et Ané, 1935–1965) 6: 89–92.

21. It is not known, however, whether Innocent IV wrote his commentary on 3.34.8. before or after initiating contact with the Mongols. It is known that he worked on the commentary while he was pope; see Gabriel Le Bras, "Innocent IV Romaniste: Examen de l'Apparatus," *Studia Gratiana* 11(1967): 305–26 at 309.

22. The most extensive study of the later history of these attempts to create peaceful relations with the peoples of Asia is Adam Knobler, "Missions, Mythologies and the Search for non-European Allies in anti-Islamic Holy War, 1291–c. 1540" (Ph.D. diss., Cambridge University, 1989).

23. Expansion along the fringes of Europe did provide some opportunity to apply the legal theories of Innocent IV and Hostiensis in the fourteenth and fifteenth centuries. For their use in connection with expansion in eastern Europe and in the Canary Islands, see Muldoon, *Popes, Lawyers*, 105–31. Concerning the conquest of the Canary Islands and their place in the overseas expansion of Spain, see; Felipe Fernández-Armesto, *Before Columbus: Exploration and Colonization from the Mediterranean to the Atlantic, 1229–1492* (Philadelphia: University of Pennsylvania Press, 1987), 153–222.

24. Spanish scholars were influenced by the debates about natural rights that

were taking place at the University of Paris at the beginning of the sixteenth century. One of the most important figures in these debates was the Scottish philosopher John Major (c.1470–c. 1540) who was a teacher of Francis Vitoria; see Hamilton, *Political Thought*, 171 and Noreña, *Studies*, 12–20, 43–45. See also Parry, *Spanish Theory of Empire*, 16–19. On the study of law, see J. Beneyto Pérez, "The Science of Law in the Spain of the Catholic Kings," *Spain in the Fifteenth Century, 1369–1516: Essays and Extracts by Historians of Spain*, ed. R. Highfield (London: Macmillan, 1972), 276–95.

25. See the work of Charles Martial de Witte, "Les bulles pontificales et l'expansion portugaise au XVe siècle," *Revue d'Histoire Ecclésiastique* 48(1953): 683–718; 49(1954): 438–61; 51(1956): 413–53, 809–36; 53(1958): 5–46, 443–71. See also Muldoon, "Papal Responsibility for the Infidel."

26. Even Columbus's activities were framed within a legal context. The capitulations, that is, the legal agreements, that he signed with Ferdinand and Isabella set out the terms under which he sailed and the rewards he would receive if successful. The failure of the monarchs to live up to the terms of the agreements as Columbus understood then led to a lengthy series of lawsuits that ended only in the reign of Philip II; see James Muldoon, "Columbus's First Voyage and the Medieval Legal Tradition," *Medievalia et Humanistica*, n. s. 19(1992): 11–26.

27. The sixteenth century saw an important revival of medieval scholastic philosophy, what some scholars term the "second scholasticism." While this movement began in Italy, its influence was most important in the Spanish universities and encompassed the major Spanish philosophers and theologians of the time. For a brief introduction to this movement, see Frederick Copleston, S.J., *History of Philosophy*, 9 vols. (Westminster, MD: Newman Press, 1948–1953), *Ockham to Suárez* (1953) 3: 335–52; Noreña, *Studies*, 68–74.

28. On Spanish universities, see; Lynch, *Spain Under the Habsburgs*, 1: 263–67.

29. Kenneth J. Pennington, "Bartolomé de Las Casas and the Tradition of Medieval Law," *Church History* 39(1970): 149–61; James Muldoon, "A Canonistic Contribution to the Formation of International Law," *The Jurist* 28(1968): 265–79.

30. "On the American Indians," Francisco de Vitoria, *Political Writings*, ed. Anthony Pagden and Jeremy Lawrance (Cambridge: Cambridge University Press, 1991), 252. This is the most recent translation of Vitoria's work and replaces the older translation issued in the *Classics of International Law Series*, Franciscus de Victoria, *De Indis et de Ivre Belli Relectiones*, ed. E. Nys (Washington, DC: Carnegie Institution, 1917; reprint ed. New York: Oceana, 1964).

31. There were, reasonably enough, canonical prohibitions against any trade in weapons and materials that could be used against Christians. These prohibitions were issued against Christians dealing with the Muslims; see Muldoon, *Popes, Lawyers*, 102.

32. This is the standard interpretation of the first voyage, but one that is not unchallenged. See Sale, *Conquest*, 23–26, for a discussion of this issue.

33. Solórzano, 2.1.8–9. The *De Indiarum Jure* is cited according to book, chapter, and paragraph. All citations are to volume 1.

34. Solórzano, 2.1.1.

35. Ibid., 2.1.3. The reference is to Lucretius, *The Way Things Are [De Rerum*

Natura], trans. Rolfe Humphries (London and Bloomington: Indiana University Press, 1968): 86. Even books that were not intended as *florilegia* could be used in this fashion. For example, when Solórzano cites the works of St. Augustine, he virtually always cites Augustine from the excerpts that Gratian included in the *Decretum*.

36. Ibid., 2.1.5.

37. Ibid., 2.1.19. The reference to the *Summa Theologica* is to 2.2., quaest. 10., art. 10. The 1777 edition has quaest. 19. The reference to the *De Regimine Principum* cites book 3, ch. 9, but there is no such book, and there is no discussion of *dominium* elsewhere in this treatise.

38. On Covarrubias, see NCE 4: 401; on Molina, see NCE 9: 1010–11.

39. Solórzano, 2.1.20–21. It was never put in print until the twentieth century; Juan López de Palacios Rubios, *De las islas del mar oceano*, trans. Agustín Millares Carlo (México: Fondo de Cultura Económica, 1954).

40. Muldoon, *Popes, Lawyers*, 140–43; and "John Wyclif and the Rights of the Infidels: The *Requerimiento* Re-examined," *Americas* 36(1980): 301–16.

41. For a translation of the *Requerimiento*, see *History of Latin American Civilization*, vol. 1, *The Colonial Experience*, ed. Lewis Hanke (Boston: Little, Brown, 1967), 123–25. For an important reading of the *Requerimiento* in its context, see Seed, "Taking Possession," 202–7.

42. Solórzano, 2.1.22.

43. The major work on Sepúlveda is J. A. Fernández-Santamaria, *The State, War and Peace*. On the importance of Sepúlveda, see the observations of T. Bentley Duncan, review, *Journal of Modern History* 50(1978): 764–66.

44. Solórzano., 2.1.28.

45. Ibid., 2.1.29. Concerning the condemnation of Sepúlveda's work see Pagden, *Fall of Natural Man*, 109–11. In addition, see Lewis Hanke, *Aristotle and the American Indians*, 86, 96–97; Helps, *The Spanish Conquest in America*, 4: 214. An important reason for royal opposition to Sepúlveda's work is that it supported the position of the encomendaros who had acquired large numbers of Indian laborers. Charles V and Philip II feared the creation of a feudal aristocracy in the Americas in which the descendants of the conquerors, ruling over a serf population, would be able to reduce royal power to the absolute minimum, if not throw it off altogether. By defending the full humanity and rationality of the Indians, the Spanish monarchs were identifying them as subjects, not serfs.

46. On the Valladolid debate, see Introduction, note 22.

47. Solórzano, 2.1.37. There is an extensive literature on Vitoria. The best introduction to Vitoria's work as it related to the debate about the New World is Anthony Pagden, *The Fall of Natural Man*, although see the critique by Brian Tierney, "Aristotle and the American Indians—Again," *Cristianesimo nella storia* 12(1991): 295–322 at 305–22.

48. Solórzano, 2.1.33, 40 [erroneously numbered 41 in the 1629 edition]. Cardinal Bellarmine was one of the most important Catholic political thinkers of the time. His views on the limited power of the pope to intervene in temporal affairs has received a great deal of attention in modern times, in the 1920s and '30s because his views on the limited nature of papal power in secular affairs were sometimes seen as

foreshadowing modern theories about the separation of church and state, even, according to some scholars, to the extent of having an influence on Thomas Jefferson's thought. Bellarmine argued that the papacy's power was limited to an "indirect" supervisory jurisdiction, operative only when the secular power has failed to act properly. Bellarmine's views on papal power were similar to those of the medieval canonists, usually labeled dualists because they recognized the existence of an autonomous secular sphere of jurisdiction exempt from papal jurisdiction. At the same time the dualists argued, like Bellarmine, that as the ultimate purpose of mankind was spiritual in nature, secular power was ultimately subordinate to the spiritual as means are to an end. There were also those canonists, known as hierocrats, who denied the autonomy of the secular power under any circumstances. For a brief introduction to the issues involved and to the literature that has appeared on the dualist-hierocrat debate, see Colin Morris, *The Papal Monarchy: The Western Church from 1050 to 1250* (Oxford: Clarendon Press, 1989), 568–69, 653–54. For a brief introduction to Bellarmine's political thought in English translation, see his *De laicis or the Treatise on Civil Government*, trans. Kathleen E. Murphy (New York: Fordham University Press, 1928; reprint ed. Westport CT: Hyperion Press, 1979); and his *Power of the Pope in Temporal Affairs*, trans. George Albert Moore (Chevy Chase, MD: Country Dollar Press, 1949); see also Franz Xaver Arnold, *Die Staatslehre des kardinals Bellarmin: un beitrag zur Rechts- und Staatsphilosophie des konfessionellen Zeitalters* (München: M. Hueber, 1934); Davis S. Schaff, "The Bellarmine-Jefferson Legend and the Declaration of Independence," *American Society of Church History Papers*, 2nd series, vol. 8 (New York and London, 1928): 237–76; John Clement Roger, *Political Philosophy of Blessed Cardinal Bellarmine* (Washington, DC: Catholic University of America Press, 1926); John Courtney Murray, "Bellarmine on the Indirect Power," *Theological Studies* 9 (1948): 491–535. Quentin Skinner, *The Foundations of Modern Political Thought*, vol. 2, *The Age of Reformation* (Cambridge: Cambridge University Press, 1978), esp. 174–80. For further discussion of Solórzano's use of Bellarmine's work, see James Muldoon, "Spiritual Conquests Compared: *Laudabiliter* and the Conquest of the Americas," *In Iure Veritas: Studies in Canon Law in Memory of Schafer Williams*, ed. Steven Bowman and Blanche Cody (Cincinnati, OH: University of Cincinnati Press, 1991), 174–86.

49. Solórzano, 2.1.30,35, 40 [41 in 1629 ed.]. On Dávila Padilla see NCE 4: 662; on Matienzo see *New Catholic Encyclopedia* 9: 462.

50. Ibid., 2.1.32. Marquardus de Susannis was the author of the *De Iudaeis et Aliis Infidelibus*, a treatise "intended to be a handbook for judges in cases involving Jewry law" but also containing "a polemic whose purpose . . . is to convince Jews and other infidels to embrace Christianity." It was a very popular and widely read work; see Kenneth R. Stow, *Catholic Thought and Papal Jewry Policy 1555–1593* (New York: Jewish Theological Seminary of America, 1977): 64–65.

51. Ibid., 2.1.48. The *Mare liberum* was placed on the Index of Forbidden Books in 1610: see *Index Librorum Prohibitorum*, new edition (Rome: Ex Typographia Polyglotta, 1881): 208. For a brief discussion of why it was placed there, see Fr. Heinrich Reusch, *Der Index de verbotenen Bücher*, 2 vols. in 3 (Bonn: Verlag von Max Cohen & Sohn, 1885), 2.1:374. For the text, see Hugo Grotius, *The Freedom of the Seas (Mare Liberum)*, trans. Ralph Van Deman Magoffin, ed. J. B.

Scott (New York: Oxford University Press, 1916). While Solórzano may be telling the literal truth here, it is also possible that he wished to save himself some difficulty with the censors by asserting that he knew of Grotius's work only at second hand. Ironically, the *De Indiarum Jure* was placed on the *Index* in 1642: see *Index Librorum Prohibitorum*: 314 and Reusch, 2. 1:374.

52. Grotius, *The Freedom of the Seas*, 13. On the his tory of the *Mare Liberum*, see C. G. Roelofsen, "Grotius and the International Politics of the Seventeenth Century," *Hugo Grotius and International Relations*, ed. Hedley Bull et al. (Oxford: Clarendon Press, 1990), 95–131 at 106–10; and W. E. Butler, "Grotius and the Law of the Sea," *Hugo Grotius and International Relations*, 209–20 at 209–12.

53. Grotius, *The Freedom of the Seas*, 16.

54. Solórzano, 2.1.50; see Frei Serafim de Freitas, *De Justo imperio asiatico dos portugeses, de iusto imperio Lusitanorum Asiatico*, 2 vols. (Lisbon: Instituto Nacional de Investigacao Cientifica, 1983).

55. "7. *spec. Law.* Legal right to possession of property (esp. real property); the evidence of such right." *Oxford English Dictionary*, 11: 78. Such usage was medieval in origin. In classical Latin, it had the related meaning of a "cause or reason alleged, a pretense, pretext." *A Latin Dictionary*, ed. Charlton T. Lewis and Charles Short (Oxford: Clarendon Press, 1879), 1875.

56. Vitoria, *Political Writings*, 252.

57. Ibid., 238.

58. Modern writers are of several minds about the sincerity of these Spanish writers. On one hand, it is quite easy to see these debates as a hypocritical facade for an evil policy, or as a means of assuaging pangs of guilt, or as the ineffectual bleatings of intellectuals who neither had nor could have any effect on the course of official Spanish policy. On the other hand, it is also possible to see these debates as conscientious attempts to grapple with serious moral and political problems. My own view is that these writers were sincere about the moral problems raised but, when dealing with them, they were constrained by a theoretical structure that was not sufficiently broad to provide an adequate basis for dealing with problems of international (or cross-cultural) relations.

59. A major reason for the impact of Vitoria's approach to the issues was the fact that many leading Spanish intellectuals had been his students. One estimate suggests "that 5,000 students passed through his lecturerooms; twenty-four of his pupils held chairs of arts or theology at Salamanca." Hamilton, *Political Thought*, 175.

60. Vitoria, *Political Writings*, 237–38.

61. Ibid., 252, 258, 264, 265, 272, 275, 276.

62. Ibid., 278, 284, 286, 287, 288, 289, 290.

63. Ibid., 275–76.

64. Elliott, *The Old World and the New*, 100; D. A. Brading, *The First America* (Cambridge: Cambridge University Press, 1991), 65.

65. In 1580, Queen Elizabeth I's government rejected any Spanish right to the Americas based on either papal grant or scattered settlements, and as late as 1623 an Englishman could write a polemic against Alexander VI's bulls to arouse anti-Spanish feelings; see Charles M. Andrews, *The Colonial Period of American History*,

4 vols., (New Haven, CT: Yale University Press, 1934–1938), 1: 20. See below, chapter 7, where Solórzano pointed out the irony of English possession of Ireland based on papal grant, the bull *Laudabiliter* of 1155 that granted Ireland to Henry II, while denying to the Spanish possession of the New World based on a similar papal grant.

66. This is a reference to the theory of the *translatio imperii*, by which the pope crowned Charlemagne in 800 and the basis upon which the papacy claimed the right to judge the fitness of any candidate for the imperial office. On the disputes about this and the other aspects of the papacy's relationship to the emperor and the empire, see Richard Koebner, *Empire* (Cambridge: Cambridge University Press, 1966), 18–43; P. A. Van Den Baar, *Die kirkliche Lehere der Translatio Imperii Romani bis zur Mitte des 13. Jahrhunderts* (Rome: Apud Aedes Universitatis Gregorianae, 1956); Werner Goez, *Translatio Imperii* (Tübingen: J. C. B. Mohr (Paul Siebeck), 1958); Franz Bosbach, "Papsttum und Universal-monarchie im Zeitalter der Reformation," *Historisches Jahrbuch* 107(1987): 44–76; Ernst Werner, "Translatio Imperii ad Turcos: Päpstliche Renovatio und Weltkaiseridee nach dem Fall Konstantinopels," *Byzantinische Forschungen* 11(1987): 465–72. Alois Dempf, *Sacrum Imperium* (München und Berlin: R. Oldenbourg, 1929; reprint ed., 1962); P. A. van den Baar, *Die kirchliche Lehre der Translatio Imperii Romani bis zur Mitte des 13. Jahrhunderts* (Rome: Apud Aedes Universitatis Gregorianae, 1956); Robert Folz, *L'idée d'empire en Occident du Ve au XIVe siècle* (Paris: Aubier, 1953). See also Lewis, *Medieval Political Ideas*, 2: 430–66.

67. Edward Peters, *The Shadow King: Rex Inutilis in Medieval Law and Literature* (New Haven, CT: Yale University Press, 1970): 135–69.

68. Patrick McGrath, *Papists and Puritans under Elizabeth I* (London: Blandford Press, 1967): 68–72, 123. For the general background to the papacy's dealings with Elizabeth I, see C. G. Bayne, *Anglo-Roman Relations 1558–1565* (Oxford: Clarendon Press, 1913; reprint ed., University Press, 1968).

Chapter Two

1. *Select Charters and Other Documents Illustrative of American History, 1606–1775*, ed. William MacDonald (New York: Macmillan, 1899), 25. It should be noted that other charters, however, recognized the existence of a resident population and asserted jurisdiction over them in terms similar to those found in *Inter caetera*. For example, the First Charter of Virginia, 1606, following the language of *Inter caetera*, restricted English occupation to lands not already possessed by Christians and assigned to the colonists the responsibility for converting and to civilizing the Indians, *Select Charters and Other Documents*, 2; see also Seed, "Taking Possession and Reading Texts," 185–90, 208–9.

2. "That unoccupied lands become the property of the individuals who become occupants of them, unless they have been taken over as a whole by a people." Grotius, *Law of War and Peace*, 191; " . . . the idea that the lands in the New World were a *vacuum domicilium*, a wasteland, open for the taking, had wide

acceptance." Francis Paul Prucha, *The Great Father: The United States Government and the American Indians*, 2 vols. (Lincoln: University of Nebraska Press, 1984), 1: 14.

3. Christopher Columbus, *The Columbus Letter of 1493*, trans. Frank E. Robbins (Ann Arbor, MI: The Clements Library Associates, 1952), 10–11.

4. Ibid., 12, 15–16.

5. Alexander VI, *Inter caetera*, in *European Treaties Bearing on the History of the United States and its Dependencies to 1648*, ed. F. G. Davenport (Washington, DC: Carnegie Institution of Washington, 1917; reprint ed., Gloucester, MA: Peter Smith, 1967), 62.

6. Concerning the attempts of the Jesuits to establish communities that would both protect the Indians and gradually acculturate them to European ways, see Philip Caraman, *The Lost Paradise: The Jesuit Republic in South America* (New York: Seabury Press, 1976).

7. There is an extensive literature about the Indians who were settled in what became known as Praying Towns as part of the process of acculturation and Christianization; see Neal Salisbury, "Red Puritans: The 'Praying Indians' of Massachusetts and John Eliot," *William and Mary Quarterly* 31(1974): 27–54; Muldoon, "The Indian as Irishman", *Essex Institute Historical Collections*, 267–89; James P. Ronda, "Generations of Faith: The Christian Indians of Martha's Vineyard," *William and Mary Quarterly* 38(1981): 369–94; Harold W. van Lonkhuyzen, "A Reappraisal of the Praying Indians: Acculturation, Conversion, and Identity at Natick, Massachusetts, 1646–1730," *New England Quarterly* 63(1990): 396–428.

8. *De Indiarum Jure*, 2.7.1.

9. Ibid., 2.7.2.

10. Ibid., 2.7.3; 1 Cor. 14: 11.

11. Ibid., 2.7.4. On the relationship between Berber and barbarian, see "Berbers," *Encyclopaedia Britannica*, 11th ed., 29 vols. (New York: Encyclopaedia Britannica, 1910–11) 3: 764; "Barbary," *The Oxford English Dictionary*, 13 vols. (Oxford: Clarendon Press, 1933), 1:665.

12. Ibid., 2.7.5.

13. Concerning the Greek conception of the barbarian, see Edith Hall, *Inventing the Barbarian: Self-Definition through Tragedy* (Oxford: Oxford University Press, 1989), 1–6, 9–12, 160–65.

14. Tacitus, *The Agricola and the Germania*, trans. H. Mattingly, revised by S. A. Handford (Harmondsworth: Penguin Books, 1970), 72–73. By describing the deleterious effects of Romanization upon the Britons, Tacitus was also indirectly alluding to the effects of contemporary Roman imperial culture on the practice of the traditional virtues associated with the Republic.

15. See Hayden White, "The Forms of Wildness: Archaeology of an Idea," *The Wild Man Within: An Image in Western Thought from the Renaissance to Romanticism*, eds. Edward Dudley and Maximillian E. Novak (Pittsburgh: University of Pittsburgh Press, 1972), 3–38, esp. 18–25.

16. Solórzano, 2.7.6–7; concerning Marcus Varro (116–27 BC), see *The Oxford Classical Dictionary*, ed. M. Cary et al. (Oxford: Clarendon Press, 1949), 937.

17. Ibid., 2.7.15.

18. Ibid., 2.7.27.

19. Ibid., 2.7.28.

20. Ibid., 2.7.29. In recent years there has been an increasing amount of interest in Acosta and his anthropological work; see Fermin del Pino Díaz, "Humanismo renacentista y origenes de la etnologia: a proposito del P. Acosta, paradigma del humanismo antropologico jésuita," in Berta Ares et al., *Humanismo y vision del otro*: 379–429; and his "La Renaissance et le Nouveau Monde: José d'Acosta, jésuite anthropologue (1540–1600)," *L'Homme* 122–24, XXXII(1992): 309–26; John H. Rowe, "Ethnography and Ethnology in the Sixteenth Century," *The Kroeber Anthropological Society Papers* 30(Spring 1964): 1–19; Pagden, *The Fall of Natural Man*, 146–200.

21. Aristotle, *Politics*, book 1, ch. 2, trans. Benjamin Jowett in *The Basic Works of Aristotle*, ed. Richard McKeon (New York: Random House, 1941), 1129.

22. Solórzano, 2.7.29.

23. Ibid., 2.7.33.

24. Ibid.

25. Ibid. The missionary was Fray Bernardo Buil, who was assigned to convert the Indians. He was also a member of the group of Catalans who opposed Columbus and who, when he returned to Spain, "circulated the most outrageous slanders against the Columbus brothers": Samuel Eliot Morison, *Admiral of the Ocean Sea*, 2 vols. (Boston: Little, Brown, 1942), 2: 166; see also Louis-André Vigneras, "Saint Thomas, Apostle of America," *Hispanic American Historical Review* 57(1977): 82–90 at 83–84; and Paulo Emilio Taviani, *Columbus: The Great Adventure*, trans. L. F. Farina and M. A. Beckwith (New York: Orion Books, 1991), 173–74, 176–77.

Morison and Taviani refer to Buil as a member of the Benedictine Order, but the papal bull that authorized him to direct missionary activities refers to him as a Frater ordinis Minorum, that is, as a Franciscan; see *America Pontificia: Primi Saeculi Evangelizationis 1493–1592*, 2 vols., ed. Josef Metzler (Vatican City: Libreria Editrice Vaticana, 1991), 1: 84–86 at 84.

26. Solórzano, 2.7.34.

27. Ibid., 2.7.36.

28. Ibid., 2.7.38.

29. Ibid., 2.7.52.

30. Davis, *Problem of Slavery*, 33–35.

31. Solórzano, 2.7.52.

32. Ibid., 2.7.56.

33. Ibid., 2.7.66.

34. Ibid., 2.7.67.

35. Ibid., 2.7.68.

36. Ibid., 2.7.69–71. Concerning the practices associated with manumission, see W. W. Buckland, *The Roman Law of Slavery* (Cambridge: University Press, 1908), 451–52.

37. Virgil, *The Aeneid*, trans. Robert Fitzgerald (New York: Random House, 1983), book 6, lines 854–57, 190.

38. Solórzano, 2.7.76–78.

39. Ibid., 2.7.85. In this case, the term *dominium* clearly has the meaning of overlordship.

40. Ibid., 2.7.86.

41. Ibid., 2.8.3.

42. Ibid., 2.8.4.

43. Ibid., 2.8.5.

44. Margaret T. Hodgen, *Early Anthropology in the Sixteenth and Seventeenth Centuries* (Philadelphia: University of Pennsylvania Press, 1964; reprint ed., 1971), 20.

45. The literary tradition may well exaggerate the extent of belief in the existence of monstrous peoples; see James Muldoon, "The Nature of the Infidel: The Anthropology of the Canon Lawyers," *Discovering New Worlds: Essays on Medieval Exploration and Imagination*, ed. Scott D. Westrem (New York: Garland, 1991), 116–25.

46. *The Columbus Letter of 1493*, 15.

47. Solórzano, 2.8.6–7.

48. Ibid. He also cited Johann Boemus to the same end. Concerning Boemus, see Anthony Grafton, *New Worlds, Ancient Texts* (Cambridge, MA: Harvard University Press, 1992): 99–101.

49. Ibid., 2.8.16–18.

50. Genesis 1, 4. All biblical citations are from *The Holy Bible*, Revised Standard Version (Toronto, New York: Thomas Nelson, 1952). On the image of Cain see Ricardo J. Quinones, *The Changes of Cain* (Princeton, NJ: Princeton University Press, 1991), 27–29.

51. According to Augustine " . . . this earthly city's foundation was laid by a murderer of his own brother." To drive the point home even further, he pointed out that Rome also was founded by a man who killed his brother. Augustine, *City of God*, trans. John Healy, 2 vols. (London: J. M. Dent, 1945), book 15, ch. 5 2: 64–65. The consequence of this view is that coercive power within society is of divine origin because of Adam's fall and the subsequent sinful aspect of human nature. "Coercive government has been made necessary through sin, and is a divinely appointed remedy for sin." R. W. Carlyle and A. J. Carlyle, *A History of Mediaeval Political Theory in the West*, 6 vols. (Edinburgh and London: William Blackwood & Sons, 1903–1936), 1: 128; see also H.-X. Arquillière, *L'augustinisme politique: essai sur la formation des théories politiques du moyen-âge*, 2nd. ed. (Paris: J. Vrin, 1955).

52. "Whole and complete, with a rounded life of its own, the polis rises to still higher dignity than that of self-sufficiency." Aristotle, *Politics*, trans. Ernest Barker (Oxford: Clarendon Press, 1946), xlviii.

53. Solórzano, 2.8.19.

54. ibid., "propter errorem, atque inscitiam".

55. Ibid., 2.8.20.

56. Guenter Lewy, *Constitutionalism and Statecraft*: 39.

57. The Jesuits in Paraguay organized the indigenous population in what they termed *reducciós* which "may perhaps best be translated as 'community.' The Spanish *reducir* . . . meant to gather into mission settlements." C. J. McNaspy, *Lost*

Cities of Paraguay: Art and Architecture of the Jesuit Reductions 1607–1767 (Chicago: Loyola University Press, 1982), 8. "To reduce" also has the meaning of 'to call back' and in this case can also mean calling the Indians back to the normal state of human existence, Aristotle's polis. See the *OED* 8: 317–18.

58. Solórzano, 2.8.22.

59. Ibid., 2.8.23.

60. Ibid., 2.8.25.

61. Ibid., 2.8.27.

62. Ibid., 2.8.28.

63. Ibid., 2.8.29.

64. On the medieval frontier and its implications see *Medieval Frontier Societies*, ed. Robert Bartlett and Angus MacKay (Oxford: Oxford University Press, 1989); also, Robert Bartlett, *The Making of Europe: Conquest, Colonization, & Cultural Change, 950–1350* (Princeton, NJ: Princeton University Press, 1993).

65. Solórzano, 2.8.30.

66. Muldoon, "The Indian as Irishman," 275–76.

67. Solórzano, 2.8.44.

68. Ibid. Cicero, *The Letters to His Friends*, trans. W. Glynn Willams, 3 vols., Loeb Classical Library (Cambridge, MA: Harvard University Press, 1927–1954), 3: 417–19.

69. Ibid., 2.8.45.

70. Ibid., 2.8.48.

71. Ibid., 2.8.49.

72. Ibid., 2.8.50.

73. Ibid., 2.8.51: "inspecta natura, & feritate Indorum, qui in primis insulis . . . reperti sunt . . . , atque hoc colore multa damna miseris Indis generaliter a militibus irrogata fuerint."

74. In saying this, Solórzano was speaking in a fashion typical of Spanish officials who opposed the conquistadores and the threat of a feudalized aristocracy that they posed to the royal government. See Haring, *The Spanish Empire in America*, 25.

75. Solórzano, 2.8.52. "cum alii, & quidem numero plures, politicam vitam agerent, & pro captu suo propriis legibus, ac Regibus civiliter gubernarentur."

76. Ibid.

77. On Castilian immigration policy, see J. H. Elliott, *Spain and Its World 1500–1700* (New Haven, CT: Yale University Press, 1989), 11–13.

78. Solórzano, 2.8.52: "& ad quaslibet artes etiam liberales addiscendas, quas etiam ante Hispanorum adventum suo more, ac modo in aliquibus regionibus plusquam mediocriter exercebant."

79. Ibid., 2.8.53, 54.

80. Ibid., 2.8.78–79. Concerning this papal letter, see Lewis Hanke, "Pope Paul III and the American Indians"; *Harvard Theological Review* 30(1939): 65–162; see also his *Aristotle and the American Indians*, esp. 19–23; and his *All Mankind is One*, 17–22. This last includes a lengthy excerpt from the bull (p. 21).

81. Ibid., 2.8.55.

82. Ibid., 2.8.64.

83. Ibid., 2.8.65.

84. Ibid., 2.8.66–69.

85. Ibid., 2.8.80.

86. Ibid., 2.8.82.

87. Ibid., 2.8.81. According to Solórzano, the references are to the last chapter of the Book of Sophonias (Zephaniah), Book 3, and to the Book of Isaiah, chs. 42 and 64. The references to Isaiah would seem to be to Isaiah 24: 16 and 66: 19. The citations from Isaiah had also been used by Columbus; see Christopher Columbus, *The Libro de las profecías*, trans. Delno C. West and August Kling (Gainesville: University of Florida Press, 1991), 168–69, 182–85. Columbus listed the reference to Sophonias but did not quote from the book, *The Libro de las profecías*, 256–57.

88. Ibid., 2.8.83.

89. Ibid., 2.8.84.

90. Ibid., 2.8.87–88. Aristotle, *Politics*, 7.9; *Works*, 1288–89.

91. Ibid., 2.8.91.

92. Ibid., 2.8.92.

93. Ibid., 2.8.95–96. Concerning the forms of writing in the Americas, see James Lockhart, *The Nahuas After the Conquest* (Stanford, CA: Stanford University Press, 1992): 326–34; on the Inca mode of recording information on *quipus*, "knotted strings of different lengths, different numbers of knots, and different colours," see Garcilaso de la Vega, El Inca, *Royal Commentaries of the Incas*, trans. Harold V. Livermore, 2 vols. (Austin: University of Texas Press, 1966), 1: xi–xii.

94. Ibid., 2.8.97.

95. Ibid., 2.8.98. This is not modern Albania but "the land . . . adjacent to the eastern Caucasus and the western Caspian . . . ." *Oxford Classical Dictionary*, 28.

96. Ibid., 2.8.99–100.

97. Ibid., 2.8.101. Strabo, *The Geography*, trans. H. L. Jones, 8 vols., Loeb Classical Library (Cambridge, MA: Harvad University Press, 1917–1932), 2: 109.

98. Ibid., 2.8.102–3.

99. Ibid., 2.8.104–5. See Garcilaso de la Vega, El Inca, *Royal Commentaries of the Incas*, 1: 561.

100. Ibid., 2.8.107–8.

101. Ibid., 2.8.110–2. Julius Caesar, *Gallic War*, trans. F. P. Long (Oxford: Clarendon Press, 1911), bk. 5, ch. 15, p.129.

102. Ibid., 2.8.109.

103. Ibid., 2.8.113–4. Concerning the Roman practice of painting the bodies of emperors, see Pliny, *Natural History*, trans. H. Rackham, W. H. S. Jones, D. E. Eichholz, 10 vols., The Loeb Classical Library (Cambridge, MA: Harvard University Press, 1949–1962), 9,book 33, ch. 36: 85–87. Solórzano cited it as Pliny, book 33, ch. 7.

104. Ibid., 2.8.115.

105. Ibid., 2.8.117.

106. Ibid., 2.8.118.

107. Ibid., 2.8.119.

108. Ibid., 2.8.125.

109. Ibid., 2.8.126.
110. Ibid., 2.8.127.
111. Ibid., 2.8.125. The reference is to Augustine, *The City of God*, 5: 17, p. 164.

Chapter Three

1. Aristotle, *Politics*, bk. 1, ch. 5; *The Basic Works*: 1132–33. Curiously, he does not cite Sepúlveda at this point.

2. The comparison with the Romans was a common one in the sixteenth and seventeenth centuries. The English, for example, described their conquest of Ireland in the same terms. See Muldoon, "The Indian as Irishman," 275–77, 279.

3. Solórzano, 2.9.1. He had provided an excerpt from this bull in 2.8.78–79.

4. Solórzano, 2.9.1–2.

5. Ibid., 2.9.3.

6. Ibid., 2.9.4.

7. Concerning Acosta and his role in the development of comparative studies, see Pagden, *The Fall of Natural Man*, esp. 146–200. Hodgen pointed out that "Acosta's *Natural and Moral History of the Indies* . . . was published and republished, translated and retranslated, before the end of the sixteenth century. . . ." Hodgen, *Early Anthropology*, 209.

8. Solórzano, 2.9.9.

9. Ibid., 2.9.10.

10. Ibid., 2.9.11.

11. Ibid., 2.9.16–17.

12. Ibid., 2.9.18.

13. Ibid., 2.9.30.

14. Ibid., 2.13.66. Here Solórzano refers to their "ancient kingdoms and empires." See also 2.12.25, 2.2.65.

15. On the meaning of *imperium*, see Koebner, *Empire*, 4.

16. Ibid., 2.14.46.

17. In addition, Solórzano discussed in various places the Roman Empire as found in Roman and canon law. He also described Christian society as the Christian Republic: Koebner, *Empire*, 2.14.9.

18. Concerning the military basis of the Aztec *Empire*, see Inga Clendinnen, "The Cost of Courage in Aztec Society," *Past & Present* 107 (May, 1985): 44–89. For an introduction to the current literature on the Aztecs and the Incas, see the thoughtful review by Benjamin Keen, "Recent Writings on the Spanish Conquest," *Latin American Research Review* 20(1985): 161–71.

19. See Pagden, *Fall of Natural Man*, 167.

20. Ibid.: 140. Cicero, *De inventione*, trans. H. M. Hubbell, Loeb Classical Library (Cambridge, MA: Harvard University Press, 1949); bk. 1, chs. 2, 3: 5–8.

21. Rowe, "Ethnography and Ethnology," 9.

22. Solórzano, 2.9.13.

23. Ibid., 2.9.16.

24. Ibid., 2.9.18.

25. Ibid., 2.9.19.

26. Ibid., 2.9.20.

27. Ibid.

28. Ibid., 2.8.52; see ch. 4, note 31.

29. Ibid., 2.9.23.

30. Ibid., 2.9.24. Very similar language is to be found in papal-royal correspondence dealing with the Portuguese invasion of the Canary Islands in the early-fifteenth century; see James Muldoon, "A Fifteenth-Century Application of the Canonistic Theory of the Just War," *Proceedings of the Fourth International Congress of Medieval Canon Law* (Vatican City: Biblioteca Apostolica Vaticana, 1976), 467–80 at 469–70.

31. Ibid., 2.9.26.

32. Ibid., 2.9.27.

33. Ibid., 2.9.29.

34. Ibid., 2.9.30.

35. Ibid., 2.9.31.

36. Ibid., 2.9.39.

37. On the early development of theories of social contract, see Carlyle and Carlyle, *History of Mediaeval Political Theory*, 3: 160–69; 5: 471–72.

38. Solórzano, 2.9.42.

39. Ibid., 2.9.47–54.

40. Ibid., 2.9.55.

41. Ibid., 2.9.56.

42. Ibid., 2.9.57.

43. Ibid., 2.9.58–59.

44. Ibid., 2.9.60.

45. Ibid., 2.9.62.

46. Ibid., 2.9.64.

47. Ibid., 2.9.65.

48. Ibid., 2.9.66–67.

49. Ibid., 2.9.71.

50. Ibid., 2.9.72–73.

51. Ibid., 2.9.75.

Chapter Four

1. The most convenient introduction to the notion of natural law is A. P. d'Entrèves, *Natural Law* (London: Hutchinson University Library, 1951). The basic work on natural law in the thinking of the canon lawyers is Rudolf Weigand, *Die Naturrechtslehre der Legisten und Dekretisten von Irnerius bis Accursius und von Gratian bis Johannes Teutonicus* (München: Hueber, 1967). Other standard works include Heinrich A. Rommen, *The Natural Law: A Study in Legal and Social History*, trans. Thomas R. Hanley (St. Louis: B. Herder, 1949); Michael B. Crowe, *The*

Changing Profile of the Natural Law (The Hague: Nijhoff, 1977); Francis Oakley, *Natural Law, Conciliarism and Consent in the Late Middle Ages* (London: Variorum, 1984).

2. *Digest*, Bk.1, tit. 1, in d'Entrèves, *Natural Law*: 25.

3. Ibid.

4. P. D. King, "The Barbarian Kingdoms," in *Cambridge History of Medieval Political Thought*, 123–53 at 141.

5. Carlyle and Carlyle, *History of Mediaeval Political Thought*, 1: 117.

6. Romans 2: 12–14. See Carlyle and Carlyle, *History of Mediaeval Political Theory*, 1: 82–83.

7. On the revival of Roman law, see Stephan Kuttner, "The Revival of Jurisprudence," *Renaissance and Renewal in the Twelfth Century*, ed. Robert L. Benson and Giles Constable (Cambridge, MA: Harvard University Press, 1982): 299–323.

8. *Decretum*, D.1.cc. 7,9 in *Corpus Iuris Canonici*, ed. A. Friedberg, 2 vols. (Leipzig: Tauchnitz, 1879, 1881; reprint ed. Graz: Akademische Druck- und Verlagsanstalt, 1959), 1.

9. *Summa Theologiae* I-II, q. 91, art. 2. The translation is from Ewart Lewis, *Medieval Political Ideas*, 2 vols. (New York: Knopf, 1954), 1: 49. There are several other anthologies that provide the text of Aquinas's discussion on the nature of law. These include *The Political Ideas of St. Thomas Aquinas*, ed. Dino Bigongiari (New York: Hafner, 1957); and *Aquinas: Selected Political Writings*, ed. A. P. d'Entrèves (Oxford: Basil Blackwell, 1954).

10. Solórzano, 2.12.

11. Ibid., 2.12.3. "Ubi refert aliqua scelera, quae ab Indis ferino more, & contra legem, & rationem naturalem perpetrabantur. . . ."

12. Ibid., 2.13.68. The reference is to *Summa Theologiae* I-II.q.94; see Lewis, *Medieval Political Ideas*, 1: 52–56.

13. Ibid., 2.13.69.

14. Ibid., 2.13.70. The reference is to Augustine, *Confessions*, bk. 2, c. 4, trans. Henry Chadwick (Oxford: Oxford University Press, 1991), 28.

15. Ibid., 2.12.1.

16. Ibid., 2.12.2. The reference is to Genesis 19.

17. Vitoria, "On the American Indians," 287–88. Curiously, although Solórzano cited more than a score of references at this point, he did not cite Vitoria.

18. Solórzano, 2.12.3.

19. *European Treaties*, p. 76. On Columbus's view of the peoples whom he encountered, see Muldoon, "Columbus's First Voyage," 16–20. Solórzano included a copy of one of these bulls, 2.24.16.

20. Solórzano, 2.12.4.

21. Ibid., 2.12.5. One would like to know how Solórzano saw the situation of Spanish peasants at the same time. An Aztec or Inca visitor to Castile might have said the same about conditions there.

22. Ibid., 2.12.6–8.

23. Aristotle, *Politics*, book 5, ch. 11, *Works*, 1258.

24. Solórzano, 2.12.12.

25. Solórzano, 2.12.9–11. There is an extensive literature on the distinction between the king and the tyrant in medieval political thought; see, for example, Carlyle and Carlyle, *History of Mediaeval Political Theory*, 3: 137–42; 5: 89–99; Jean Dunbabin, "Government," *The Cambridge History of Medieval Political Thought c. 350–c. 1450*, ed. J. H. Burns (Cambridge: Cambridge University Press, 1988), 477–519 at 493–98.

26. Solórzano, 2.12.20.

27. Ibid., 2.12.21–22.

28. Vitoria, "On the American Indians," 275–76.

29. Solórzano, 2.12.23–24.

30. Ibid., 2.12.25.

31. Ibid., 2.12.26.

32. Ibid., 2.12.35.

33. Ibid., 2.12.39. The question of cannibalism among the inhabitants of the Americas has received a great deal of attention in recent years. Kirkpatrick Sale has argued that the occasions of cannibalism were greatly exaggerated from the very beginning of Spanish contacts with the New World; see *Conquest*, esp. 129–40 and the accompanying bibliographical notes.

34. Ibid., 2.12.56, 59.

35. Ibid., 2.12.61.

36. Ibid., 2.12.62.

37. Ibid., 2.12.63.

38. Ibid., 2.12.64–72. For example, he cited Cicero and Quintillian, among others.

39. Ibid., 2.12.101.

40. Ibid., 2.12.102.

41. Ibid., 2.12.106.

42. Ibid., 2.12.112.

43. Ibid., 2.12.114.

44. Ibid., 2.13.1.

45. Ibid., 2.13.2.

46. Ibid., 2.13.3.

47. Ibid., 2.13.5.

48. Ibid., 2.13.6.

49. Ibid., 2.13.8.

50. Ibid., 2.13.12.

51. Ibid., 2.13.22.

52. Ibid., 2.13.32.

53. Ibid., 2.13.36.

54. Ibid., 2.13.68.

55. Ibid., 2.13.73.

56. Ibid., 2.13.75–76.

57. Ibid., 2.13.77.

58. Ibid., 2.14.2.

59. Ibid., 2.14.4.

60. Ibid., 2.14.5.

61. Ibid., 2.14.7.
62. Ibid., 2.14.9.
63. Ibid., 2.14.13.
64. Ibid., 2.14.16.
65. Ibid., 2.14.18.
66. Ibid., 2.14.19.
67. Ibid., 2.14.24.
68. Ibid., 2.14.29. The obvious case of Christian toleration of the practices of non-Christians in the Middle Ages was Spain with its large subject populations of Jews and Muslims. On the nature of the relations between the Catholic monarchs of the Spanish kingdoms and their Jewish and Muslim subjects, the so-called *convivencia*, see J. N. Hillgarth, *The Spanish Kingdoms 1250–1516*, 2 vols. (Oxford: Clarendon Press, 1976–78), 2: 126–69.
69. Solórzano, 2.14.30.
70. Ibid., 2.14.31.
71. Ibid., 2.14.33.
72. Ibid., 2.14.34.
73. Ibid., 2.14.38.
74. Ibid., 2.14.53.
75. Ibid., 2.14.54–55.
76. Ibid., 2.14.61–64.
77. Ibid., 2.14.70.
78. Ibid., 2.14.71–72.
79. Ibid., 2.14.74.
80. Ibid., 2.14.76–92.
81. Ibid., 2.14.93.
82. Ibid., 2.14.101.
83. Ibid., 2.14.109.
84. Ibid., 2.14.111.
85. Ibid., 2.14.112–13.
86. Ibid., 2.14.114.
87. Ibid., 2.15.3.
88. Ibid., 2.15.26.
89. Ibid., 2.15.47.
90. Ibid., 2.15.48.
91. Ibid., 2 15.50.
92. Ibid., 2.15.52.
93. Ibid., 2.15.53.

Chapter Five

1. Solórzano, 2.22. The precise nature of the grant Alexander VI made in *Inter caetera* has been the subject of some controversy; see H. Van der Linden, "Alexander VI and the Demarcation of the Maritime and Colonial Domains of Spain and Portugal, 1493–94," *American Historical Review* 22(1916–17): 1–20;

E. Staedler, "Die 'donatio Alexandrina' und die 'divisio mundi' von 1493," *Archiv für katholisches kirchenrecht* 117(1937): 363–402, and "Die urkunde Alexanders VI zur westindischen Investitur der Krone Spanien von 1493," *Archiv für Urkunden-forschung* 15(1937): 145–58; Luis Weckmann, "The Alexandrine Bulls of 1493: Pseudo-Asiatic Documents," *First Images of America*, ed. Fredi Chiappelli, 2 vols. (Berkeley: University of California Press, 1976), 1: 201–9.

2. The most extensive work on the deep roots of *Inter caetera* in medieval papal thought and practice is Luis Weckmann, *Las Bulas Alejandrinas de 1493 y la Teoriá Política del Papado Medieval* (México: Editorial Jus, 1949). Weckmann summarized his conclusions in "Alexandrine Bulls," *New Catholic Encyclopedia* 1: 306.

3. Solórzano, 2.22.1.

4. Samuel Eliot Morison, *The European Discovery of America: The Northern Voyages* (New York: Oxford University Press, 1971), 159–60.

5. Ibid., 435.

6. The legal advisors of Henry VII and Francis I may also have pointed out to their respective employers the cliché that to be valid, a law must be enforceable and enforced. Seeing *Inter caetera* as a law, the lawyers could simply point out that the division of the world between Portugal and Castile was unenforceable and thus not binding on any other ruler who chose to support voyages of discovery. As late as the early eighteenth century, the Spanish were claiming a monopoly of the New World based on *Inter caetera*. Charles M. Andrews suggested that Henry VII may have had some hesitation about infringing on the Spanish monopoly, at least with regard to lands that the Spanish actually occupied; see Andrews, *Colonial Period*, 1: 19–20. When French explorers were attempting to establish a permanent base on the Mississippi River, the Spanish monarch, Philip V, complained to Louis XIV that such activity was a violation of the bull's terms. Louis XIV responded that "he was bound, as a son of Holy Church, to convert the Indians and keep out the English heretics." Francis Parkman, *Half Century of Conflict*, Centenary edition, 2 vols. (Boston: Little, Brown, and Company, 1927), 1: 305.

7. Luther, for example, publicly burned volumes of the canon law to demonstrate his opinion of the law and the place of the pope in it; see Preserved Smith, *The Life and Letters of Martin Luther* (Boston: Houghton Mifflin, 1911), 100–101.

8. This did not mean, however, that Protestant rulers rejected similar claims for themselves. The charters that English kings granted to the colonists of North America employed much of the same language as well as the same claims contained in *Inter caetera*. See, for example, the charters for Virginia and Massachusetts in *English Historical Documents*, vol. IX, *American Colonial Documents to 1776*, ed. Merrill Jensen (New York: Oxford University Press, 1955): 65–84. Both charters forbade the colonists from taking possession of land already held by a Christian ruler and insisted that the conversion of the Indians to Christianity was an important goal of the settlement. The language in each case is almost identical with that of *Inter caetera*; see Seed, "Taking Possession": 201–2, 208–9.

9. Andrews, *Colonial Period*, 1: 20. Until Grotius's *Mare liberum*, which appeared in 1609, there seems to have been no extended Protestant critique of *Inter caetera*. Protestants may have believed that their fundamental assault on the papacy's pretensions was sufficient to destroy the underlying basis of Alexander VI's actions.

10. Solórzano, 2.22.2.

11. Ibid., 2.22.4.

12. For the history of the image of the two swords, see Carlyle and Carlyle, *History of Mediaeval Political Theory*, 4: 333–36. There is a very good introduction to the issues involved in Lewis, *Medieval Political Ideas*, 2: 506–615. Most recently, see I. S. Robinson, "Church and Papacy," *Cambridge History of Medieval Political Thought c. 350–c. 1450*, 252–305 at 300–305; and J. A. Watt, "Spiritual and Temporal Powers," *Cambridge History of Medieval Political Thought c. 350–c. 1450*, 367–423 at 370–74. The origin of the usage is in the writings of Bernard of Clairvaux (1090–1153); for the text, see Brian Tierney, *The Crisis of Church & State 1050–1300*: 92–94. John Calvin, whose thought was deeply indebted to medieval thinkers, also used the image of the sword but without mentioning Bernard; see Charles A. M. Hall, *With the Spirit's Sword* (Richmond, VA: John Knox Press, 1968): 174–76; and Ralph C. Hancock, *Calvin and the Foundations of Modern Politics* (Ithaca, NY: Cornell University Press, 1989), 55–61.

13. Solórzano, 2.22.4.

14. *Decretum*, D. 22, c. 1, *Omnes*, and c. 25, q. 1., c. 5, *Violatores*.

15. In the next chapter, 2.23.119–20, Solórzano excerpted approximately two-thirds of the bull's text, beginning with the discussion of the two swords; for a translation of the bull, see Tierney, *Crisis*, 188–89.

16. While Solórzano appears to have seen *Unam sanctam* as an extreme assertion of papal power, it may be argued that he, along with many others, failed to appreciate the fact that the substance of the letter was not as extreme as its rhetoric might have suggested. See James Muldoon, "Boniface VIII's Forty Years of Experience in the Law," *Jurist* 31(1971): 449–77; and "Boniface VIII as Defender of Royal Power: *Unam Sanctam* as a Basis for the Spanish Conquest of the Americas," *Popes, Teachers, and Canon Law in the Middle Ages*, ed. James Ross Sweeney and Stanley Chodorow (Ithaca, NY: Cornell University Press, 1989), 62–73.

17. Solórzano, 2.22.5.

18. The *Decretum*, D. 96, ch. 14, contains part of the Donation, although Gratian, the original compiler, had not included it. There is an extensive literature on the Donation; see D. Maffei, *La donazione di Cosantino nei giuristi medievali* (Milan: Giuffrè, 1964). For an introduction to Lorenzo Valla's famous criticism of the document that demonstrated that it was a forgery, see Lorenzo Valla, *The Profession of the Religious and the Principal Arguments from The Falsely-Believed and Forged Donation of Constantine*, trans. and ed., Olga Zorzi Pugliese (Toronto: Centre for Reformation and Renaissance Studies, 1985). For the text of the Donation, see *Documents of the Christian Church*, 2nd ed., ed. Henry Bettenson (New York: Oxford University Press, 1963), 135–40.

19. Solórzano, 2.22.5.

20. Ibid., 2.22.6.

21. Ibid., 2.22.7.

22. Ibid., 2.22.11.

23. On Dante's political views, see Thomas G. Bergin, *Dante* (Boston: Houghton Mifflin Company, 1965), 177–94.

24. Solórzano, 2.22.12.

25. Muldoon, *Popes, Lawyers*, 124–31. The text of the *consilia* has been published: see *Monumenta Henricina* V (Coimbra: Comissao Executiva das Comemoracoes do V Centinário da Morte do Infante D. Henrique, 1963), 285–343. I wish to thank Dr. Anthony Pagden for this reference. There is a brief notice about Rosellis in DDC 7: 731–32.

26. Solórzano, 2.22.13.

27. *Venerabilem* was included in the *Decretales*, 1.6.34, *Corpus Iuris Canonici*, vol. 2. There is a translation in Tierney, *Crisis*, 133–34. Innocent III had produced *Venerabilem* as a result of the civil war in Germany following the death of Henry VI in 1197. The materials which he gathered in the course of the struggle and on the basis of which he developed the theory of papal-imperial relations spelled out in the bull formed a single papal register and provides an interesting insight into the way in which a pope reached a decision in an important legal-political matter. Innocent III, *Regestum super negotio Romani Imperii*, ed. F. Kempf (Rome: Pontificia Università Gregoriana, 1947).

28. Solórzano, 2.22.14. The reference is to the *Decretum*, D. 63, c. 22, Adrianus.

29. Ibid., 2.22.15.

30. Ibid., 2.22.16. The basic work on Gallicanism is Victor Martin, *Les origines du Gallicanisme*, 2 vols. (Paris: Bloud & Gay, 1939).

31. The fundamental book on the conciliar movement is Brian Tierney, *Foundations of the Conciliar Theory* (Cambridge: Cambridge University Press, 1955).

32. Solórzano, 2.22.17.

33. Ibid., 2.22.18.

34. Ibid., 2.22.20.

35. Ibid., 2.22.21. For the literature on the *translatio*, see Chapter 1, note 72.

36. Ibid., 2.22.24.

37. Ibid., 2.22.25–26, 28. On Bartolus, see C. N. S. Woolf, *Bartolus of Sassoferrato* (Cambridge: Cambridge University Press, 1913).

38. Ibid., 2.22.26.

39. Ibid., 2.22.27. As noted previously, Huss was also condemned for asserting that *dominium* depended upon grace, a view that was in turn based on the ancient Donatist heresy. Muldoon, *Popes, Lawyers*, 110–12.

40. Ibid., 2.22.28.

41. Ibid., 2.22.29.

42. Ibid., 2.22.30. The empire was not in fact a papal fief, although Solórzano and others referred to it as such. On one famous occasion in the twelfth century, when a papal representative did refer to the Empire as a *beneficium*, a word that could be translated as "fief", the assembled German nobles responded violently to the suggestion; see Morris, *Papal Monarchy*, 191–92. Excerpts from the basic documents are in Tierney, *Crisis*, 105–9. For a brief discussion of the events commemorated in the fresco, see Morris: 186–87.

43. Solórzano, 2.22.31. For a more complete picture of Henry IV's submission to Rome, see Mark Greengrass, *France in the Age of Henri IV* (London: Longman, 1984), 68–85.

44. Ibid., 32.

45. In reality, the situation was rather different. Henry IV had authorized further French penetration of Canada in spite of *Inter caetera* and there was, according to one historian, "a verbal agreement . . . between Spain and France, whereby the continual state of war between the two countries in the Americas would be allowed to continue without endangering the peace in Europe." Henry Folmer, *Franco-Spanish Rivalry in North America, 1524–1763* (Glendale, CA: Arthur H. Clark, 1953): 125, 128.

46. Solórzano, 2.22.34.

47. Ibid.

48. Ibid. 2.22.35.

49. Ibid., 2.22.37–38. Louis the Pious's renunciation was also in the *Decretum*, D. 63, c. 30, *Ego Lodovicus*.

50. Ibid., 2.22.39. The figure of 342 years could in fact only refer to Charlemagne's accession to the Frankish throne in 771, not his death in 814. These canons were in fact not Sigebert's creations. They appear to have been created around 1084 to support the claims of bishops of Ravenna against the increasing power of the reforming papacy of the eleventh and twelfth centuries and reflect "the Ravennese case against the Gergorian [sic] papacy." Sigebert was one of the leading opponents of the Gregorian reform movement and supported "the traditional rights of the church of Liège and the authority of the Salian emperor" against Gregorian claims of papal superiority. On the other hand, he "sympathized with the objectives of the papal reform movement." I. S. Robinson, *Authority and Resistance in the Investiture Contest* (New York: Holmes & Meier, 1978), 160, 175.

51. Solórzano, 2.22.39. The reference is to D. 63, c. 34, *Sacrorum*. Solórzano provided the text of this short canon at this point.

52. Ibid., 2.22.40–41.

53. Ibid., 2.22.42.

54. Ibid., 2.22.43.

55. Ibid., 2.22.45.

56. Ibid., 2.22.46.

57. On Innocent IV's reputation, see Muldoon, *Popes, Lawyers*, 126. Frederick Maitland, it might be added, described Innocent IV as "the greatest lawyer that ever sat upon the chair of Peter." Muldoon, *Popes, Lawyers*, x. The most recent study of Innocent IV's thought is Alberto Melloni, *Innocenzo IV: La concezione e l'esperienza della cristianità come regimen unius personae* (Genoa: Marietti, 1990).

58. Solórzano, 2.22.47.

59. 2.22.50–51.

60. Ibid., 2.22.50–51.

61. Ibid., 2.22.52. The decretal involved was 4.17.13, *Per venerabilem*. On this decretal, see Brian Tierney, "'Tria Quippe Distinguit Iudicia . . ?' A Note on Innocent III's Decretal *Per venerablem*," *Speculum* 37(1962): 48–59.

62. Solórzano, 2.22.54.

63. Ibid., 2.22.56. Concerning Gregory VII's battle with Henry IV, see Karl F. Morrison, "Canossa: A Revision," *Traditio* 18(1962): 121–48.

64. Ibid., 2.22.57. Solórzano identifies him as Ferdinand V, clearly a typographical error for Ferdinand II. Concerning the acquisition of Navarre by Ferdinand, see Merriman, *Rise*, 2: 340–49.

65. Ibid., 2.22.58.

66. Concerning this and other papal criticisms of medieval Spanish rulers, see: Elena Lourie, "Free Moslems in the Balearics Under Christian Rule in the Thirteenth Century," *Speculum* 45(1970): 624–49, esp. 628–29; Hillgarth, *The Spanish Kingdoms*, 1: 167–71.

Chapter Six

1. Solórzano, 2.23.1.

2. Ibid.

3. Ibid., 2.10.41.

4. Ibid., 2.23.2.

5. Ibid., 2.23.3.

6. Ibid., 2.23.4. Ambrosius Catharinus (c. 1484–1553) was a Dominican theologian and bishop: see *New Catholic Encyclopedia* 1: 377.

7. Ibid., 2.23.5.

8. Ibid.

9. Ibid.

10. Ibid.

11. It has been suggested that Innocent III sought to develop the papal policy of obtaining feudal overlordship of various kingdoms in order to have another means of exercising power over Christian rulers: see A. Luchaire, *Innocent III*, 6 vols. (Paris: Hachette, 1905–1908), 5, *Les Royautés vassales de Saint-Siège*. On the other hand, Carlyle and Carlyle, *History of Mediaeval Political Theory*, 5: 183–86, argue that Innocent III did not rely on feudal overlordship in any significant way. Innocent III certainly did see the pope as the supreme arbiter of disputes between Christian rulers. Concerning his complicated relations with King John of England, see C. R. Cheney, *Pope Innocent III and England* (Stuttgart: Hiersemann, 1976). On the pope as arbiter and mediator, see Walter Ullmann, "The Medieval Papal Court as an International Tribunal," *Virginia Journal of International Law* 11(1971): 356–71. For a convenient introduction to the scholarly debate about Innocent's conception of his role and power, see *Innocent III: Vicar of Christ or Lord of the World?* ed. James M. Powell (Boston: D. C. Heath, 1963).

12. Solórzano, 2.23.10.

13. Concerning Benzoni, see the article in the *New Catholic Encyclopedia* 2: 317. Solórzano's description of Benzoni as a heretic would seem to have been based on the fact that Benzoni's record of his travels in the New World "supplied the main ammunition to the foreign detractors of Spain who instigated the so-called Black Legend." Bartolomé de Las Casas, *History of the Indies*, trans. and ed. Andrée Collard (New York: Harper & Row, 1971), xi, n. 2, "Heretic" was, after all, about the worst epithet that Solórzano could hurl at anyone.

14. See also Susan Milbrath, "Old World Meets New: Views Across the Atlantic," *First Encounters: Spanish Explorations in the Caribbean and the United States, 1492–1570*, ed. Jerald T. Milanich and Susan Milbrath (Gainesville: University Presses of Florida, 1989); 183–210 at 196. For a brief excerpt from Benzoni, see *The Black Legend*, ed. Charles Gibson (New York: Knopf, 1969); 78–89. Solórzano,

2.23.11. Garcilaso de la Vega, however, identifies the ruler as Atahuallpa and terms this story "fabulous and may be set down to the false and flattering reports given to the historians." *Royal Commentaries*, 2: 688–89.

15. This took place in 1562. See Samuel Eliot Morison, *The European Discovery of America: The Southern Voyages* (New York: Oxford University Press, 1974), 593–95.

16. Solórzano, 2.23.12.

17. On the history of the *Mare liberum* see J. B. Scott, "Introduction" to Grotius, *The Freedom of the Seas*, v–vi. This edition has the Latin original and the English translation on facing pages. It was a response to a treatise defending Portuguese control of the Indian Ocean by Frei Serafin de Freitas, *Do justo império Asiático dos Portugueses*.

18. Solórzano, 2.23.13. Solórzano has correctly identified the chapters of the *Mare Liberum* that deal with papal claims to jurisdiction over infidels, suggesting that he may have actually seen the text. Cardinal Sandoval, the inquisitor general of Spain, issued a list of forbidden books in 1612; see George Haven Putnam, *The Censorship of the Church of Rome*, 2 vols. (New York: G. P. Putnam Sons, 1906–1907), 1: 282–85.

19. Ibid., 2.23.15.

20. Ibid., 2.23.17.

21. Ibid., 2.23.18.

22. Ibid., 2.23.19.

23. Ibid., 2.23.20.

24. Ibid., 2.23.22. Concerning Jerome, see *New Catholic Encyclopedia* 7: 872–74.

25. Ibid., 2.23.23.

26. Ibid., 2.23.25.

27. Ibid., 2.23.27–28.

28. Ibid., 2.23.29. By phrasing the question of Christ's and the Apostles' possession of goods in these terms, Solórzano could emphasize their poverty without denying them the right to possess goods. In this way he avoided the problem that rocked the Franciscan order in the late Middle Ages, the problem of whether Christians, especially the clergy, could legitimately own property. The extremists held that Christ and His Apostles did not possess property, and so neither should the Church. The extreme position was eventually condemned as heretical, but continued to surface among those who opposed the Church. On the issue of Christ's poverty, see John Moorman, *A History of the Franciscan Order from Its Origins to the Year 1517* (Oxford: Oxford University Press, 1968), 307–19.

29. Ibid., 2.23.30.

30. Ibid., 2.23.34.

31. Ibid., 2.23.35.

32. Ibid., 2.23.37–38.

33. Ibid., 2.23.39. A convenient introduction to Bernard of Clairvaux's thought on the two swords, along with excerpts from his writings, is Tierney, *Crisis*, 88, 92–94. In addition, see I. S. Robinson, "Church and Papacy," in *The Cambridge History of Medieval Political Thought, c. 350–c. 1450*: 252–305 at 300–305.

34. Ibid., 2.23.42.

35. Ibid., 2.23.44. Solórzano takes this phrase from the *Decretum*, D. 96 c. 10 *Duo sunt*. There is an extensive modern literature on the meaning of this phrase; see Robinson, "Church and Papacy," 288–300. For an excerpt from the text, see Tierney, *Crisis*, 13–14.

36. Ibid., 2.23.45. The decretal *Solitae* is in the *Decretales*, 1.33.6.

37. Solórzano, 2.23.50.

38. Ibid., 2.23.51.

39. Ibid., 2.23.52.

40. Ibid., 2.23.54.

41. Ibid., 2.23.55.

42. Ibid., 2.23.53.

43. Ibid., 2.23.59.

44. Ibid., 2.23.71.

45. Ibid., 2.23.77.

46. Ibid., 2.23.89.

47. Ibid., 2.23.91.

48. Ibid., 2.23.92.

49. Ibid., 2.23.104.

50. Ibid., 2.23.109. Concerning Scotus, see *New Catholic Encyclopedia* 10: 783.

51. Ibid., 2.23. 112.

52. Ibid., 2.23.113.

53. Ibid., 2.23.115.

54. Ibid., 2.23.114. The reference is to Jeremiah 1:10.

55. Ibid., 2.23.115.

56. Ibid., 2.23.117.

57. Ibid., 2.23.118.

58. Ibid., 2.23.119.

59. Ibid., 2.23.120.

60. Ibid., 2.23.127.

61. Ibid., 2.23.128.

62. Ibid., 2.23.129.

63. Ibid., 2.23.132.

64. Ibid., 2.23.133. He cites Ausonius, epig. 20 as a source, although it would appear that it is from one of Aesop's fables. It would also seem to be the same story that Shakespeare's Henry V used in response to the French demand for his surrender on the eve of Agincourt. See William Shakespeare, *Henry V*, ed. Gary Taylor (Oxford: Oxford University Press, 1984), 4.3, lines 91–95 and explanatory note.

65. Ibid., 2.23.138–139.

66. Ibid., 2.23.141.

67. Ibid., 2.23.142. In the 1777 edition, this paragraph is erroneously numbered 132.

68. Solórzano, 2.23.143.

69. Innocent IV, *Commentaria, ad* 2.2.10.

70. Solórzano, 2.23.146.

71. Ibid., 2.23.150.

72. Ibid., 2.23.153.

73. Ibid., 2.23.157.

74. Ibid., 2.23.158.

75. Ibid., 2.23.159.

76. Ibid., 2.23.160.

77. Ibid., 2.23.161.

78. Ibid., 2.23.163.

79. Ibid., 2.23.164. He again cited Innocent III's decretal 2.2.10, *Licet*, at the beginning of his list of citations here. For a brief excerpt from this letter, see Tierney, *Crisis*: 138.

80. Ibid., 2.23.165.

81. Ibid., 2.23.166.

82. Ibid., 2.23.167. The argument is from 1.33.6, *Solitae*.

83. Ibid., 2.23.168.

84. Ibid., 2.23.171–72.

85. The terms "dualist" and "hierocratic" came into widespread use with the work of Walter Ullmann, who argued that the medieval popes and the canon lawyers who served them were hierocrats. Ullmann's views have not been generally accepted by those who work in the field of canon law studies. For an introduction to the debate, see Francis Oakley, "Celestial Hierarchies Revisited: Walter Ullmann's Vision of Medieval Politics," *Past & Present* 60 (August, 1973): 3–48. For some more recent observations, see James Burns, "Introduction," *Cambridge History of Mediaeval Political Thought c. 350–c. 1450*, 1–8; and Jeannine Quillet, "Community, Counsel and Representation," ibid., 520–72 at 555.

86. The standard English edition is Marsiglio of Padua, *The Defender of the Peace*, trans. Alan Gewirth (New York: Columbia University Press, 1956). See the important review of this volume by Brian Tierney, *The Catholic Historical Review* 43(1957): 186–87.

87. Of course, the Protestants rejected not only any papal jurisdiction in temporal matters but in spiritual ones as well, and demanded the abolition of the papal office; see, for example, Martin Luther, "To the Christian Nobility of the German Nation," trans. Charles M. Jacobs, revised by James Atkinson, *Three Treatises*, 2nd rev. ed. (Philadelphia: Fortress Press, 1970), 1–112 at 12–16. In the Act in Restraint of Appeals, April, 1533, Henry VIII similarly rejected papal overlordship in temporal affairs; see R. Koebner, "'The Imperial Crown of this Realm:' Henry VIII, Constantine the Great, and Polydore Vergil," *Bulletin of the Institute of Historical Research* 26(1953): 29–52.

Chapter Seven

1. E. N. van Kleffens, *Hispanic Law Until the End of the Middle Ages* (Edinburgh: Edinburgh University Press, 1968), 36–38.

2. Solórzano, 2.24.1.

3. Ibid., 2.24.2. On Baldus, see J. P. Canning, *The Political Thought of Baldus de Ubaldis* (Cambridge: Cambridge University Press, 1987).

4. Ibid., 2.24.4.

5. Ibid., 2.24.5.

6. Ibid., 2.24.6–7.

7. Ibid., 2.24.8.

8. Ibid., 2.24.9.

9. Ibid., 2.24.11.

10. Ibid., 2.24.12.

11. Ibid., 2.24.13.

12. Ibid., 2.24.14.

13. Ibid., 2.24.15. The 1777 edition has an obvious typographical error that dates *Inter caetera* as 1403, not 1493. The phrase *plenitudo potestatis* was one of the most important in the development of the theory of papal power; see Robinson, "Church and Papacy," 282–88; Pennington, "Law, Legislative Authority and Theories of Government, 1150–1300," *The Cambridge History of Medieval Political Thought c. 350–c. 1450*, 424–53 at 430–36; Morris, *Papal Monarchy*, 205–10.

14. The Latin texts of all these bulls, along with English translations, are to be found in *European Treaties*. The first version of *Inter caetera* is doc. 5: 56–63. In addition, there is the bull *Eximiae Devotionis*, May 3, 1493, and a second bull that begins *Inter Caetera*, May 4, 1493. Gardiner cites Solórzano as providing an early printed version of these latter bulls that Alexander VI issued: *European Treaties*: doc. 6: 64, doc. 7: 72. There is a recent new edition of these bulls, *America Pontificia*, 1: 71–83.

15. Solórzano, 2.24.16; *European Treaties*, doc. 7: 71–78.

16. Ibid., 2.24.24; *European Treaties*, doc.6: 64–70, doc. 8: 79–83.

17. Solórzano, 2.24.18. He states that the line was to be 340 leagues west of the Cape Verde Islands. The text of this treaty is in *European Treaties*, doc. 9: 84–100. Concerning Solórzano and the treaty, see Angel Losada, "Repercusiones europeas del tradado de Tordesillas," in *El tratado de Tordesillas y su proyeccion* (Valladolid: Seminario de Historia de America, Universidad de Valladolid, 1973), 217–65, at 222, 226–27, 260–63.

18. Solórzano, 2.24.19. The phrasing of this argument might suggest that Solórzano believed that the pope possessed all power, spiritual and temporal. In fact, however, he clearly linked *dominium* and jurisdiction to his responsibility for the spiritual welfare of all mankind.

19. Ibid., 2.24.20.

20. Ibid., 2.24.22.

21. Ibid., 2.24.24.

22. For an interesting comparison of Catholic and Protestant views on missions to infidels, see Kenneth Scott Latourette, *A History of the Expansion of Christianity*, vol. III, *Three Centuries of Advance* (New York: Harper & Brothers, 1939), 24–42.

23. Solórzano, 2.24.25.

24. Ibid., 2.24.27 contains the text of *Laudabiliter* derived from Caesar Baronius, *Annales ecclesiastici*, 12 vols. in 4 (Cologne, 1609), 4: ad an. 1159.

25. Ibid., 2.24.26. There is an extensive literature on *Laudabiliter*, dealing with several problems arising from it including the question of its authenticity. For a recent discussion of *Laudabiliter*, see Muldoon, "Spiritual Conquests Compared."

26. A convenient introduction to Weckmann's views can be found in two of his

articles: "Alexandrine Bulls," *New Catholic Encylopedia* 1: 306; and "The Alexandrine Bulls of 1493: Pseudo Asiatic documents," *First Images of America: The Impact of the New World on the Old*, ed. Fredi Chiappelli, 2 vols. (Berkeley: University of California Press, 1976), 1: 201–10. For Weckmann's views on the relationship between medieval society and the world that the Spanish created in the Americas, see his *La herencia medieval de Mexico*, 2 vols. (México: Colegio de México, centro de Estudios Historicos, 1984).

27. The canon lawyers do not seem to have taken the Donation very seriously; see Muldoon, *Popes, Lawyers*, 55–56.

28. For the background to the bull, see Edmund Curtis, *A History of Ireland*, 6th ed. (London: Methuen & Co., 1950; reprint ed. 1966), 47–65. John Watt, *The Church and the Two Nations in Medieval Ireland* (Cambridge: Cambridge University Press, 1970), 35–51; and Robert Bartlett, *Gerald of Wales 1146–1223* (Oxford: Clarendon Press, 1982), 158–77.

29. *Irish Historical Documents, 1172–1922*, ed. Edmund Curtis and R. B. McDowell (London: Methuen & Co., 1943; reprint ed. New York: Barnes & Noble, 1968), 17.

30. Ibid.

31. On the title of the ruler of Ireland, see Curtis, *History of Ireland*, 66–71, 167–73. The text of the act making Henry VIII King of Ireland is in *Irish Historical Documents*, 77–78.

32. Solórzano, 2.24.28 and 1.3.21, 22.

33. Solórzano, 1.3 is devoted in its entirety to the Portuguese discoveries.

34. Solórzano, 2.24.28. The texts of these two bulls are in *European Treaties*, docs. 1, 2: 9–32.

35. There was a long history of papal bans on trade in materials of war between Christians and Moslems; see the text in *European Treaties*, 16–18.

36. Solórzano, 2.24.29.

37. Ibid.

38. This order of events might help to explain why Ferdinand and Isabella requested papal letters from Alexander VI only after Columbus returned from his first voyage.

39. Ibid., 2.24.30–31.

40. Cortés, *Letters from Mexico*, 20, esp. note 27.

41. Solórzano, 2.24.31. "Et eadem formula data est ab Imperatore Carolo V. Francisco Pizarro anno 1533. ubi ad conquisitionem huius Regni Peruani missus fuit, & caeteris subinde Ducibus, qui ad ejusmodi expeditiones delegabantur." For a discussion of Pizarro's use of the document in the course of the conquest, see John Hemming, *The Conquest of the Inca* (New York: Harcourt Brace Jovanovich, 1970), 41, 88, 128, 130.

42. Ibid., 2.24.32. The English translation, except where otherwise noted, is from Lewis Hanke, *History of Latin American Civilization*, 2 vols. (Boston: Little, Brown and Company, 1967): 123–25.

43. Solórzano, 2.24.32; Hanke, *History of Latin American Civilization*, 124.

44. Ibid.

45. Muldoon, "John Wyclif and the Rights of the Infidels," 316.

46. Solórzano, 2.24.34. The reference is to the *Digest*, 41.2.11.

47. Hillgarth, *The Spanish Kingdoms*, 2 vols. 2: 564–69.

48. Solórzano, 2.24.35.

49. Ibid.

50. Ibid., 2.24.36.

51. Ibid., 2.24.39.

52. Ibid., 2.24.41.

53. Ibid., 2.24.42.

54. Ibid., 2.24.43.

55. Ibid., 2.24.51.

56. Ibid., 2.24.92.

57. Ibid., 2.24.93.

58. Ibid., 2.24.94. The role of the cardinals in the daily administration of the Church was a major point of debate in the fourteenth and fifteenth centuries. For the outlines of this debate, see Stephan Kuttner, "Cardinalis: The History of a Canonical Concept," *Traditio* 3(1945): 129–214; and Tierney, *Foundations of the Conciliar Theory*, 68–84.

59. Ibid., 2.24.99.

60. Ibid., 2.24.100.

61. Ibid., 2.24.101.

62. In defining law, Aquinas argued that to be a law, a statement must be enforced. The words alone do not make a law. *Summa Theologiae* I-II, q. 90, art. 4; Aquinas, *Selected Political Writings*, 111–13.

63. In fact, they made no known formal objection until the fourteenth century: see James Muldoon, "The Remonstrance of the Irish Princes and the Canon Law Tradition of the Just War," *American Journal of Legal History* 22(1978): 309–25. For a study of the Remonstrance in a broader context, see J. R. S. Phillips, "The Irish Remonstrance of 1317: An International Perspective," *Irish Historical Studies* 27(1990): 112–29.

64. Concerning the conciliar movement, see Antony Black, "The Conciliar Movement," 573–87.

Chapter Eight

1. Stephan Kuttner, *Harmony from Dissonance; An Interpretation of Medieval Canon Law* (Latrobe, PA: Archabbey Press, [c.1960]).

2. Aquinas, *Selected Political Writings*, 12–13.

3. Dante, *Monarchy and Three Political Letters*, trans. Donald Nicholl and Colin Hardie (New York: Noonday Press, n.d.), 8–10.

4. Lewis, *Medieval Political Ideas*, 2: 502–5.

5. Vitoria, "On the American Indians," *Political Writings*, 252–64.

6. Solórzano, 2.21.1. The distinction between *auctoritas* and *potestas* was an ancient one, first stated in a letter of Pope Gelasius I (492–496). In the opinion of one modern scholar, the "political theology of the Middle Ages was dominated by a single *sententia*," the paragraph in which Gelasius stated the relationship between

these two kinds of power. See Robinson, "Church and Papacy," 288–300. For the text of the pope's letter, see Tierney, *Crisis*, 13–14.

7. On the medieval papal-imperial conflict, see Lewis, *Medieval Political Ideas*, 2: 430–505.

8. On Charles's abdications, see Karl Brandi, *The Emperor Charles V*, trans. C. V. Wedgwood (London: J. Cape, 1939), 629–37.

9. Solórzano, 2.21.2. Cortés, *Letters from Mexico*, xxvii, 48.

10. Gaines Post, "Blessed Lady Spain — Vincentius Hispanus and Spanish National Imperialism in the Thirteenth Century," *Speculum* 29(1954): 198–209.

11. Solórzano, 2.21.8–10. Starting with James I (1603–1625), the King of England was also not only King of Ireland, but King of Scotland as well. In the Church, multiple officeholding was a serious problem. Henry VIII's adviser, Cardinal Wolsey, was at one and the same time archbishop of York, abbot of St. Albans, and bishop of Winchester, among other offices held; see Jasper Ridley, *The Statesman and the Fanatic* (London: Constable, 1982), 227.

12. Ibid., 2.21.15.

13. Ibid., 2.21.16.

14. Ibid., 2.21.17.

15. Ibid., 2.21.18.

16. Ibid., 2.21.19. Solórzano gives two citations from the Roman law at this point, of which the first, *Digest*, lib. 14, tit. 2, *Deprecatio*, contains the emperor Antoninus's description of himself as "Ego quidem mundi dominus." The statement from Justinian is in the *Authentica*, coll. 5, tit. 24, m. 69, *Haec Considerantes: Corpus Iuris Civilis*, 2 vols. (Geneva: Apud Petrum & Iacobum Chouët, 1626).

17. Ibid., 2.21.21.

18. Ibid., 2.2.24.

19. Ibid., 2.21.25. The reference is to *Decretum*, C. 7 q. 1. c. 41, *In apibus*. Aquinas also used the same image in his *De Regimine Principum*, bk. 1, ch. 2, Aquinas, *Selected Political Writings*, 12–13.

20. Ibid., 2.21.27.

21. Ibid., 2.21.29.

22. Ibid., 2.21.30.

23. Ibid., 2.21.31.

24. For the medieval view of the Roman Empire's role as provider of peace and stability, see Donna Mancusi-Ungaro, *Dante and the Empire* (New York: Peter Lang, 1987); and A. P. d'Entrèves, *Dante as a Political Thinker* (Oxford: Clarendon Press, 1965), 26–51.

25. Solórzano, 2.21.32.

26. Ibid., 2.21.35.

27. Ibid., 2.21.37.

28. Ibid., 2.21.38.

29. Ibid., 2.21.39.

30. Ibid.

31. Ibid., 2.21.40.

32. Ibid., 2.21.41.

33. Ibid., 2.21.42.

34. Ibid., 2.21.43.

35. Ibid., 2.21.44.

36. Ibid., 2.21.46.

37. Ibid., 2.21.48.

38. Ibid., 2.21.49.

39. Ibid., 2.21.53.

40. Ibid., 2.21.58.

41. Ibid., 2.21.60.

42. Ibid., 2.21.62.

43. Ibid., 2.21.64 (2.21.65 in 1629 ed.).

44. Ibid., 2.21.70 (2.21.71 in 1629 ed.).

45. Ibid., 2.21.71 (2.21.72 in 1629 ed.). The description of rulers as possessing the same powers as the emperor was a medieval legal expression for attributing sovereignty to European rulers. On the history and use of the basic concept, see Helmut G. Walther, *Imperiales Königtum. Konziliarismus und Volkssouveränität* (Munich: Wilhelm Fink Verlag, 1976), 65–111.

46. Ibid., 2.21.73 (2.21.74 in 1629 ed.).

47. Ibid., 2.21.74–75 (2.21.75–76 in 1619 ed.).

48. Ibid., 2.21.76 (2.21.77 in 1629 ed.). Because of the confusion that the term "empire" caused and because of the fear that the imperial title could be used against Spanish independence of the Holy Roman Empire, it is not quite accurate to say, as Brading does, that the sixteenth- and seventeenth-century Spanish monarchs erected their conception of government on "the old medieval idea of the universal Christian empire." Brading, *First America*, 225. What the Spanish, and later the English, lacked was a political and governmental language that could comprehend the worldwide colonial systems being created without terming them empires. While then and now we refer to the Spanish and to the British "empires", in fact, legally and constitutionally no such entities existed. It would be more accurate to say that the Spanish were building on the notion of a universal Christian society.

49. Solórzano, 2.25. title [of this section] .

50. Ibid., 2.25.3.

51. Ibid., 2.25.4.

52. Ibid., 2.25.5.

53. The pope could do these things in his capacity as ruler of the papal state where he was, in effect, a secular prince. He could not do so, however, in his spiritual capacity.

54. Solórzano, 2.25.9.

55. Ibid., 2.25.11.

56. Ibid., 2.25.13.

57. Ibid., 2.25.14. In writing this, Solórzano was no doubt thinking of the Edict of Nantes of 1594, by which the French King, Henry IV, had granted legal recognition to the Huguenots, followers of Calvin, as the price of ending the religious wars in France. The Huguenots did attempt to establish settlements in the New World, but these failed, in part at least because the French government did not support such settlements. Like the Spanish, the French wanted overseas colonization restricted to Catholics. Concerning Huguenot attempts at colonization and the

official French position toward them, see Francis Parkman, *Count Frontenac and New France Under Louis XIV*, Centenary edition (Boston: Little, Brown, 1927), 416–17; and, more recently, Marc-André Bédard, "La présence protestante en Nouvelle-France," *Revue d'Histoire de l'Amérique Française* 31 (1978): 325–49.

58. Solórzano, 2.25.15. Strictly speaking, Christopher Columbus did not approach these monarchs, his brother Bartholomew did; see Morison, *The Southern Voyages*, 39.

59. Solórzano, 2.25.17.

60. Ibid., 2.25.21.

61. Ibid., 2.25.25. According to Solórzano, Pope John VIII (872–882) sent two letters with this title to King Alfonso in 853. The correct date was 876. One was addressed to "Adelfonso regi christianissimo." See the *Regesta Pontificum Romanorum*, ed. Philip Jaffé, 2nd ed., 2 vols. (Leipzig: Veit, 1885, 1888), 1: 387, nos. 3035, 3036.

62. Solórzano, 2.25.26.

63. Ibid., 2.25.27. In 1496 Pope Alexander VI gave Ferdinand and Isabella "the title of 'Catholic Monarchs' for their aid against the French. . . ." Hillgarth, *The Spanish Kingdoms*, 2: 398. The reference to the Visigothic King Reccared may well reflect the practice of linking the Spanish monarchy at the end of the fifteenth century with its Visigothic forebears, a practice that began under Ferdinand; see *The Spanish Kingdom*, 204–205.

64. Ibid., 2.25.31–32. On the history of the "king's touch," see Marc Bloch, *The Royal Touch; Sacred Monarchy and Scrofula in England and France*, trans. J. E. Anderson (London: Routledge & Kegan Paul, 1973).

65. Solórzano, 2.25.30.

66. Ibid., 2.25.33.

67. Ibid., 2.25.34–35.

68. Ibid., 2.25.36.

69. Ibid., 2.25.37. The reference here is to the final chapter of the Gospel of Mark and to bk. 16, ch. 11, where Christ's injunction to preach to all men everywhere is found. For purposes of the argument that critics of the Spanish monopoly in the New World had offered, Solórzano takes this to mean that all Christians, not just the clergy, have the obligation to preach the Gospel. Therefore the leaders of Christian kingdoms have a special responsibility in this work.

70. Ibid., 2.25.38.

71. Ibid., 2.25.40.

72. Ibid., 2.25.41.

73. Ibid., 2.25.43.

74. Ibid., 2.25.44–45.

75. Ibid., 2.25.46.

76. Ibid., 2.25.47.

77. Ibid., 2.25.48. He refers his reader to the discussion of this issue in the first part of this volume, 1.6.68. On the series of fifteenth-century disputes that marked Castilian-Portuguese relations in the fifteenth century and the place of Columbus's voyages in that, see Fernández-Armesto, *Before Columbus*, 203–7.

78. Ibid., 2.25.49.

79. Ibid., 2.25.50.

80. Ibid., 2.25.51–52.

81. Ibid., 2.25.53–54.

82. Ibid., 2.25.55–56.

83. Ibid., 2.25.57.

84. Ibid., 2.25.59–60. The reference is to Aristotle's *Politics*, bk. 2, ch. 5, *Works*; 1150–54.

85. Ibid., 2.25.62.

86. Henry Charles Lea pointed out long ago that the "ostensible object of the Spanish conquests in the New World was the propagation of the faith." That being the case, establishing inquisitorial tribunals in the Americas was a necessary and logical thing to do: Henry Charles Lea, *The Inquisition in the Spanish Dependencies* (New York: Macmillan, 1908), 191. "As early as 1508, bishops in Havana and Puerto Rico were informing Madrid that the New World was being filled with *hebreo cristanos* (Hebrew Christians), *nuevo cristianos* (New Christians), *conversos* (converts), *Moriscos* (Muslim converts), and other heretics in spite of several decrees barring their entry." Seymour B. Liebman, *The Inquisitors and the Jews in the New World* (Coral Gables, FL: University of Miami Press, 1974), 18. See also Richard E. Greenleaf, *The Mexican Inquisition of the Sixteenth Century* (Albuquerque: University of New Mexico Press, 1969); William Monter, *Frontiers of Heresy: The Spanish Inquisition from the Basque Lands to Sicily* (Cambridge: Cambridge University Press, 1990). For a detailed discussion of the Inquisition's operations in one specific area, see Inga Clendinnen, *Ambivalent Conquests: Maya and Spaniard in Yucatan 1517–1570* (Cambridge: Cambridge University Press, 1987).

87. Solórzano, 2.25.63.

88. Ibid., 2.25.65.

89. Ibid., 2.25.67.

90. Ibid., 2.25.68. Columbus observed his sailors cheating the peoples whom he encountered on his first voyage and claimed to have intervened to stop such practices. See Christopher Columbus, *Journals and Other Documents on the Life and Voyages of Christopher Columbus*, trans. and ed. Samuel Eliot Morison (New York: The Heritage Press, 1963), 67.

91. Solórzano, 2.25.69–70.

92. Ibid., 2.25.71.

93. Ibid., 2.25.73.

94. See Ernest Barker, *From Alexander to Constantine* (Oxford: Clarendon Press, 1956), 6–7.

95. On Dante's imperial vision, see Dante, *Monarchy*, 29–31.

96. One measure of Solórzano's ambition is the fact that the *De Indiarum Jure* was placed on the Roman Index because of the author's enthusiastic defense of Spanish royal control of ecclesiastical administration. To the papacy, Solórzano appeared to suggest that the moral qualities of the Spanish monarchs alone would have justified Spanish possession of the Americas, even without papal permission. The condemnation referred specifically to the discussion of the monarchy's rights with regard to church administration in Book III; see Javier Malagón and José M. Ots Capdequí, *Solórzano*, 71–72.

Conclusion

1. J. H. Elliott, *Imperial Spain*, 296.

2. Concerning "mirror of the prince" literature and Machiavelli's place in that tradition, see Allan H. Gilbert, *Machiavelli's Prince and Its Forerunners* (Durham, NC: Duke University Press, 1938; reprint ed., New York: Barnes & Noble, 1968).

3. Bireley: 1. Solórzano knew of Machiavelli as a teacher of evil (1.16.89).

4. Ibid.: 3. Solórzano cited at least two of the six anti-Machiavellian writers that Bireley discusses, Justus Lipsius and Giovanni Botero. The index lists seven references to Lipsius and three to Botero.

5. Recently there has appeared strong criticism of the contemporary emphasis on realism in international affairs, a position associated most notably with the work of Professor Hans Morgenthau. A critic wrote that Morgenthau taught a "Machiavellian approach to international relations." He in turn called for a return to the legal-positivist approach to international relations that developed in the United States in the two decades before the First World War. See Francis Anthony Boyle, *World Politics and International Law* (Durham, NC: Duke University Press, 1985), 15. One of the leading figures in the formation of this legal-positivist approach to international affairs was James Brown Scott, who was also one of the leading proponents in citing the importance of the Spanish scholastics in the development of international law and was subsequently one of President Woodrow Wilson's advisers at Versailles after World War I.

6. Vitoria, *Political Writings*, xiv; Crowe, *Changing Profile*, 74, 215.

7. One might argue that these writers were more sophisticated than Hugo Grotius and the legal thinkers who followed in his footsteps, because the later writers tended to ignore the human dimension of the encounter between Europeans and non-Europeans.

8. Grafton, *New Worlds*, 248.

9. For a discussion of the medieval underpinnings, the "medieval mental geology," that underlay the world view of Columbus and his contemporaries, see Valerie Flint, *The Imaginative Landscape of Christopher Columbus* (Princeton, NJ: Princeton University Press, l992): 116.

10. One might also argue that the supporters of the movement to encourage world peace through world law of the first four decades of the twentieth century had a similar view.

11. It is worth noting here that in the sixteenth century, there was developing within the Russian Orthodox Church another theory of *translatio imperii*, this time the *translatio* of the seat of empire from Constantinople, which had fallen to the Turks in 1453, to Moscow. This theory in turn led to the development of a Russian sense of historical mission in defense of true Christianity. See Mikhail Agursky, *The Third Rome: National Bolshevism in the USSR* (Boulder, CO: Westview Press, 1987), 6–7.

12. A similar union of spiritual and economic goods was to be found in Pope Urban II's (1088–99) call for the first crusade in 1095; see *The First Crusade*, ed. Edward Peters (Philadelphia: University of Pennsylvania Press, 1971), 3–4.

13. See Richard Rosecrance, *The Rise of the Trading State: Commerce and Conquest in the Modern World* (New York: Basic Books, 1986), 72–79.

14. Edward N. Luttwak, "Wrong Place, Wrong Time," *The New York Times*, July 22, 1993: A23. A forceful argument favoring the re-establishment of colonial governments in Africa and elsewhere is Paul Johnson, "Wanted: A New Imperialism," *National Review* 44(Dec. 14, 1992): 28–34.

Bibliography

Primary Sources

Abercrombie, William. *Magna Carta for America*. Philadelphia: American Philosophical Society, 1986.
America Pontificia: Primi Saeculi Evangelizationis 1493–1592. 2 vols., ed. Josef Metzler. Vatican City: Libreria Editrice Vaticana, 1991.
Andreae, Johannes. *In quinque decretalium libros novella commentaria*. Venice: 1581. Reprint ed., Turin: Bottega d'Erasmo, 1963.
Aquinas, Thomas. *The Political Ideas*, ed. Dino Bigongiari. New York: Hafner Publishing Co., 1957.
———. *Aquinas: Selected Political Writings*, ed. A. P. d'Entrèves. Oxford: Basil Blackwell, 1954.
Aristotle. *The Basic Works*, ed. Richard McKeon. New York: Random House, 1941.
———. *The Politics*, trans. Ernest Barker. Oxford: Clarendon Press, 1946.
Augustine. *The City of God*, trans. John Healey. London: J. M. Dent, 1945.
Baronius, Caesar. *Annales ecclesiastici*, 12 vols. in 4, Cologne, 1609.
Bellarmine, Robert. *De laicis or the Treatise on Civil Government*, trans. Kathleen E. Murphy. New York: Fordham University Press, 1928. Reprint ed., Westport, CT: Hyperion Press, 1979.
———. *Power of the Pope in Temporal Affairs*, trans. George Albert Moore. Chevy Chase, MD: Country Dollar Press, 1949.
Bettenson, Henry. *Documents of the Christian Church*. 2nd ed. New York: Oxford University Press, 1963.
Bland, Richard. *An Enquiry into the Rights of the British Colonies*. Williamsburg: Alexander Purdie, 1766. Reprinted London: J. Almon, 1769.
Caesar, Julius. *Gallic War*, trans. F. P. Long. Oxford: Clarendon Press, 1911.
Cicero. *De inventione*, trans. H. M. Hubbell. Loeb Classical Library. Cambridge, MA: Harvard University Press, 1949.
Columbus, Christopher. *The Libro de las profecías*, trans. Delno C. West and August Kling. Gainesville: University Presses of Florida, 1991.
———. *The Columbus Letter of 1493*, trans. Frank E. Robbins. Ann Arbor, MI: Clements Library Associates, 1952.
———. *Journal and Other Documents on the Life and Voyages of Christopher Columbus*, trans. and ed. Samuel Eliot Morison. New York: The Heritage Press, 1963.
Corpus Iuris Civilis. 2 vols. Geneva: Apud Petrum & Iacobum Chouët, 1626.
Corpus Iuris Canonici, ed. A. Friedberg. 2 vols. Leipzig: Bernard Tauchnitz, 1879–1881. Reprint ed. Graz: Akademische Druck–U. Verlagsanstalt, 1959.
Cortés, Hernan. *Letters from Mexico*, trans. and ed. A. R. Pagden. New York: Grossman Pubs., 1971.

Dante. *Monarchy and Three Political Letters*, trans. Donald Nicholl and Colin Hardie. New York: Noonday Press, n.d.

Davenport, F. G., ed. *European Treaties Bearing on the History of the United States and Its Dependencies to 1648*. Washington, DC: Carnegie Institution of Washington, 1917. Reprint ed. Gloucester, MA: Peter Smith, 1967.

Domat, Jean. *The Civil Law in Its Natural Order*, trans. William Strahan. 2 vols. London: J. Bettenham, 1722.

Douglas, David C. and George W. Greenaway, eds. *English Historical Documents*. Vol. II, 1042–1189. 2nd ed. New York: Oxford University Press, 1981.

Freitas, Frei Serafim de. *Do Justo imperio asiatico dos portugeses, de iusto imperio Lusitanorum Asiatico*. 2 vols. Lisbon: Instituto Nacional de Investigacao Cientifica, 1983.

Grotius, Hugo. *De Jure Belli ac Pacis Libri Tres* [*The Law of War and Peace*], trans. Francis W. Kelsey. The Classics of International Law. Washington, DC: Carnegie Endowment for International Peace, 1925. Reprint ed. Indianapolis, IN: Bobbs-Merrill, 1962.

——. *The Freedom of the Seas*, trans. Ralph Van Deman Magoffin, ed. J. B. Scott. New York: Oxford University Press, 1916.

Index Librorum Prohibitorum, new edition. Rome: Ex Typographia Polyglotta, 1881.

Innocent III. *Regestum super negotio Romani Imperii*, ed. F. Kempf. Rome: Pontificia Università Gregoriana, 1947.

Irish Historical Documents, 1172–1922, ed. Edmund Curtis and R. B. McDowell. London: Methuen & Co., 1943. Reprint ed. New York: Barnes & Noble, 1968.

Jensen, Merrill, ed. *English Historical Documents*. Vol. IX, *American Colonial Documents to 1776*. New York: Oxford University Press, 1955.

Las Casas, Bartolomé de. *History of the Indies*, trans. and ed. André Collard. New York: Harper & Row, 1971.

——. *In Defense of the Indians*, trans. and ed. Stafford Poole, C.M. DeKalb: Northern Illinois University Press, 1974.

Luther, Martin. "To the Christian Nobility of the German Nation," trans. Charles M. Jacobs, rev. James Atkinson. *Three Treatises*. 2nd rev. ed. Philadelphia: Fortress Press, 1970: 1–112.

MacDonald, William, ed. *Select Charters and Other Documents Illustrative of American History, 1606–1775*. New York: Macmillan, 1899.

Marsiglio of Padua. *The Defender of the Peace*, trans. Alan Gewirth. New York: Columbia University Press, 1956.

Monumenta Henricina V. Coimbra: Comissao Executiva das Comemoracoes do V Centinário da Morte do Infante D. Henrique, 1963.

Otis, James. "The Rights of the British Colonies Asserted and Proved." *Pamphlets of the American Revolution*, ed. Bernard Bailyn, vol. 1. Cambridge, MA: Belknap Press, 1965: 419–82.

Palacios Rubios, Juan López de. *De las islas del mar oceano*, trans. Agustín Millares Carlo. México: Fondo de Cultura Económica, 1954.

Peters, Edward, ed. *The First Crusade*. Philadelphia: University of Pennsylvania Press, 1971.

Pliny. *Natural History*, trans. H. Rackham, W. H. S. Johns, D. E. Eichholz. 10 vols. Loeb Classical Library. Cambridge, MA: Harvard University Press, 1949–1962.

Shakespeare, William. *Henry V*, ed. Gary Taylor. Oxford: Oxford University Press, 1984.

Smith, Adam. *An Inquiry into the Nature and Causes of the Wealth of Nations*. New York: Modern Library, 1937.

Solórzano Pereira, Juan de. *De Indiarum Jure sive de justa Indiarum Occidentalium Inquisitione, Acquisitione, & Retentione*. 2 vols. Madrid: Ex typographia Francisci Martinez, 1629–1639.

———. *De Indiarum Jure sive de justa Indiarum Occidentalium Inquisitione, Acquisitione, & Retentione*. 2 vols. Madrid: In typographia regia, 1777.

———. *Política indiana*. Biblioteca de autores españoles desde la formacion del lenguaje hasta nuestros dias, ed. Miguel Angel Ochoa Brun. 5 vols. Madrid: Ediciones Atlas, 1972.

Tacitus. *The Agricola and The Germania*, trans. H. Mattingly, rev. S. A. Handford. Harmondsworth: Penguin Books, 1970.

Valla, Lorenzo. *The Profession of the Religious and the Principal Arguments from the Falsely-Believed and Forged Donation of Constantine*, trans. and ed. Olga Zorzi Pugliese. Toronto: Centre for Reformation and Renaissance Studies, 1985.

Vega, Garcilaso de la, El Inca. *Royal Commentaries of the Incas*, trans. Harold V. Livermore. 2 vols. Austin: University of Texas Press, 1966.

Virgil. *The Aeneid*, trans. Robert Fitzgerald. New York: Random House, 1983.

Vitoria, Francisco de. *Political Writings*, ed. Anthony Pagden and Jeremy Lawrance. Cambridge: Cambridge University Press, 1991.

White, Joseph M., ed. *A New Collection of Laws, Charters and Local Ordinances of the Governments of Great Britain, France and Spain relating to the concessions of land in their respective colonies; together with the laws of Mexico and Texas on the same subject*. 2 vols. Philadelphia: T. & J. W. Johnson, 1839.

SECONDARY WORKS

Acton, John Emmerich. "Inaugural Lecture on the Study of History." *Lectures on Modern History*. Reprint ed. London: Collins, 1960.

Agursky, Mikhail. *The Third Rome: National Bolshevism in the USSR*. Boulder, CO: Westview Press, 1987.

Andrews, Charles M. *The Colonial Period of American History*, 4 vols. New Haven, CT: Yale University Press, 1934–1938.

Andrien, Kenneth J. "Corruption, Inefficiency, and Imperial Decline in the Seventeenth-Century Viceroyalty of Peru." *Americas* 41 (1984): 1–20.

Ares, Berta, Jesus Bustamante, Francisco Castilla, and Fermin del Pino. *Humanismo y vision del otro en la España moderna: cuatro estudios*. Madrid: Consejo Superior de Investigaciones Científicas, 1992.

Arnold, Franz Xaver. *Die Staatslehre des kardinals Bellarmin: un beitrag zur Rechts- und Staatsphilosophie des konfessionellen Zeitalters*. München: M. Hueber, 1934.

Arquillière, H.-X. *L'augustinisme politique: essai sur la formation des théories politiques du moyen-âge.* 2nd ed. Paris: J. Vrin, 1955.

Axtell, James. *The Invasion Within: The Contest of Cultures in Colonial North America.* New York: Oxford University Press, 1985.

Barker, Ernest. *From Alexander to Constantine.* Oxford: Clarendon Press, 1956.

Barnes, Harry Elmer. *A History of Historical Writing.* 2nd rev. ed. Norman: University of Oklahoma Press, 1937. reprint ed. New York: Dover Publications, 1962.

Bartlett, Robert. *Gerald of Wales 1146–1223.* Oxford: Clarendon Press, 1982.

——. *The Making of Europe: Conquest, Colonization, & Cultural Change, 950–1350.* Princeton, NJ: Princeton University Press, 1993.

Bartlett, Robert and Angus MacKay. *Medieval Frontier Societies.* Oxford: Oxford University Press, 1989.

Bayne, C. G. *Anglo-Roman Relations 1558–1565.* Oxford: Clarendon Press, 1913. Reprint ed. Oxford: Clarendon Press, 1968.

Bell, Aubrey F. G. "Liberty in Sixteenth-Century Spain," *Bulletin of Spanish Studies* 10 (1933): 164–79.

Bergin, Thomas G. *Dante.* Boston: Houghton Mifflin, 1965.

Bireley, Robert. *The Counter-Reformation Prince: Anti-Machiavellianism or Catholic Statecraft in Early Modern Europe.* Chapel Hill: University of North Carolina Press, 1990.

Black, Anthony. "The Individual and Society." In Burns, *Cambridge History of Medieval Political Thought c. 350–c. 1450,* 588–606.

Bloch, Marc. *The Royal Touch: Sacred Monarchy and Scrofula in England and France,* trans. J. E. Anderson. London: Routledge & Kegan Paul, 1973.

Bosbach, Franz. "Papsttum und Universalmonarchie im Zeitalter der Reformation." *Historisches Jahrbuch* 107 (1987): 44–76.

Boyle, Francis Anthony. *World Politics and International Law.* Durham, NC: Duke University Press, 1985.

Brading, D. A. *The First America.* Cambridge: Cambridge Univerity Press, 1991.

Brandi, Karl. *The Emperor Charles V,* trans. C. V. Wedgwood. London: J. Cape, 1939.

Breisach, Ernst. *Historiography: Ancient, Medieval, & Modern.* Chicago: University of Chicago Press, 1983.

Brundage, James. *Medieval Canon Law and the Crusader.* Madison: University of Wisconsin Press, 1969.

Buckland, W. W. *The Roman Law of Slavery.* Cambridge: Cambridge University Press, 1908.

Burke, Peter. "Tacitism, Sceptisism [sic], and Reason." In Burns and Goldie, *Cambridge History of Political Thought 1450–1700:* 479–98.

Bull, Hedley, Benedict Kingsbury, Adam Roberts, ed. *Hugo Grotius and International Relations.* Oxford: Clarendon Press, 1990.

Burns, J. H., ed. *Cambridge History of Medieval Political Thought c. 350–c. 1450.* Cambridge: Cambridge University Press, 1988.

——. "Introduction." In J. H. Burns, *Cambridge History of Medieval Political Thought c. 350–c. 1450:* 1–8.

Burns, J. H. and Mark Goldie, eds. *Cambridge History of Political Thought 1450–1700.* Cambridge: Cambridge University Press, 1991.

Butler, W. E. "Grotius and the Law of the Sea." *Hugo Grotius and the Law of the Sea*: 209–20.

Butterfield, Herbert. *The Whig Interpretation of History*. London: G. Bell, 1931. Reprint ed., 1963.

Canning, J. P. *The Political Thought of Baldus de Ubaldis.* Cambridge: Cambridge University Press, 1987.

Caraman, Philip. *The Lost Paradise: The Jesuit Republic in South America*. New York: Seabury Press, 1976.

Carlyle R. W. and A. J. Carlyle. *A History of Mediaeval Political Theory in the West*. 6 vols. Edinburgh and London: William Blackwood & Sons, 1903–1936.

Cheney, C. R. *Pope Innocent III and England*. Stuttgart: Hiersemann, 1976.

Clendinnen, Inga. *Ambivalent Conquests: Maya and Spaniard in Yucatan 1517–1570*. Cambridge: Cambridge University Press, 1987.

———. "The Cost of Courage in Aztec Society." *Past & Present* 107 (May 1985): 44–89.

Cohen, Jeremy. *The Friars and the Jews: The Evolution of Medieval Anti-Semitism*. Ithaca, NY: Cornell University Press, 1982.

Crosby, Alfred W. *The Columbian Exchange: Biological and Cultural Consequences of 1492*. Westport, CT: Greenwood Press, 1972.

———. *Ecological Imperialism: The Biological Expansion of Europe, 900–1900*. Cambridge: Cambridge University Press, 1986.

Copleston, Frederick S. J. *History of Philosophy*. 9 vols. Westminster, MD: Newman Press, 1948–1953. Vol. 3, *Ockham to Suárez*, 1953.

Crowe, Michael B. *The Changing Profile of the Natural Law*. The Hague: Martinus Nijhoff, 1977.

Curtis, Edmund. *A History of Ireland*. 6th ed. London: Methuen & Co., 1950. Reprint ed., 1966.

Davis, David Brion. *The Problem of Slavery in Western Culture*. Ithaca, NY: Cornell University Press, 1966.

Deane, Herbert A. *The Political and Social Ideas of St. Augustine*. New York: Columbia University Press, 1963.

Dempf, Alois. *Sacrum Imperium*. München und Berlin: R. Oldenbourg, 1929. Reprint ed., 1962.

D'Entrèves, A. P. *Dante as a Political Thinker*. Oxford: Clarendon Press, 1965.

———. *Natural Law*. London: Hutchinson University Library, 1951.

Dictionnaire de droit canonique, ed. R. Naz. 7 vols. Paris: Letouzey et Ané, 1935–1965.

Dunbabin, Jean. "Government." In Burns, *Cambridge History of Medieval Political Thought c. 350–c. 1450*, 477–519.

Duncan, T. Bentley. Review. *Journal of Modern History* 50(1978): 764–66.

Elliott, John H. *Imperial Spain, 1469–1716*. New York: St. Martin's Press, 1963. Reprint ed. New York: New American Library, 1966.

———. *The Count-Duke of Olivares: The Statesman in an Age of Decline*. New Haven, CT: Yale University Press, 1986.

———. "The Decline of Spain." *Past & Present* 20(Nov. 1961): 52–75. Reprinted *Crisis in Europe, 1560–1660*, ed. T. H. Aston. New York: Basic Books, 1965.

——. *The Old World and the New, 1492–1650*. Cambridge: Cambridge University Press, 1970.

Encyclopaedia Britannica. 11th ed., 29 vols. New York: Encyclopaedia Britannica, 1910–1911.

Encyclopedia universal ilustrada Europeo-Americana. Bilbao, Madrid, Barcelona: Espasa-Calpe, 1930–1933.

Fernández-Armesto, Felipe. *Before Columbus: Exploration and Colonization from the Mediterranean to the Atlantic, 1229–1492*. Philadelphia: University of Pennsylvania Press, 1987.

Fernández Santamaria, J. A. *Reason of State and Statecraft in Spanish Political Thought, 1595–1640*. Lanham, MD: University Press of America, 1983.

——. *The State, War and Peace: Spanish Political Thought in the Renaissance, 1516–1559*. Cambridge: Cambridge University Press, 1977.

Flint, Valerie. *The Imaginative Landscape of Christopher Columbus*. Princeton, NJ: Princeton University Press, 1992.

Folz, Robert. *L'idée d'empire en Occident du Ve au XIVe siècle*. Paris: Aubier, 1953.

Folmer, Henry. *Franco-Spanish Rivalry in North America, 1524–1763*. Glendale, CA: Arthur H. Clark, 1953.

Garrett, William R. "Religion, Law and the Human Condition." *Sociological Analysis* 47(1987): 1–34.

Gibson, Charles, ed. *The Black Legend*. New York: Knopf, 1969.

Gierke, Otto. *Political Theories of the Middle Age*, trans. F. W. Maitland. Cambridge: Cambridge University Press, 1900.

Gil Fernández, Luis. *Panorma social del humanismo español (1500–1800)*. Madrid: Editorial Alhambra, 1981.

Gilbert, Allan H. *Machiavelli's Prince and Its Forerunners* Durham, NC: Duke University Press, 1938. Reprint ed., New York: Barnes & Noble, 1968.

Goez, Werner. *Translatio Imperii*. Tübingen: J. C. B. Mohr (Paul Siebeck), 1958.

"Good Guy or Dirty Word?" *Time*, November 26, 1990, 79.

Góngora, Mario. *Studies in the Colonial History of Spanish America*, trans. Richard Southern. Cambridge: Cambridge University Press, 1975.

Gordley, James. *The Philosophical Origins of Modern Contract Doctrine*. Oxford: Clarendon Press, 1991.

Grafton, Anthony. *New Worlds, Ancient Texts*. Cambridge, MA: Harvard University Press, 1992.

——. "Humanism and Political Theory." In Burns, *Cambridge History of Medieval Political Thought c. 350–c. 1450*: 9–29.

Greengrass, Mark. *France in the Age of Henri IV*. London: Longman, 1984.

Greenleaf, Richard E. *The Mexican Inquisition of the Sixteenth Century*. Albuquerque: University of New Mexico Press, 1969.

Hall, Charles A. M. *With the Spirit's Sword*. Richmond, VA: John Knox Press, 1968.

Hall, Edith. *Inventing the Barbarian: Self-Definition Through Tragedy*. Oxford: Oxford University Press, 1989.

Hamilton, Bernice. *Political Thought in Sixteenth-Century Spain: A Study of the Political Ideas of Vitoria, de Soto, Suárez, and Molina*. Oxford: Oxford University Press, 1963.

Hancock, Ralph C. *Calvin and the Foundations of Modern Politics*. Ithaca, NY: Cornell University Press, 1989.

Hanke, Lewis. *All Mankind is One*. DeKalb: Northern Illinois University Press, 1974.

———. "A Modest Proposal for a Moratorium on Grand Generalizations: Some Thoughts on the Black Legend." *Hispanic American Historical Review* 51 (1971): 112–27.

———. *Aristotle and the American Indians: A Study in Race Prejudice in the Modern World*. Bloomington: Indiana University Press, 1959.

———, ed. *History of Latin American Civilization*. 2 vols. Boston: Little, Brown, 1967.

———. "More Heat and Some Light on the Spanish Struggle for Justice in the Conquest of America." *Hispanic American Historical Review* 44(1964): 293–340.

———. "Pope Paul III and the American Indians." *Harvard Theological Review* 30(1939): 65–162.

———. *The Spanish Struggle for Justice in the Conquest of America*. Philadelphia: University of Pennsylvania Press, 1949.

Haring, C. H. *The Spanish Empire in America*. New York: Oxford University Press, 1947.

Headly, John M. *Luther's View of Church History*. New Haven, CT: Yale University Press, 1963.

Helps, Sir Arthur. *The Spanish Conquest in America and its Relation to the History of Slavery and to the Government of the Colonies*. 4 vols. Reprint ed. New York: AMS Press, 1966.

Hemming, John. *The Conquest of the Inca*. New York: Harcourt Brace Jovanovich, 1970.

Hillgarth, J. N. *The Spanish Kingdoms 1250–1516*. 2 vols. Oxford: Clarendon Press, 1976–1978.

Himmelfarb, Gertrude. *Lord Acton: A Study in Conscience and Politics*. Chicago: University of Chicago Press, 1952.

———. *Victorian Minds*. New York: A. A. Knopf, 1968.

Hodgen, Margaret T. *Early Anthropology in the Sixteenth and Seventeenth Centuries*. Philadelphia: University of Pennsylvania Press, 1964. Reprint ed., 1971.

Index Librorum Prohibitorum, new edition. Rome: Ex Typographia Polyglotta, 1881.

Israel, J. I. and Henry Kamen. "Debate: The Decline of Spain: A Historical Myth?" *Past & Present* 91 (May 1981): 170–85.

Jaffé, Philip, ed. *Regesta Pontificum Romanorum*. 2nd ed., 2 vols. Leipzig: Veit, 1885, 1888.

Johnson, Herbert A. *Imported Eighteenth-Century Law Treatises in American Libraries, 1700–1799*. Knoxville: University of Tennessee Press, 1978.

Johnson, James Turner. *Ideology, Reason, and the Limitation of War*. Princeton, NJ: Princeton University Press, 1975.

———. *The Just War Tradition and the Restraint of War*. Princeton, NJ: Princeton University Press, 1981.

Johnson, Paul. "Wanted: A New Imperialism." *National Review* 44(Dec. 14, 1992): 28–34.

Kagan, Richard L. *Students and Society in Early Modern Spain*. Baltimore: Johns Hopkins University Press, 1974.

——. "Universities in Castile 1500–1810." In *The University in Society*, ed. Lawrence Stone. 2 vols. Princeton, NJ: Princeton University Press, 1974, 2: 355–405.

Kamen, Henry. "The Decline of Spain: A Historical Myth?" *Past & Present* 81 (Nov. 1978): 24–50.

——. John TePaske and Herbert S. Klein. "Debate: The Seventeenth-Century Crisis in New Spain: Myth or Reality?" *Past & Present* 97 (Nov. 1982): 144–61.

Kantorowicz, Ernst. *The King's Two Bodies: A Study in Mediaeval Political Theology*. Princeton, NJ: Princeton University Press, 1957.

Kedar, B. Z. "Canon Law and the Burning of the Talmud." *Bulletin of Medieval Canon Law* n.s. 9(1979): 79–82.

Keen, Benjamin. "The Black Legend Revisited: Assumptions and Realities." *Hispanic American Historical Review* 49(1969): 703–19.

——. "Main Currents in United States Writings on Colonial Spanish America, 1884–1984." *Hispanic American Historical Review* 65(1985): 657–82.

——. "Recent Writings on the Spanish Conquest." *Latin American Research Review* 20(1985): 161–71.

——. "The White Legend Revisited: A Reply to Professor Hanke's 'Modest Proposal'." *Hispanic American Historical Review* 51(1971): 336–55.

Kelley, Donald R. "Law." In Burns and Goldie, *Cambridge History of Political Thought 1450–1700*: 66–94.

Kennedy, Paul. *The Rise and Fall of the Great Powers: Economic Change and Military Conflict from 1500 to 2000*. New York: Random House, 1987.

King, P. D. "The Barbarian Kingdoms." In Burns, *Cambridge History of Medieval Political Thought c. 350–c. 1450*, 123–53.

Kisch, Guido. *Studien zur humanistischen Jurisprudenz*. Berlin and New York: Walter de Gruyter, 1972.

Kleffens, E. N. van. *Hispanic Law Until the End of the Middle Ages*. Edinburgh: Edinburgh University Press, 1968.

Knobler, Adam. "Missions, Mythologies and the Search for Non-European Allies in Anti-Islamic Holy War, 1291–c. 1540." University of Cambridge dissertation, 1989.

Koebner, Richard. *Empire*. Cambridge: Cambridge University Press, 1966.

——. " 'The Imperial Crown of This Realm': Henry VIII, Constantine the Great, and Polydore Vergil." *Bulletin of the Institute of Historical Research* 26(1953): 29–52.

Kristeller, Paul Oskar. "The European Diffusion of Italian Humanism." *Renaissance Thought and the Arts*. Princeton, NJ: Princeton University Press, 1990, 69–88.

——. "The Moral Thought of Renaissance Humanism," *Renaissance Thought and the Arts*, 20–68.

Kuttner, Stephan. "Cardinalis: The History of a Canonical Concept." *Traditio* 3(1945): 129–214.

——. *Harmony from Dissonance: An Interpretation of Medieval Canon Law*. Latrobe, PA: Archabbey Press [c.1960].

———. "The Revival of Jurisprudence." *Renaissance and Renewal in the Twelfth Century*, ed. Robert L. Benson and Giles Constable. Cambridge, MA: Harvard University Press, 1982, 299–323.

Latourette, Kenneth Scott. *A History of the Expansion of Christianity*. Vol. III, *Three Centuries of Advance*. New York: Harper & Brothers, 1939.

Lea, Henry Charles. *The Inquisition in the Spanish Dependencies*. New York: Macmillan, 1908.

Le Bras, Gabriel. "Innocent IV Romaniste: Examen de l'Apparatus." *Studia Gratiana* 11(1967): 305–26.

Levin, David. *History as Romantic Art: Bancroft, Motley, Prescott, and Parkman*. Stanford, CA: Stanford University Press, 1959.

Lewis, Charlton T. and Charles Short, eds. *A Latin Dictionary*. Oxford: Clarendon Press, 1879.

Lewis, Ewart. *Medieval Political Ideas*. 2 vols. New York: Knopf, 1954.

Lewy, Guenter. *Constitutionalism and Statecraft During the Golden Age of Spain: A Study of the Political Philosophy of Juan de Mariana, S.J.* Geneva: Librairie E. Droz, 1960.

Lhoest, Brigitte F. P. "Spanish American Law: A Product of Conflicting Interests." *Itinerario* 16(1992): 21–34.

Liebman, Seymour B. *The Inquisitors and the Jews in the New World*. Coral Gables, FL: University of Miami Press, 1974.

Linden, H. Vander. "Alexander VI and the Demarcation of the Maritime and Colonial Domains of Spain and Portugal, 1493–94." *American Historical Review* 22(1916–1917): 1–20.

Lockhart, James. *The Nahuas After the Conquest*. Stanford, CA: Stanford University Press, 1992.

Lonkhuyzen, Harold W. van. "A Reappraisal of the Praying Indians: Acculturation, Conversion, and Identity at Natick, Massachusetts, 1646–1730." *New England Quarterly* 63(1990): 396–428.

Lourie, Elena. "Free Moslems in the Balearics Under Christian Rule in the Thirteenth Century." *Speculum* 45(1970): 624–49.

Luchaire, A. *Innocent III*. 6 vols. Paris: Hachette, 1905–1908. Vol. 5, *Les Royautés vassales de Saint-Siège*.

Luttwak, Edward N. "Wrong Place, Wrong Time." *New York Times* (July 22, 1993): A23.

Lynch, John. *Spain Under the Habsburgs*, 2 vols., 2nd ed. New York: New York University Press, 1984.

Maccarrone, Michele. *Chiesa e stato nella dottrina di papa Innocenzo III*. Rome: Facultas Theologica Pontificii Athenaei Lateranensis, 1940.

McGrath, Patrick. *Papists and Puritans Under Elizabeth I*. London: Blandford Press, 1967.

MacLachlan, Colin M. *Spain's Empire in the New World: The Role of Ideas in Institutional and Social Change*. Berkeley: University of California Press, 1988.

McNaspy, C. J. *Lost Cities of Paraguay: Art and Architecture of the Jesuit Reductions 1607–1767*. Chicago: Loyola University Press, 1982.

Madariaga, Salvador de. *El Auge del Imperio Español en America*. 2nd ed. Buenos Aires: Editorial Sudamericana, 1959.

——. *El Ocaso del Imperio Español en America*. 2nd ed. Buenos Aires: Editorial Sudamerica, 1959.

——. *The Rise of the Spanish American Empire*. New York: Macmillan, 1947.

Maffei, Domenico. *La donazione di Cosantino nei giuristi medievali*. Milan: Giuffrè, 1964.

Malagón, Javier and José M. Ots Capdequí. *Solórzano y la Política indiana*. 2nd ed. México: Fondo de Cultura Económica, 1983.

Maltby, William S. *The Black Legend in England: The Development of Anti-Spanish Sentiment, 1558–1660*. Durham, NC: Duke University Press, 1971.

Mancusi-Ungaro, Donna. *Dante and the Empire*. New York: Peter Lang, 1987.

Martin, David. *Tongues of Fire: The Explosion of Protestantism in Latin America*. Oxford: Basil Blackwell, 1990.

Martin, Victor. *Les origines du Gallicanisme*. 2 vols. Paris: Bloud & Gay, 1939.

Melloni, Alberto. *Innocenzo IV: La concezione e l'esperienza della cristianità come regimen unius personae*. Genoa: Marietti, 1990.

Merriman, Roger Bigelow. *The Rise of the Spanish Empire in the Old World and in the New*. 4 vols. New York: Macmillan, 1918–34. Reprint ed. New York: Cooper Square, 1962.

Milbrath, Susan. "Old World Meets New: Views Across the Atlantic." *First Encounters: Spanish Explorations in the Caribbean and the United States, 1492–1570*, ed. Susan Milbrath and Jerald T. Milanich. Gainesville: University Presses of Florida, 1989: 183–210.

Monter, William. *Frontiers of Heresy: The Spanish Inquisition from the Basque Lands to Sicily*. Cambridge: Cambridge University Press, 1990.

Moorman, John. *A History of the Franciscan Order from Its Origins to the Year 1517*. Oxford: Oxford University Press, 1968.

Morford, Mark. *Stoics and Neostoics: Reubens and the Circle of Lipsius*. Princeton, NJ: Princeton University Press, 1991.

Morison, Samuel Eliot. *Admiral of the Ocean Sea*. 2 vols. Boston: Little, Brown, 1942.

——. *The European Discovery of America: The Northern Voyages*. New York: Oxford University Press, 1971.

——. *The European Discovery of America: The Southern Voyages*. New York: Oxford University Press, 1974.

Morris, Colin. *The Papal Monarchy: The Western Church from 1050 to 1250*. Oxford: Clarendon Press, 1989.

Morrison, Karl F. "Canossa: A Revision." *Traditio* 18 (1962): 121–48.

Muldoon, James. "Boniface VIII's Forty Years of Experience in the Law." *The Jurist* 31 (1971): 449–77.

——. "Boniface VIII as Defender of Royal Power: *Unam Sanctam* as a Basis for the Spanish Conquest of the Americas." *Popes, Teachers, and Canon Law in the Middle Ages*, eds. James Ross Sweeney and Stanley Chodorow. Ithaca, NY: Cornell University Press, 1989, 62–73.

——. "Columbus's First Voyage and the Medieval Legal Tradition." *Medievalia et Humanistica* n.s. 19(1992): 11–26.

——. "The Columbus Quincentennial: Should Christians Celebrate It?" *America* (October 27, 1990): 300–303.

——. "The Contribution of the Medieval Canon-Lawyers to the Formation of International Law." *Traditio* 28(1972): 483–97.

——. "A Fifteenth-Century Application of the Canonistic Theory of the Just War." *Proceedings of the Fourth International Congress of Medieval Canon Law*, Vatican City: Biblioteca Apostolica Vaticana, 1976, 467–80.

——. "The Indian as Irishman." *Essex Institute Historical Collections* 111(1975): 267–89.

——. "John Wyclif and the Rights of the Infidels: The *Requerimiento* Re-examined." *The Americas* 36(1980): 301–16.

——. "The Nature of the Infidel: The Anthropology of the Canon Lawyers." *Discovering New Worlds: Essays on Medieval Exploration and Imagination*, ed. Scott D. Westrem. New York: Garland, 1991, 116–25.

——. "Papal Responsibility for the Infidel: Another Look at Alexander VI's Inter Caetera." *Catholic Historical Review* 64(1978): 168–84.

——. *Popes, Lawyers, and Infidels: The Church and the Non-Christian World, 1250–1550*. Philadelphia: University of Pennsylvania Press, 1979.

——. "The Remonstrance of the Irish Princes and the Canon Law Tradition of the Just War." *American Journal of Legal History* 22(1978): 309–25.

——. "Spiritual Conquests Compared: *Laudabiliter* and the Conquest of the Americas." *In Iure Veritas: Studies in Canon Law in Memory of Schafer Williams*, ed. Steven Bowman and Blanche Cody. Cincinnati, OH: University of Cincinnati Press, 1991: 174–86.

Murray, John Courtney. "Bellarmine on the Indirect Power." *Theological Studies* 9(1948): 491–535.

Nalle, Sara T. "Literacy and Culture in Early Modern Castile." *Past & Present* 125 (Nov. 1989): 65–96.

The New Catholic Encyclopedia. 17 vols. New York: McGraw-Hill, 1967.

Noonan, J. T., Jr. "Who was Rolandus." *Law, Church and Society: Essays in Honor of Stephan Kuttner*, ed. Kenneth Pennington and R. Somerville. Philadelphia: University of Pennsylvania Press, 1977, 21–48.

Noreña, Carlos G. *Studies in Spanish Renaissance Thought*. The Hague: Martinus Nijhof, 1975.

Oakley, Francis. "Celestial Hierarchies Revisited: Walter Ullmann's Vision of Medieval Politics." *Past & Present* 60(August 1973): 3–48.

——. *Natural Law, Conciliarism and Consent in the Late Middle Ages*. London: Variorum, 1984.

Ortiz, Antonio Domínguez. *The Golden Age of Spain, 1516–1659*, trans. James Casey. New York: Basic Books, 1971.

Oxford Classical Dictionary, ed. M. Cary et al. Oxford: Clarendon Press, 1949.

The Oxford English Dictionary. 13 vols. Oxford: Clarendon Press, 1933.

Pagden, Anthony. *The Fall of Natural Man: The American Indian and the Origins of Comparative Ethnology*. Cambridge: Cambridge University Press, 1982.

Parkman, Francis. *Count Frontenac and New France Under Louis XIV*, Centenary edition. Boston: Little, Brown, 1927.

——. *Half Century of Conflict*. Centenary edition. 2 vols. Boston: Little, Brown, and Company, 1927.

Parry, J. H. *The Spanish Seaborne Empire*. New York: Knopf, 1970.

——. *The Spanish Theory of Empire in the Sixteenth Century*. Cambridge: Cambridge University Press, 1940. Reprint ed. New York: Octagon Books, 1974.

Pennington, Kenneth. "The Legal Education of Pope Innocent III." *Bulletin of Medieval Canon Law* n.s. 4(1974): 70–77.

——. "An Earlier Recension of Hostiensis's Lectura on the Decretals." *Bulletin of Medieval Canon Law* n.s. 17(1987): 77–90.

Pérez, J. Beneyto. "The Science of Law in the Spain of the Catholic Kings." *Spain in the Fifteenth Century, 1369–1516: Essays and Extracts by Historians of Spain*, ed. R. Highfield. London: Macmillan, 1972, 276–95.

Peters, Edward. *The Shadow King: Rex Inutilis in Medieval Law and Literature*. New Haven, CT: Yale University Press, 1970.

Phillips, J. R. S. "The Irish Remonstrance of 1317: An International Perspective." *Irish Historical Studies* 27(1990): 112–29.

Phillips, William D., Jr. *Slavery from Roman Times to the Early Transatlantic Trade*. Minneapolis: University of Minnesota Press, 1985.

Pino Díaz, Fermin del. "Humanismo renacentista y origenes de la etnologia: a proposito del P. Acosta, paradigma del humanismo antropologico jésuita." In Ares et al., *Humanismo y vision del otro*: 379–429.

——. "La Renaissance et le Nouveau Monde: José d'Acosta, jésuite anthropologue (1540–1600)." *L'Homme* 122–24, XXXII(1992): 309–26.

Poole, Stafford, C. M. "Institutionalized Corruption in the Letrado Bureaucracy." *Americas* 38(1981–82): 149–71.

Powell, James M., ed. *Innocent III: Vicar of Christ or Lord of the World?* Boston: D. C. Heath, 1963.

Prescott, W. H. *The History of the Conquest of Mexico*. 2 vols. London: George Routledge and Sons, n. d. [1878].

Prucha, Francis Paul. *The Great Father: The United States Government and the American Indians*. 2 vols. Lincoln: University of Nebraska Press, 1984.

Putnam, George Haven. *The Censorship of the Church of Rome*. 2 vols. New York: G. P. Putnam's Sons, 1906–1907.

Quillet, Jeannine. "Community, Counsel and Representation." *In Burns, Cambridge History of Medieval Political Thought c. 350–c. 1450*, 520–73.

Quinones, Ricardo J. *The Changes of Cain*. Princeton, NJ: Princeton University Press, 1991.

Reusch, Fr. Heinrich. *Der Index de verbotenen Bücher*. 2 vols. in 3. Bonn: Verlag von Max Cohen & Sohn, 1885.

Ricard, Robert. *The Spiritual Conquest of Mexico*, trans. Lesley Byrd Simpson. Reprint ed. Berkeley: University of California Press, 1982.

Ridley, Jasper. *The Statesman and the Fanatic*. London: Constable, 1982.

Robinson, I. S. *Authority and Resistance in the Investiture Contest*. New York: Holmes & Meier, 1978.

———. "Church and Papacy." *Cambridge History of Medieval Political Thought*: 252–305.

Roelofsen, C. G. "Grotius and the International Politics of the Seventeenth Century." *Hugo Grotius and International Relations*, 95–131.

Roger, John Clement. *Political Philosophy of Blessed Cardinal Bellarmine*. Washington, DC: Catholic University of America Press, 1926.

Rommen, Heinrich A. *The Natural Law: A Study in Legal and Social History*, trans. Thomas R. Hanley. St. Louis: B. Herder, 1949.

Ronda, James P. "Generations of Faith: The Christian Indians of Martha's Vineyard." *William and Mary Quarterly* 38(1981): 369–94.

Rosecrance, Richard. *The Rise of the Trading State: Commerce and Conquest in the Modern World*. New York: Basic Books, 1986.

Rowe, John H. "Ethnography and Ethnology in the Sixteenth Century." *The Kroeber Anthropological Society Papers* 30(Spring, 1964): 1–19.

Russell, Frederick H. *The Just War in the Middle Ages*. Cambridge: Cambridge University Press, 1975.

Sale, Kirkpatrick. *The Conquest of Paradise: Christopher Columbus and the Columbian Legacy*. New York: Knopf, 1990.

Salisbury, Neal. "Red Puritans: The 'Praying Indians' of Massachusetts and John Eliot." *William and Mary Quarterly* 31(1974): 27–54.

Saunders, Jason Lewis. *Justus Lipsius: The Philosophy of Renaissance Stoicism*. New York: The Liberal Arts Press, 1955.

Scammell, G. V. Review. *English Historical Review* 103(1988): 108–10.

Schaff, Davis S. "The Bellarmine-Jefferson Legend and the Declaration of Independence." American Society of Church History Papers. New York and London, 1928, 2nd series, vol. VIII, 237–76.

Scott, James Brown. *The Spanish Origin of International Law: Francisco de Vitoria and His Law of Nations*. Oxford: Clarendon Press, 1934.

Seed, Patricia. "Taking Possession and Reading Texts: Establishing the Authority of Overseas Empires." *William and Mary Quarterly* 49(1992): 183–209.

Skinner, Quentin. *The Foundations of Modern Political Thought*. Vol. 2, *The Age of Reformation*. Cambridge: Cambridge University Press, 1978.

Smith, Preserved. *The Life and Letters of Martin Luther*. Boston: Houghton Mifflin, 1911.

Sparks, Carol. "England and the Columbian Discoveries: The Attempt to Legitimize English Voyages to the New World." *Terrae Incognitae* 22(1990): 1–12.

Staedler, E. "Die 'donatio Alexandrina' und die 'divisio mundi' von 1493," *Archiv für katholisches kirchenrecht* 117(1937): 363–402.

———. "Die urkunde Alexanders VI zur westindischen Investitur der Krone Spanien von 1493." *Archiv für Urkundenforschung* 15(1937): 145–58.

Stoetzer, O. Carlos. *The Scholastic Roots of the Spanish American Revolution*. New York: Fordham University Press, 1979.

Strading, R. A. *Europe and the Decline of Spain: A Study of the Spanish System, 1580–1720*. Boston: Allen & Unwin, 1981.

——. *Philip IV and the Government of Spain 1621–1665*. New York: Cambridge University Press, 1988.

TePaske, John J. and Herbert S. Klein. "The Seventeenth-Century Crisis in New Spain: Myth or Reality?" *Past & Present* 90 (Feb. 1981): 116–35.

Thompson, James Westfall. *A History of Historical Writing*, 2 vols. New York: Macmillan, 1942.

Tierney, Brian. "Aristotle and the American Indians—Again." *Cristianesimo nella storia* 12(1991): 295–322.

——. *The Crisis of Church and State, 1050–1300*. Englewood Cliffs, NJ: Prentice Hall, 1964.

——. *Foundations of the Conciliar Theory*. Cambridge: Cambridge University Press, 1955.

——. *Religion, Law, and the Growth of Constitutional Thought, 1150–1650*. Cambridge: Cambridge University Press, 1982.

——. Review. *Catholic Historical Review* 43 (1957): 186–87.

——. "'Tria Quippe Distinguit Iudicia . . .' A Note on Innocent III's Decretal *Per venerablem.*" *Speculum* 37 (1962): 48–59.

Twigg, Graham. *The Black Death: A Biological Reappraisal*. New York: Schocken Books, 1985.

Ullmann, Walter. *Medieval Papalism*. London: Methuen & Co., 1949).

Van Den Baar, P. A. *Die kirhliche Lehere der Translatio Imperii Romani bis zur Mitte des 13. Jahrhunderts*. Rome: Apud Aedes Universitatis Gregorianae, 1956.

Vigneras, Louis-André. "Saint Thomas, Apostle of America." *Hispanic American Historical Review* 57(1977): 82–90.

Walther, Helmut G. *Imperiales Königtum. Konziliarismusund Volkssouveränität*. Munich: Wilhelm Fink Verlag 1976.

Watt, John. *The Church and the Two Nations in Medieval Ireland*. Cambridge: Cambridge University Press, 1970.

Weckmann, Luis. "The Alexandrine Bulls of 1493: Pseudo-Asiatic Documents." *First Images of America*, ed. Fredi Chiappelli. 2 vols. Berkeley: University of California Press, 1976: 201–9.

——. *Las Bulas Alejandrinas de 1493 y la Teoriá Política del Papado Medieval*. México: Editorial Jus, 1949.

——. *La herencia medieval de México*. 2 vols. México: Colegio de Mexico, Centro de Estudios Historicos, 1984.

——. *The Medieval Heritage of Mexico*, trans. Frances M. Lopez-Morillas. New York: Fordham University Press, 1992.

Weigand, Rudolf. *Die Naturrechtslehre der Legisten und Dekretisten von Irnerius bis Accursius und von Gratian bis Johannes Teutonicus*. München: Hueber, 1967.

Werner, Ernst. "Translatio Imperii ad Turcos: Päpstliche Renovatio und Weltkaiseridee nach dem Fall Konstantinopels." *Byzantinische Forschungen* 11(1987): 465–72.

West, Delno. "Christopher Columbus and his Enterprise to the Indies: Scholarship of the Last Quarter Century." *William and Mary Quarterly* 49(1992): 254–77.

White, Hayden. "The Forms of Wildness: Archaeology of an Idea." *The Wild Man*

Within: An Image in Western Thought from the Renaissance to Romanticism, ed. Edward Dudley and Maximillian E. Novak. Pittsburgh: University of Pittsburgh Press, 1972, 3–38.

Williams, Robert A. Jr., *The American Indian in Western Legal Thought: The Discourses of Conquest*. New York: Oxford University Press, 1990.

Witte, Charles Martial de. "Les bulles pontificales et l'expansion portugaise au XVe siècle." *Revue d'Histoire Ecclésiastique* 48(1953): 683–718; 49(1954): 438–61; 51(1956): 413–53, 809–36; 53(1958): 5–46, 443–71.

Woolf, C. N. S. *Bartolus of Sassoferrato*. Cambridge: Cambridge University Press, 1913.

Ziegler, Philip. *The Black Death*. New York: John Day Co., 1969.

Index

Abelard, Peter, 143
Acosta, Joseph, 28, 43, 44, 58, 61, 65, 67–71,
 73, 74, 80, 83, 94, 111, 168
Acton, Lord, 3, 4
Adam, 52, 78, 97
Adrian I, 101
Adrian IV, 132, 133, 136, 141
Adrianus, 105
Aeneid, 173
African, Africans, 1, 47, 55, 176
Alans, 54
Albanians, 61
Alexander the Great, 47
Alexander VI, 4, 22, 23, 29, 37, 40, 57, 82,
 97, 98, 109, 111–114, 118, 126, 127–132,
 140, 156–158, 161–163, 166, 171, 172
Alfonso V, 135, 156
Alfonso VIII, 156
Ambrosius, Catharinus, 111
Amorites, 92
Anabaptists, 160
Anastasius I, 116
Aquinas, Thomas, 26, 29, 41, 48, 79, 81, 90,
 107, 114, 115, 119, 143, 144, 167, 170
arbitristas, 8
Aristotle, Aristotelian, 27, 43, 46, 48, 52, 53,
 59, 63, 64, 66, 68–72, 83, 84, 88, 94, 151,
 158, 160, 162, 167
Asturians, 55
Atabalibam, 113
Atahualpa, 84
Athenians, 53
Augustine, Augustinian, 20, 50–52, 59, 64,
 81, 87, 90, 151
Augustus, 148
Azores, 130
Aztecs, 2, 3, 24, 45, 48, 69, 70, 83, 94, 146

Bacchus, 63
Baldus de Ubaldis, 128
baptism, 2, 17, 18, 40, 72, 90, 93, 114, 131,
 173, 174

barbarians, definition of, 40–44, 47, 50, 53–
 56, 67, 69, 173, 175
Baronius, Caesar, 105, 168
Bartolus, 103, 123
Basques, 55
Bellarmine, Robert, 28, 99, 105, 107, 108,
 112, 114, 115, 128, 131
Benzoni, Girolamo de, 113, 114
Bernard of Clairvaux, 89, 116, 124
Bireley, Robert, 166
Black Legend, 5, 9, 169, 174
Boniface VIII, 99, 101, 108, 119, 120, 133,
 141, 163, 172
Bozius, Thomas, 44, 45, 131
Britons, 54, 62, 91, 172
Brundage, James, 16
Bry, Theodore de, 113

Cabot, John, 97
Caesar, Caesars, 148, 149
Cain, 52
Calixtus III, 134, 135, 136
Calvin, John, 99, 100, 131, 155
Canaanites, 92
Canary Islands, 101
cannibals, cannibalism, x, 39, 45, 73, 80–82,
 85, 91, 92
Canossa, 108
Cantabrians, 62
Cape Verde Islands, 130
Caribs, 69, 85
Carolingian, 54, 148
Carthaginians, 92
Caspian Sea, 61
Cassian, John, 81
Castilians, 15, 21, 22, 24, 57, 98, 112, 126,
 129, 130, 138, 140, 158, 161, 171, 173
Ceuta, 135
Charlemagne, 37, 54, 101, 104–106, 148,
 172, 173
Charles I (Aragon), 147
Charles I (Castile), 136, 146, 147

Charles I (England), 134
Chile, Chileans, 68, 69
China, Chinese, 21, 23, 67–69, 71, 75
Chrysostom, John, 90
Cicero, 46, 53, 55, 70, 71, 88, 167
City of God, 52
Clement V, 120
Columbus, Christopher, x, 1–4, 22–25, 27,
    39, 40, 45, 51, 82, 85, 129, 146, 155, 158,
    165, 167, 170
comos polis, 162
conquest, legitimacy of, 1, 3, 5, 6, 11–14, 17,
    22–32, 34–37, 39, 40, 45–50, 60, 61, 63,
    64, 66, 74, 75, 79–82, 84–86, 88, 89, 91,
    96, 98, 101, 107, 111, 114, 115, 127, 129,
    131, 136, 143, 144, 146, 147, 149, 152,
    153, 157, 164, 165, 170, 171, 174
Conrad, 148
Constantine, 12, 14, 132, 148, 172
conversion, converts, 1, 2, 12, 14, 15, 17, 22,
    27, 28, 32, 44, 45, 47, 54, 57, 58, 64, 73,
    87, 90, 93, 95, 96, 109, 112, 128, 153–163,
    173, 174
Corpus iuris civilis, 144
Cortés, Hernán, 136, 146
Council for New England, 38
Council of Constance, 103
Covarrubias, Diego de, 26
crusade, crusader, 15, 16

Dante, 100, 103, 144, 162
David, King, 122
Decretum, 79, 99, 101, 104–106, 143, 148
Defensor Pacis, 125
De Indis, 13, 31, 33, 82, 144
De las Islas del Mar Oceano, 26
De Monarchia, 100, 144, 162
De Regimine Principum (*On Kingship*), 26,
    144
Diodorus Siculus, 83
Dominicans, 5, 27, 28, 34
dominum, 17, 19, 20, 21, 26, 27, 30, 31, 48–
    50, 64, 66, 68–75, 79, 80, 84, 94, 96, 97,
    110, 114, 115, 117, 118, 122, 123, 128,
    131, 132, 137–139, 143, 152, 167, 171,
    172
dominus mundi, 111, 114, 147, 148, 153, 162
Donation of Constantine, 100, 132, 148
Donatists, 20, 97
Dudum Siquidem, 130
Duns Scotus, 118

East Indies, 67, 126, 128, 135, 171, 175
ecocide, 1
Einhard, 54
Elizabeth I, 36, 37, 98, 108
Elliott, John H., 7, 165
empire, definition, 40, 42, 46, 48, 61, 62, 69,
    70, 89, 111, 117, 122, 128, 147, 151–153,
    155, 156, 172
Epicurus, 88
Ethiopians, 45, 54, 60
Eugenius III, 89, 124
Eugenius IV, 101, 114, 140
Eximiae devotionis, 130

Ferdinand I, 146
Ferdinand of Aragon, 22, 23, 26, 27, 97, 104,
    108, 109, 128–130, 136, 137, 139, 146, 156
Fortunatus, 54
Francis I, 35, 97
Franciscans, 21
Franks, 54, 148
Freitas, Seraphinus de, 29, 113, 128

Gallican Church, 102
Gallicians, 55
Gaul, Gauls, 55
Gelasius, 116
Genesis, 52, 71, 83
Germans, 54, 55, 101, 102, 109, 146–148, 151
Goths, 54, 156, 172, 173
Grafton, Anthony, 167
Gratian, 79, 105, 106, 143
Greek, Greeks, 25, 41, 42, 53, 59, 71, 151,
    162, 167
Gregory I, 12
Gregory VII, 105, 108
Grotius, Hugo, 6, 13, 29, 113, 114, 128, 164,
    165, 168, 169, 174–176
Guiccardini, Francisco, 131

Henry II, 132, 133, 134, 141
Henry IV (France), 104
Henry IV (Germany), 105, 108
Henry VII, 97, 98, 134
Henry VIII, 134
Henry the Navigator, 134
heretics, 20, 103, 106, 108, 113, 114, 120,
    134, 139, 155, 157, 160, 161, 172
Herodotus, 51, 83
Herrera, Antonio de, 45
Herules, 54

Historia del Mondo Nuovo, 113
History of the Conquest of Mexico, 3
Holy Roman Empire, 100, 102, 144, 146,
    147, 163
Hostiensis (Henry of Susa), 19–22, 26, 28,
    117, 137, 149
Huguenots, 113, 160
human rights, x, 175, 176
human sacrifice, x, 80, 82, 85, 86, 92
Hungarians, 54
Huss, John, 20, 103

Iberians, 62
idolatry, x, 80, 81, 85–88, 90, 92, 93
imperator, imperatores, 62, 63
imperium, 40, 42, 46, 48, 61, 62, 69, 70, 89,
    111, 117, 122, 128, 155, 156, 172
Incas, 24, 45, 48, 62, 69, 70, 83, 94, 146
Index of Forbidden Books, 101, 164
Indians, 2–6, 10, 12, 24, 26–28, 30, 31, 33,
    34, 36, 39, 40, 42–46, 47, 49, 52, 54–64,
    66, 67, 69, 70–76, 79, 80–89, 91–94, 96,
    97, 111–113, 125, 129, 131, 136–138, 143,
    151, 153–155, 157–163, 172, 173, 175
infidels, 16–23, 26, 29–31, 33–37, 44, 45, 64,
    69, 76, 80, 82, 84, 86–99, 110–112, 114,
    117, 118–121, 128, 131, 134–136, 138,
    139, 144, 147, 149, 153, 154, 157–161,
    170, 173, 174
In memoriam, 105
Innocent II, 103
Innocent III, 16, 17, 20, 101, 107, 112, 116,
    119–121
Innocent IV, 16, 17–22, 27, 28, 31, 37, 82,
    87, 90, 91, 93, 96, 101, 106, 107, 110, 121,
    128, 133, 134, 137, 164, 170, 171, 172
In synodo, 105
Inter caetera, 22, 23, 36, 38, 40, 49, 97, 98,
    109, 111, 112, 118, 127, 129–131, 133,
    134–136, 140, 141, 163, 172, 173
international order, 36, 95
international relations, 21, 24, 128, 169
international society, 165
Investiture Controversy, 36, 98, 132, 133,
    141
Ireland, Irish, 55, 132–134, 141, 173
Isabella of Castile, 4, 22, 23, 26, 97, 104, 128,
    129, 130, 136, 137, 156
Isidore of Seville, 78
Israel, Israelites, 83, 91, 92
ius civile, 78

ius gentium, 78
ius naturale, 78, 162

James I, 38
James (Apostle), 58
Japan, Japanese, 23, 67–69, 71, 75
Jeremiah, 119
Jerome, 114, 120, 148, 152
Jesuit, Jesuits, 10, 40, 44, 56, 65, 67
Jews, 17, 18, 76, 86, 114, 117, 134
John I (Portugal), 134
John VIII, 155
John of England, 112, 134
John of Navarre, 108
Josephus, 83
Julius Caesar, 62
Julius II, 108, 139
just war, 13, 15, 16, 47, 120
Justinian, 147

Kennedy, Paul, 8
kingdom, definition, 43, 48, 68, 69, 147,
    151–153
Kuttner, Stephen, 143

Las Casas, Bartolomé de, 1, 5, 6, 10, 22, 27,
    28, 35, 58, 66, 107, 120, 121, 128, 155,
    165, 169
Latin, Latins, 25, 53
Laudabiliter, 132–134, 141
law of nature, 72, 81, 82, 88, 89
law, civil, 78
law, eternal, 79
law, international, 5, 6, 9, 17, 29, 30, 164,
    168, 169
law, natural, x, 17–19, 34, 71, 77–83, 85–95,
    111, 114, 128, 140, 149, 161
Leo III, 37
lex naturae, 81
liberal arts, 57, 72
Licet, 121
line of demarcation, 130, 138, 158
Lothair, 103
Louis IV, the Bavarian, 101, 103
Louis XI, 156
Louis the Pious, 105
Lucan, 60
Luther, Martin, 131, 155

Machiavelli, Machiavellian, x, 166
Maiolo, Simon, 51

Mandeville, John, 167
Marcellinus, Ammianus, 56
Mare Liberum, 29, 113
Mariana, Juan de, 10, 56
Marsilius of Padua, 125
Martin V, 134
Martyr, Peter, 43
Matienzo, Juan, 29
Meruit, 120
Mexico, Mexicans, 2, 28, 43, 44, 48, 60, 62, 68, 69, 83, 85, 136, 146
mirror of the prince, 165, 166
missionaries, 1, 2, 5, 12, 14, 17, 18, 21, 22, 28, 34, 45, 57–59, 71, 86, 97, 112, 130, 131, 134, 137, 138, 154, 167, 172, 173
Molina, Luis de, 26
monstrous creatures, people, 51, 67
Montezuma, 69, 85
Muslims, 15, 16, 19, 21, 120, 134, 135, 146, 152

National Council of Churches, 1
Navarre, 26, 108, 109, 139
Nicholas V, 134, 135
Novit, 124

Olivares, Count-Duke, 7
Orosius, 87
Otto the Great, 14

Padilla, Agustín Dávila, 28
Palacios Rubios, Juan López de, 26, 139
Pannonians, 54
papal power, 28, 35–37, 90, 96, 98–100, 102–112, 114–123, 125–129, 131–135, 138–142, 147, 158–160, 171, 173
Papal State, 100, 110
Paraguay, 40
Parkman, Francis, 3
Parry, J. H., 9
Paul III, 58, 67
Paul (Apostle), 41, 79, 81, 93, 111, 114
Persians, Persian Empire, 151
Peru, Peruvians, 8, 14, 43, 44, 48, 60, 62, 68, 69, 83–85, 113, 114, 120, 136, 137
Peter of Aragon, 87
Peter (Apostle), 99, 100, 102, 115, 116, 118, 122, 124, 133, 137, 138, 143, 150
Peter's Pence, 133
Philip II (France), 112
Philip II (Spain), 6, 7, 8, 27, 108, 146

Philip IV (France), 99, 101, 103, 141
Philip IV (Spain), 7
Phoenicians, 60
Pius II (Aeneas Sylvius), 144, 156
Pius V, 37, 87, 108
Pizarro, Francisco, 136
Plato, 46, 74
Plautus, 53
plenitudo potestatis, 140
Pliny, 83
Poles, 54, 91
polis, 69, 70, 94, 162
Política indiana, 10
Polo, Marco, 167
Polybius, 148, 151
Pontius Pilate, 123
Praying Towns, 2
Prescott, W. H., 3
Protestants, 2, 6, 12, 13, 28, 30, 35–37, 98–100, 113, 131, 134, 141, 169, 171, 174
Puritans, 40

Qur'an, 19
Quod super his, 16, 18, 21, 26, 82, 111, 128

Reccared, 156
Recopilación de leyes de las Indias, 8
Regnans in excelsis, 108
Requerimiento, 26, 27, 136–139
respublica, respublicae, republic, 43, 44, 48, 52, 67–70, 72, 73, 80, 87, 89, 119, 152
Roman Empire, 41, 47, 48, 54, 92, 146–151, 163, 172
Romans, 41, 42, 47, 48, 59, 62–64, 66, 71, 91, 92, 111, 148, 151, 162, 167, 173
Romanus Pontifex, 135
Rosellis, Antonio de, 101
Royal Commentaries of the Inca, 61
Russians, 54

Sale, Kirkpatrick, 1
Sancho II, 37
Sandoval, Cardinal, 114
Sarmatians, 54
Saxons, 54
Scott, James Brown, 5, 6, 168
Scythians, 53, 55
Seneca, 54, 60
Sepúlveda, Juan Ginés de, 5, 27, 40, 46, 63, 66

Sigebert, 105
Sixtus IV, 108
Sixtus V, 108
slavery, natural, 27, 46, 48, 56, 63, 66, 72, 73, 78
slaves, slavery, 1, 4, 46, 47, 55, 63, 66, 75, 76, 78, 80, 89, 117, 135, 137
Sodom, 82
Solitae, 116, 119
Solórzano, Juan de Pereira, background, education, career, 8, 12–15, 24–30, 38, 165, 167, 170
Solórzano, natural slavery, 45–48, 52, 65, 66, 72
Solórzano, papal power, 37, 39, 95–102, 104, 106–114, 116–129, 131, 134, 136, 139–141, 147, 153, 154, 158, 163
Solórzano, placed on Roman Index, 164
Solórzano, reputation, 8, 9, 11, 168
Solórzano, writings, 9–12
Somalia, ix, 176
South Africa, ix
Spanish Armada, 108
Spenser, Edmund, 55, 132, 133, 141, 173
Strabo, 54, 55, 61, 83
Suárez, Francis, 6, 73, 168
Sublimis Deus, 67
Suevi, 54
Summa Theologica, 26, 143
Sussanis, Marquardus de, 29
Sylvester, 100

Tacitus, 41, 54, 61
The Prince, 166
Thracians, 61

Tierney, Brian, xi
Tlaxcalan, 58
translatio imperii, transfer of the empire, 37, 102, 148, 151, 163, 172
Treaty of the Pyrenees, 8
Treaty of Tordesillas, 130
two swords, 99, 100, 106, 116, 117, 119, 124, 150

Unam sanctam, 99, 100, 101, 103, 108, 119, 141
United Nations, ix
United States, ix, x, 9

Vargas, Francisco à, 28
Vega, Garcilaso de la, 61, 62
Venerabilem, 101
Vespucci, Amerigo, 43
Vettones, 61
Viet Nam, x
Virgil, 47, 172
Visigoths, 152, 156
Vitoria, Francis, 6, 13, 22–24, 28, 29, 31–36, 40, 82, 84, 107, 110, 114, 115, 144, 157, 166, 167–169, 171, 175, 176

Waldensians, 160
Weckmann, Luis, 132
West Indies, 24, 44, 46, 126, 138, 171
White Legend, 5
White, Joseph M., 9
world order, 12–14, 19, 30, 135, 143, 144, 162–165, 168–172, 174–176
writing, Indian interest in, use of, 60, 61, 68

This book has been set in Linotron Galliard. Galliard was designed for Mergenthaler in 1978 by Matthew Carter. Galliard retains many of the features of a sixteenth-century typeface cut by Robert Granjon but has some modifications that give it a more contemporary look.

Printed on acid-free paper.